The Politics of Education in Turkey

The Politics of Education in Turkey

Islam, Neoliberalism and Gender

Zühre Emanet

I.B.TAURIS
LONDON • NEW YORK • OXFORD • NEW DELHI • SYDNEY

I.B. TAURIS
Bloomsbury Publishing Plc
50 Bedford Square, London, WC1B 3DP, UK
1385 Broadway, New York, NY 10018, USA
29 Earlsfort Terrace, Dublin 2, Ireland

BLOOMSBURY, I.B. TAURIS and the I.B. Tauris logo
are trademarks of Bloomsbury Publishing Plc

First published in Great Britain 2023
Paperback edition published 2025

Series design by Adriana Brioso
Cover image: Turkish children play volleyball on the street in Konya, Turkey, 2009.
(© Oleg Znamenskiy/Alamy Stock Photo)

A catalogue record for this book is available from the British Library.

A catalog record for this book is available from the Library of Congress.

ISBN: PB: 978-0-7556-3673-0
         ePDF: 978-0-7556-3670-9
        eBook: 978-0-7556-3671-6

Series: Contemporary Turkey

Typeset by Integra Software Services Pvt. Ltd.

To the living memory of Ayşe…

Contents

List of Figures   viii
Preface   ix
Acknowledgements   xiv
Abbreviations   xvi

1   Introduction   1
2   The contested terrain: Education in Turkey from the republic
    to the AKP   15
3   Politics of marketing education   41
4   Culture wars: Fragments from 'lived culture' of Talip and Zinnur   75
5   Controlling gazes and faces of surveillance   105
6   Fashioning gender: Nurturing mothers vs punitive fathers   123
7   Conclusion   147

Appendix   157
Notes   161
References   173
Index   194

Figures

1   Atatürk Corner in a Year Three classroom at Zinnur School   80
2   Atatürk Corner in a Year Two classroom at Zinnur School   81
3   Atatürk Corner in a Year Seven classroom at Zinnur School   81
4   Atatürk Corner in a Year Eight classroom at Zinnur School   82
5   The walls of Zinnur School I   83
6   The walls of Zinnur School II   83
7   Office board in the office of the deputy head Ruhi in Zinnur I   86
8   Office board in the office of the deputy head Ruhi in Zinnur II   87
9   A poster by Year Seven pupil Büşra   99
10 A poster by Year Six pupil Nevra   100
11 A poster by Year Seven pupil Zehra   100
12 'We want freedom for headscarves in the public space …'
    '10 Million Signature'   117

Preface

In the early years of the 2010s, I had devoted myself to the ethnography of two schools in a low-income district of Istanbul and the surrounding educational institutions including, for-profit Islamic dormitories among others, examining schooling in ways that exposed the logic of marketization and Islamization of education. I also took note of the constant changes in education policy in the shadow of turbulent political turmoil. Those were the years when I had no idea of what lay ahead of me. In the two years following my return from the field, my multi-sited ethnographic study turned out to be an account of a key transitional moment in the recent history of power struggles under the Justice and Development Party (*Adalet ve Kalkınma Partisi*, AKP) that culminated in a failed coup on 15 July 2016 followed by regime change from a parliamentary system to an executive presidency that saw President Recep Tayyip Erdoğan consolidate political power. My scholarly interest in the subject was abruptly interrupted for a long while after the diagnosis of a malignant brain tumour in one of my adored younger sisters and her loss in 2018. Of all this, I can say that the one event which prompted me to turn my PhD dissertation into this book was the first days of the 2016–17 school year following the failed coup attempt on 15 July 2016. I could clearly see, in retrospect, that my fieldwork had captured the heyday of the political alliance between the AKP and the Fethullah Gülen community-dubbed Fethullahist Terror Organization (*Fethullahçı Terör Örgütü*, FETÖ) after the coup attempt that they were held responsible for, an alliance that left a massive footprint in the field of education. Now, once again, the entire field and its key players were being redefined.

Students and pupils in Turkey began the 2016–17 school year with a week-long commemoration of the events leading to the failure of the coup attempt on 15 July 2016. The Ministry of National Education (*Milli Eğitim Bakanlığı*, MEB) issued a Circular Letter specifying every aspect of the commemoration, in terms of both content and form (MEB 2016a). The same speeches, poems and narrations were delivered in all schools across the country; pupils watched the same videos and read the same booklets within a time frame specified by the MEB. A close look at some of the selected content should suffice to illustrate that this week was a watershed in social engineering efforts to define the national imaginary. First of all, poems, speeches and narrations were an essential part of the content of the ceremonies. *Vatan* ('Homeland') by right-wing literary figure Arif Nihat Asya, with the lines '[y]ou found happiness, with my faith … I made you a homeland, oh lands … I'll mark you five times with my forehead …', was recited (EBA 2016: 8). Selected lines from the poem *Diyarbekir Kalesinden Notlar* ('Notes from Diyarbakır Fortress') by Ahmed Arif were also read out: 'These are vipers and traitors; these are the ones who are after our food and bread. You shall recognise them. You shall recognise them and grow up' (EBA 2016: 5). The popular Islamist poet favoured by the AKP Necip Fazıl Kısakürek and Nazım Hikmet's poem *Davet* ('Invitation'), which is highly praised among the nationalists, were read one after the other (EBA 2016: 2). President Recep Tayyip Erdoğan was referred to as commander-in-chief during the ceremony and his address to the country when he appeared on television via Facetime on the night of the attempted coup was read (EBA 2016: 6). In the head teachers' compulsory speech, there was a reference to 19th of May 1919 which was set as the start of the Turkish War of Independence against imperialist occupation forces, their internal and external allies, and the Ottoman Empire (EBA 2016: 3). Through these diverse components, some relating to the Kemalist period, others to favoured Islamist sources, the MEB tried to cobble together a narrative of national unity to justify what the AKP government, or more precisely the party-state, called the 'victory of democracy'.

Secondly, booklets, were distributed 'free of charge' to pupils in the first class of the school year (MEB 2017). The content of these booklets was clearly designed to 'teach' children of all ages the official party-state account of the night of 15 July. It contained various sections such as 'Dictionary of July 15' and 'Timeline of the Night of July 15' (MEB 2016b). Throughout the booklet were photos of the people taking to the streets and the military tank that became an icon of the 'resistance' of 'the people' to the failed coup attempt. 'They had the means because they had faith [*iman varsa imkan da vardı*]' was one of the slogan-like catch phrases (MEB 2016b). In the section where the events of the night of 15 July were presented hour by hour in the form of a timeline, the frightening night was outlined. The terms democracy, parliament, coup, junta, and FETÖ were briefly explained in the 'July 15 Dictionary' section. For example, it said that FETÖ '… refers to the Fethullahist terrorist organisation that exploits people's religious sentiments with its perverted views. It is also defined as a parallel state structure because it unjustly establishes itself in state institutions by stealing exam questions and using public institutions, especially in the fields of education, justice, and security, for its own interests and purposes'

(MEB 2016b). Democracy, on the other hand, was defined as a social order in which the rule of law prevails, and which is based on the equality and freedom of citizens (MEB 2016b). Massive purges, mass arrests and show trials occurred throughout the summer. And even before the school bells rang, the Decree-Law no. 672 of 1 September 2016 on the measures concerning public officials taken under the state of emergency dismissed about 40,000 of state employees, including 28,163 from the MEB and 2,346 academics (Official Gazette 2016), signalling the transition to authoritarianism.

Thirdly, another striking compulsory content of the commemoration was videos uploaded to the digital education portal called Education Information Network (*Eğitim Bilişim Ağı*, EBA). It was mandatory for teachers to make parents watch these videos as well. In this respect, I saw a similarity between schools and the mosques which played a central role in reaching out to the masses on the night of 15 July. In one of these videos, President Erdoğan reads out the national anthem against the background of a rather graphic compilation of footage of the night of violence on the 15th of July, which saw hundreds of deaths and injuries. Pupils in low-income households, where televisions are at the centre of living rooms, were likely already exposed to extensive and repetitive visual media coverage of violence, torture, via television channels, in which violence was presented as heroic and – one might even say – fetishized. It was now time to recapitulate the events with 'age-appropriate' content as the circular put it – as if that were possible in schools.

In another video, an authoritative male narrator with a deep voice presented the history of Turkey in bullet points including visuals from battles, bombings and more (MEB 2016c). According to this account, there were three important turning points in the country's history: the Gallipoli campaign (1915–16) under the Ottoman state, 30 August (1922) marking the victory against invading forces in the Turkish War of Independence and 15 July 2016. The inclusion of Victory Day in the founding moments of the country and the emphasis on the historical role of Mustafa Kemal were a drastic change, as the two major Islamic powers, the AKP and the Gülen community, had struggled for more than a decade to upstage the republican national imaginary through 'de-Atatürkification' (Kandiyoti & Emanet 2017). The honouring of the martyrs of the Turkish War of Independence did not last long. A year after the first commemoration of the failed coup in schools, in the 2017–18 school year, these lines were on the MEB website:

> On that night, when everyone took to the streets to defend their faith, their homeland, their nation, democracy and the rule of law, and an unprecedented heroic epic was written against the coup plotters, the 'Spirit of Çanakkale

[*Çanakkale Ruhu*]' was revived a century later, bringing to life a story of resistance and resurrection that has gone down in history in golden letters.

(MEB 2017)

The 'spirit of Gallipoli' had three essential components for the AKP government: Islamic unity independent of sub-national identities, a strong connection to the Ottoman past and an implicit and occasionally explicit allusion to *jihad*.

As a feminist researcher, teacher and school ethnographer, I knew very well that what I have selectively described so far reveals only half of the story. The other half is the 'lived culture' in Raymond Williams' sense (2001), which means we can only speculate about its reception in classrooms or schools. Moreover, as this book argues, the local context of schools is crucial to an understanding of 'lived culture'. The media coverage of this commemoration offered only glimpses of this culture. In one school, for example, preschool children dramatized 15 July with cardboard tanks (CNNTurk 2016); in another, primary school pupils were given wooden weapons to hold a 'democracy watch', as people did after the night of 15 July (Evrensel 2016). Among the most graphic images I gleaned from media coverage were the photos of young pupils and their teacher holding nooses (meant for execution by hanging) and saluting in the classroom (Duvar 2016). Clearly, the first week of the 2016–17 school year raises difficult questions about violence and children's rights, especially in a context that has sought to meet internationally established standards for children's rights and eliminate violence in all forms.

The memorization of 15 July in schools, in my opinion, served the purpose of enforced forgetting or, more precisely, 'repressive erasure' in Paul Connerton's sense. In his essay 'Seven Types of Forgetting', Connerton explains that '[r]epressive erasure can be employed to deny the fact of a historical rupture as well as bring about a historical break' (2008: 60–1). By commemoration of 15 July, 'repressive erasure' was not used to deny the existence of a historical rupture, but to cause one. In other words, this commemoration was imposed or forced on children to forget the recent past of collaboration with Gülenist forces which was at its apex during my fieldwork years, influencing curriculum content, teachers' orientations and educational materials. For many students, if not all, this literally meant the 'erasure' of their teachers, tutorial colleges, schools, books, songs, cartoons and more. Books were burnt in their thousands; teachers were dismissed, and schools were closed. The number of dismissed civil servants reached up to around 125,678 by 2019 (TCCB 2021: 23). In post-15 July Turkey, the AKP undermined democracy, used the state of emergency which lasted until 2018 as an opportunity to reshape the education sector and introduced education policies to create a 'sanctioned' community through *imam-hatip* schools. After these devastating changes, one of the main arguments regarding education was that education was Islamized and that Turkey, with its so-called 'secular' education system, could no longer be considered an 'exception' in the Middle East. What lies behind this argument, in my opinion, is continuation of what I call as deep 'obsession' with *imam-hatip* schools, while Islamization had already been taking place in secular track schooling for a long time as this book illustrates. Such argument only serves to make entrenched inequalities, the extent of Islamization and its devastating gendered effects invisible as this book intends to suggest. Above all, this book is an attempt to 'remember' and not to give in to 'coerced forgetting'.

Acknowledgements

I would like to thank the teachers, mothers and pupils of the two schools where I conducted my ethnography. I am indebted to the women who worked in various positions and institutions throughout the district. I would also like to thank many experts in the field of education for their reflections. I thank Prof. Çiğdem Kağıtçıbaşı who is now no longer with us, and Prof. Rıfat Okçabol. I have benefitted a lot from their reflections during my fieldwork.

I would like to thank the reviewers of the manuscript for their feedback, which has helped me immensely. I have also benefitted from the support of the editors Yasmin Garcha and Rory Gormley at Bloomsbury Publishing – it was a pleasure to work with them. I would like to thank Yasmin Garcha for her kindness, warmth and thoughtfulness, which have been invaluable in the darkness of the pandemic. I would also like to thank Sevgi Adak for her encouragement to write this book, which has given me strength. I am indebted to the series editor, Ceren Lord, for her warmth, intellectual wisdom and the encouragement and friendship that came with it.

I would like to express my sincere gratitude to my supervisor, Prof. Deniz Kandiyoti, for her unfailing positive encouragement during and after the completion of my PhD. Deniz *Hocam* has played a formative role in my ethnographic work and intellectual development. Her wisdom, generosity, kindness and love for her students have always been a constant source of inspiration and strength. I have to say that without her support I probably would not have been able to write this book while I was going through the grieving process. I think it is hard to adequately thank Deniz *Hocam* for such a support, which *literally* made this book possible.

I am grateful to the student community at the School of Oriental and African Studies (SOAS), University of London. I have benefitted greatly from the thought-provoking and intellectually invigorating discussions among my fellow students from the Global South and North. I have been fortunate to be a member of this community. I have also benefitted from the companionship within the Centre for Gender Studies. I would like to thank my dear peers Christianne F. Collantes, Rouba Mhaissen, Elena Zambelli, Alaya Forte and Valeria Dessi for their friendship. Sharing food, ideas, hopes and laughter has always given me warmth. Valeria Dessi has always been a source of inspiration and joy. I am immensely grateful to Prof. Nadje Sadig Al-Ali for her guidance, intellect, humanity and mentorship that have shaped my entire graduate life. I consider myself very fortunate to be her student.

I am indebted to Prof. Laleh Khalili and Prof. Benjamin C. Fortna for their sharp questions which guided me in the initial stages of this work. I am indebted to the great anthropologists Prof. Esra Özyürek and Prof. Yael Navaro for their insightful comments and suggestions, from which I have benefitted in turning my thesis into a book. I was fortunate to have had extraordinary scholars on my supervisory committee and viva. I would also like to thank Prof. Linda Herrera, Prof. André Elias Mazawi and Dr. Roozbeh Shirazi for their very valuable comments and insights on some selected sections in a chapter of this book. I would also like to thank Dr. Mary Lou O'Neil, who played an important role in my decision to pursue an academic career.

I am grateful to my many friends. I would like to thank Dr. Pınar Çakıroğlu for her warm friendship throughout the PhD and afterwards. I would also like to thank Dr. Prem Kumar for his intellectual curiosity and restlessness, which have been a source of inspiration. I would like to thank Dr. Merve Kütük-Kuriş for her kind and thoughtful support during critical times. Our intellectual discussions are always precious. I would like to thank Dr. Fatih Çağatay Cengiz for his intellect, his irony, his constant encouragement and his generosity.

I would like to thank my dear half-father, grandfather, sailor and worker Halil, who is now no longer with us. He played a crucial role in my life carrying me everywhere like a handbag – be it to the mosque, the teahouse, the highlands, the deep forests or the open sea. All my sisters, my beloved sisters, I thank you. I want to thank Ayşegül for always checking me. I thank Bilge for being a 'fairy'. I would like to thank Zerrin for her love. I would like to thank my dear nephew Hayat for always keeping our spirits high. I am in debt to my brother Murat for his unfailing support through thick and thin. Oğuz, thank you for being *abi* and my source of strength and joy. My young parents Münevver and Mehmet Ali, without your love nothing would have been possible. I dedicate this book to the living memory of my dear late sister, the love of our lives, Ayşe (*aklı güzel kalbi güzel kardeşim*).

Abbreviations

AÇEV	Anne Çocuk Eğitim Vakfı (The Mother Child Education Foundation)
ADD	Atatürkçü Düşünce Derneği (Atatürkist Thought Association)
AKP	Adalet ve Kalkınma Partisi (Justice and Development Party)
CCTV	Closed-Circuit Television
CHP	Cumhuriyet Halk Partisi (Republican People's Party)
ÇYDD	Çağdaş Yaşamı Destekleme Derneği (Association for the Support of Modern Life)
DİB	Diyanet İşleri Başkanlığı (Presidency of Religious Affairs)
DP	Demokrat Parti (Democrat Party)
EBA	Eğitim Bilişim Ağı (Education Information Network)
EFA	Education for All
ERG	Eğitim Reform Girşimi (Education Reform Initiative)
EU	European Union
FETÖ	Fethullahçı Terör Örgütü (Fethullahist Terorist Organization)
HKO	Haydi Kızlar Okula (Hey Girls, Let's Go to School)
IMF	International Monetary Fund
MDG	Millenium Development Goals
MEB	Milli Eğitim Bakanlığı (Ministry of National Education)
MHP	Milliyetçi Hareket Partisi (Nationalist Movement Party)
MİT	Milli İstihbarat Teşkilatı (National Intelligence Service)
MOBESE	Mobil Elektronik Sistem Entegrasyonu (Mobile Electronic System Integration)
MSP	Milli Selamet Partisi (National Salvation Party)

MÜSİAD	Müstakil Sanayici ve İş Adamları Derneği (Independent Industrialists' and Businessmen's Association)
NATO	The North Atlantic Treaty Organization
NGO	Non-governmental organization
OAB	Okul Aile Birliği (Parent Teacher Association)
OECD	Organization for Economic Co-operation and Development
PE	Physical Education
PISA	Programme for International Student Assessment
PKK	Partiya Karkerên Kurdistanê (Kurdistan Workers' Party)
RP	Refah Partisi (Welfare Party)
SBM	School Based Management
SBS	Seviye Belirleme Sınavı (Level Determination Exam)
TBMM	Türkiye Büyük Millet Meclisi (Turkish Grand National Assembly)
TEFBİS	Türkiye'de Eğitimin Finansmanı ve Eğitim Harcamaları Bilgi Yönetim Sistemi (Information Management System of Education Financing and Education Expenses)
TÖS	Türkiye Öğretmenler Sendikası (Turkish Teachers' Union)
TRT	Türkiye Radyo ve Televizyon Kurumu (Turkish Radio and Television Corporation)
TSK	Türk Silahlı Kuvvetleri (Turkish Armed Forces)
TTKB	Talim Terbiye Kurulu Başkanlığı (Board of Education and Discipline)
TÜRGEV	Türkiye Gençlik ve Eğitime Hizmet Vakfı (Foundation of Youth and Education in Turkey)
UN	United Nations
UNICEF	United Nation's Children Fund
WB	World Bank
YİBO	Yatılı İl Bölge Okulları (Regional Boarding Primary Schools)

1

Introduction

The freshly appointed deputy head of Talip School, a pseudonym for one of the two schools where I spent over a year doing fieldwork in Istanbul's Bahçelik district (also a pseudonym), Ahmet, in his early thirties, said to me as we drank tea in his office, 'What is the difference between these children [pupils in Talip] and those children [pupils in other schools in the district], ha?' He liked to ask rhetorical questions to clarify his own ideas and feelings, otherwise he kept silent. What he meant was that he deplored the inequalities among the schools in the district. As a visiting teacher/researcher at the school, I spent significant amounts of time in his always busy office which gave me the opportunity to see Talip from the vantage point of all the male deputy head teachers and, to some extent, the head teacher.

Ahmet's lively office contained a relatively large library. Three stacks of thick, miscellaneous editions of *Safahat* ('Stages') penned by Mehmet Akif Ersoy (1873–1936), who was one of the leading pan-Islamic intellectuals of the late Ottoman and early republican periods, poet and author of the Turkish national anthem, were displayed prominently. Mehmet Akif Ersoy was not necessarily among Ahmet's favourite poets, but he wanted to publicize the school in the politicized local educational market where Ersoy was promoted as the embodiment of the 'Muslim' nation, a role model for future generations and a 'hero' of the Turkish War of Independence (1919–23). *Safahat*'s placement on the most visible shelf was intended to demonstrate the school's allegiance to the upper echelons of the district bureaucracy and towards the Justice and Development Party (*Adalet ve Kalkınma Partisi*, AKP) led Bahçelik municipality, which had access to a pool of local, national and global networks through its privileged relations with the ruling party.

Ahmet's library also featured books on what he referred to as 'corporate manipulation methods', 'subliminal communication' and 'marketing'. This did not surprise me knowing that Ahmet wanted to create an image for Talip that made it marketable. Although some of the teachers in Talip criticized the mismatch between the rhetoric and practice of primary education in Turkey by referring to the fact that free education was supposed to be a constitutional right, Ahmet avoided these discussions. For him they were 'waste of time', and he was more concerned with 'the realities' as he called them. As a self-made man, Ahmet's ambition was to create a 'better school' for pupils for whom he felt compassion because of the poverty he had been exposed to in his own childhood. Ahmet was not alone; his account reflected the concrete results of how the shortfalls in state provision in primary education combined with the introduction of neoliberal education policies, in particular the School-Based Management (SBM) system, to create a local education market. In order to survive financially, schools like Talip also had to toe the line of local political priorities of the AKP-led municipality, which was itself part of a broader project of social engineering and cultural transformation.

This book examines *lived culture*, which according to Raymond Williams (2001: 66) is a 'culture of a particular time and place' and 'fully accessible only to those who live in that time and place', in two state primary schools based on my ethnographic research conducted in the Bahçelik district of Istanbul during the 2012–13 school year. I aim to demonstrate the joint effects on state education of neoliberal reforms and Islamization policies from the vantage point of Talip, an underprivileged and overcrowded school and Zinnur, a better-connected and better-run school in the same district. On the one hand, there has been a neoliberal consolidation process, which started with the implementation of structural adjustment policies in the 1980s and took a more radical turn under the AKP. On the other hand, the alleged secular character of state education has been compromised through a process of Islamization of curricular and extra-curricular content and activities. My main intention is to show how these two processes are intertwined and feed upon each other challenging key premises of republican education, that of gender equality among the others. While the recent developments in the country, especially the period following the failed coup of 15 July 2016, are beyond the remit of this book, I aim to shed light on a very significant moment in the process of radical transformation of the country's education system.

Adapting to the realities of a shifting field

There were several key turning points that have given my research agenda its final shape. Initially, I was curious about the extent to which the increasing Islamization of the public sphere coupled with neoliberal educational policies was having an impact on the socialization of gender in secular-track state primary schools. I had intended to compare a secular-track state primary school with a for-profit private school affiliated to an Islamic community in order to explore whether this might reveal significant aspects of the public-private and secular-religious dichotomy in education. I was particularly interested in finding out how these contexts might influence socialization into gender roles and expectations. I was also sceptical about the assumed 'secularity' of state primary schools. At the time, attention was mainly focused on the growing number of students in state-funded Sunni Islamic schools, namely the *imam-hatip* (prayer leader and preacher) schools (Kağıtçıbaşı 2010). This information was taken as an almost exclusive indicator of Islamization in education. My own working hypothesis, based on my reading of developments as a former teacher and teachers' union member, was at odds with the assumed divide between secular-track schools and *imam-hatip* schools. At that stage evidence for my working hypothesis about the blurring of boundaries between these institutions was still thin on the ground.

While I was conducting my preliminary research, the controversial Education Act No. 6287, widely referred to as the 4+4+4 education reform, was enacted in March 2012, amending various laws as well as the Primary Education Act of 1997. Behind this otherwise hodgepodge education law was the intention to mainstream *imam-hatip* schools, which would make secular-track state schools redundant in the long run. This is because the 4+4+4 education reform introduced a new system of education levels consisting of three levels (primary, lower secondary and upper secondary), each lasting four years. The division of the previously eight-year and uninterrupted basic education schools into two separate schools allowed for the opening of the lower secondary level of *imam-hatip* schools – they were previously reached at *lycée* level (upper secondary). In addition, the subjects of the Qur'an and the Life of Muhammad, the Prophet were included as electives in the secular-track lower secondary curriculum, further blurring the distinction between *imam-hatip* schools and ostensibly 'secular' schools. With this law, which I explain in detail in Chapter 2, my tentative assumptions turned into reality, and I rapidly started to find some answers to my questions. Nevertheless, I was interested in analysing neither the curriculum nor the expansion of *imam-hatip* schools per se. I was just sure that I wanted to do research in both primary and lower secondary schools. This is simply because, it was not possible to split the previously continuous eight-year primary schools into two separate schools (primary and lower secondary) within a few months. This made my research unique in that I was thrust into an environment where I had to *de facto* study both primary and what had become 'lower secondary' schools in an atmosphere of uncertainty and chaos where teachers were not prepared for the changes.

The second significant change to my agenda occurred when I began to map the full complexity of the educational landscape in Bahçelik district. During the second month of the school year, I became aware of the fact that the budgetary shortfalls of state primary education led to the expansion of public and private education service providers. More importantly, I discovered that the school was not the exclusive domain of gender socialization alongside the family but that there were several parallel institutional domains, which were just as crucial to understanding how educational provision operates in the locality. These discoveries led me to expand the scope of my ethnography to include what I call 'adjunct institutions'. Almost all types of facilities where the municipality of Bahçelik offered educational support services to the pupils of the two schools, including libraries, education and cultural centres run by the municipality namely *bilgi evi* (house of knowledge), became part of my study (Chapter 3). I also witnessed the mobilization of pupils' mothers through municipal projects (Chapter 6). Mothers were thrust to the forefront of this complex landscape as teachers' helpers and fundraisers (Chapter 3). This prompted me to attend numerous events, commemorations and meetings involving mothers. Furthermore, I paid visits to Qur'an courses provided by the Presidency of Religious Affairs (*Diyanet İşleri Başkanlığı*, DİB) and for-profit dormitories owned by Islamic communities in which some pupils of both schools lived. What I found in and around both schools led me to untangle one of the key puzzles of this study: how the mutual interactions between Islamization and neoliberalization play out through the placement of Islamic actors in key positions that regulate both access to resources and the selection of educational content, including materials that effect gender socialization in schools.

The third change arose from my gradual recognition of the sharp difference between official national curriculum and *lived culture* (Williams 2001) of schools. On the one hand, while the national curriculum still conveyed a conventional narrative of the republican achievements and ideals, on the other, a counter-narrative denigrating secularism and Kemalist reforms was constructed and disseminated through a wide network of 'adjunct institutions' and cultural products in the form of books, songs, documentaries and more in schools. Therefore, I immersed myself in the songs they sing, the posters they designed, the films they watched, various play forms they invented, in short, the cultural products that influence them (Chapter 4). I was interested in finding answers to how pupils comply with or challenge the established rules in schools as well as 'adjunct institutions'. This approach also revealed the limitations of focusing on textbooks or the official curriculum – commonly used in educational research in

Turkey – as a guide to understanding educational culture in general and gender socialization in schools, in particular. Furthermore, what I found on the ground at the micro-level, in both schools in Bahçelik district, did not always correspond to the discussions and debates at the national level. While at the national level there seemed to be a relentless culture war over the structure and content of education between secular and Islamic constituencies, at the local level, the AKP government had already challenged the allegedly 'dominant' official ideology of the state through the activities of the AKP-led Bahçelik municipality.

The last turning point was occasioned by the power struggle and eventual breakup between the AKP government and its erstwhile ally the Gülen community (*cemaat*) which is market-oriented Islamist movement led by Muslim preacher Fethullah Gülen. The period of my fieldwork coincided with the heyday of the Gülen community's prominence in the field of education, both as a private provider of educational services and as a multi-media networked actor that targeted children. By that stage, the AKP in alliance with the Gülen community had succeeded in marginalizing voices and actors representing secular constituencies and interests in the education sector, and the reconfigured policy domain only featured these dominant players for a while. Eventually, AKP had become reliant on the Gülen community's established expertise in the education sector and offered it a privileged status in return. This became more comprehensible following the breakup of the alliance and criminalization of the Gülen community after the failed coup of 15 July 2016 when AKP started passing 'new slate' legislation aiming to push Gülen community actors out of the field and to purge its cadres (Kandiyoti & Emanet 2017). From the vantage point of state primary education, one could argue that the power struggle between the AKP and the Gülen community became a contest over whose values, institutions and interests would dominate the education system which had previously mainly featured secular vs religious constituencies. This book reveals, among other things, the genesis of the dynamics which eventually led to a process of re-centralization of education and attempts to bring into under total government control.

Bahçelik: The setting of the schools

One of the mothers at Zinnur School described Bahçelik as a district that was 'among one of the most *varoş* districts of Istanbul'. *Varoş* has become the key term to describe working-class migrants to Istanbul since the late 1980s and especially during the 1990s (Erman 1997, 2001; White 2002). It began to be employed in an attempt to distinguish the districts engorged by an influx of migrants from Anatolia since the 1990s from the rest of the city. Tahire Erman explains that definitions of *varoş* and *varoşlu* (people living in *varoş*) were constructed by media in 1990s: 'The *varoşlu* are the economically deprived (the deprivation may be relative or absolute) and impoverished lower classes who tend to engage in criminal activities and radical political actions directed against the state. They are the political Islamists, the nationalist Kurds, the radical leftist Alevis who challenge the political authority of the state and disturb the social order of society' (2001: 996). Jenny B. White in her brilliant ethnographic work on vernacular politics of Ümraniye district of Istanbul argues, '*varoş*, like *gecekondu*, implies an entire universe of characteristics, from appearance to lifestyle and beliefs, but a *varoş* is not easily mapped or visually distinguished by location or architectural characteristics. It refers rather diffusely to any urban residential location of working-class and lower-middle class pious residents, that is, the place of Black Turks' (2013: 118).

Across the decades the term *varoş* has accrued new meanings. Youth subcultures in the district also used the term, albeit in a different way. For instance, 'you are a *varoş* my girl, you are just a *Kezban*, [*Varoşsun kızım, Kezbanın tekisin*]', whispered a young secondary school female pupil into the ear of her peer in a minibus which was packed with people, like a train compartment of the Piccadilly line during rush hour in London. *Kezban* seemed to be an attempt to name a particular type of lower-class femininity. The word 'poverty' was hardly ever mentioned when making totalizing assumptions about the lives of the inhabitants of the *varoş* and the youth and children raised in these districts.[1] All the diverse lower-class contexts across the city were subsumed under this umbrella term *varoş*, including in Bahçelik.[2]

Bahçelik looked like a collage of diverse microcosms. As one of the teachers in Zinnur, Üzeyir, candidly spelt out:

This is the 'below stairs' of the city [*burası şehrin merdiven altıdır*]. There used to be sheep here, and now you see tall buildings everywhere. Different groups live in each neighbourhood. Neighbourhood Akasya [pseudonym] is famous for its beggars, Karanfil [pseudonym] is full of Kurds, in Hatmi [pseudonym] live Alevis … In another neighbourhood Kurds and immigrants from the Black Sea live side by side. In some of these neighbourhoods, children start working at the age of nine … Some pupils literally raise themselves and some of them parent their parents [*ailesine velilik yapıyorlar*]. In other neighbourhoods, the culture is completely different because they have money. Some families have made good money by selling their land … Two schools that are next to each other can differ by ninety per cent.

These imaginary boundaries between the districts of Istanbul – even between the neighbourhoods that Üzeyir depicted – were not based on economic differences but more importantly on socio-political distinctions.

Bahçelik was among those districts that had become a hotbed for Islamist movement, namely National Outlook (*Milli Görüş*), which was led by Necmettin Erbakan (1926–2011), the mentor of the first generation of AKP leaders. National Outlook movement mobilized informal and formal networks to address the needs of the inhabitants of any given district which is known as 'social municipality' approach.[3] The AKP-led district municipality of Bahçelik not only inherited the long experience of this approach and enlisted many of its former followers, but also tried to access to the influx of resources coming from local, national and global donors.

Zinnur School: Relative privilege in a low-income area

The Zinnur School building was in the middle of one of the neighbourhoods of Bahçelik where boundaries between the residential and industrial areas were blurred. In its vicinity, workers, company owners and chief executive officers rub shoulders – metaphorically, if not literally. Nonetheless, the school was one of the leading primary schools in the district, displaying its pupils' scores on a hoarding on the facade of the school with the caption 'Our Source of Pride' ('*Gurur Tablomuz*') at the top. Majority of pupils in Zinnur were from low-income families. Yet, the reputation of the school attracted many lower-middle class families, although they were in the minority. The address-based registry system mandates that state primary schools register those living in the vicinity of the school; however, parents often make generous donations to schools to be able to exercise choice. The number of pupils in the school – around 1000 – was increasing due to the school's reputation as well as the 4+4+4 education reform that was introduced just a few months before I started my fieldwork.

Talip School: 'We can only save a few'

Talip was what I call a 'titan' school with more than 3000 pupils. Due to its poor physical infrastructure, it was a double-shift school. The texture of Talip's catchment area was very different from Zinnur's: a neighbourhood where residential buildings, schools, clothes shops, electronics stores, Qur'an courses, mosques, workshops, restaurants and bakeries were side by side. Moreover, the high-traffic boulevard adjoining the school added to this atmosphere of 'perfect chaos'. Only the high grey walls with barbed wire fences, the Turkish flag and the Atatürk bust distinguished the school from the surrounding apartment buildings whose closeness to classrooms could act as a distraction to pupils.

Many Talip teachers repeatedly referred to the story of 'The Star Thrower' by Loren Eiseley (1978) in which a little boy seeing a vast beach littered with starfish after a storm attempt to throw them back in the ocean to save them from certain death. An old man calls this boy out to explain what he was doing and says: 'But there must be tens of thousands of starfish on this beach. I'm afraid you won't really be able to make much of a difference' (Straube 2011). And the boy smiles and replies, 'It made a difference to that one!' (Straube 2011).[4] This story provides significant insights into the atmosphere of the school in general. Some of the teachers said: 'We can only save/rescue a few'. Either a teacher selects you – 'throws you into the ocean' – or, to extend the metaphor, you 'die when the sun gets high'. They did not use the words poverty and social class but romanticized their own role as a teacher in a school where most of the pupils came from low-income households. Moreover, there were substantial numbers of pupils who were qualified for conditional educational assistance programmes and were benefitting from monthly cash payments in the school. For some teachers, however, the everyday life of schooling was framed by the mere fact of working 'in an "uncivilized" part of Istanbul' or '*varoş*', as these teachers daily put it. They created an imaginary Bahçelik, 'the threatening "*varoş*"'where lived 'the terrorists', 'the poor', 'the thieves', 'the radical Islamists', 'the Kurds', 'the peasants from the Black Sea region', 'the AKP voters', 'the followers of *tariqas* [*tarikatçılar*]'. The economic, social and political background of the parents of the pupils fuelled their stereotypes and prejudices. It was clear to me that these teachers perceived pupils in Talip as the children of the 'threatening' Other (Chapter 3).

Proving my credentials: Accessing a difficult field

In Zinnur School, I obtained a post as a contracted temporary teacher with the permission of the high-ranking district officials and references from my former colleagues. With a degree from the Faculty of Education (a licence to teach) and five years of teaching experience as regular staff between 2001 and 2006, I had the credibility and confidence to act as a teacher/participant observer. However, what helped my case was that alongside the fact that I was only a 'contract' teacher with a fixed-term appointment my application coincided with the chaos that the transition to the 4+4+4 education system created which meant that my lack of political capital and connections mattered less.

During the first few months, most of the permanent staff dismissed me and were seldom interested in my research. The group of teachers dubbed the 'smokers' group' (who had to congregate outside) eventually welcomed me, after testing me. On the third day of school, Bahtiyar, finding out about my research topic, said, 'Do not misunderstand me but a PhD is something that only spinsters would do.' I knew I was being tested. His biased sexist perception, according to him, did not come out of thin air. Bahtiyar like most of the teachers had had some sort of friction with their instructors – some of them female – in the course of their university education. The authority that some of these university instructors craved alienated those students who expected to be treated as individuals rather than 'upper secondary school pupils', as he put it. Bahtiyar was testing whether I would treat him as an equal or in a patronizing way.

Although most of the male teachers were eager to understand the details of my research by means of 'testing' me, it was a challenge to get closer to the female teachers. The majority were dismissive towards me to the extent that initially some barely greeted me. I grasped that it would take some time before my presence became normalized. I was learning that the first rule of being a researcher/teacher was patience and humility. My presence was taken seriously only after the teachers, pupils and parents acknowledged my commitment to my work as a teacher. I put the interests of my pupils first and decided to give priority to all the tasks that were required of me before scribbling in or managing my fieldwork notes. I was responsible for more than 200 pupils and this number reached more than 300 after the head teacher İsmail pressed me to offer elective courses as well. I had twenty hours of class contact and extra weekly planning sessions, attended staff meetings and parent-teacher meetings, and marking and reporting on pupils' progress were among some of the tasks I undertook. Additionally, although officially I was not supposed to perform 'guard duty' (*nöbet*), which literally meant patrolling a floor in the school building during breaks, I had to take on this task (Chapter 5).

In Talip School, I was mostly a visitor during the first term, and I also conducted participant observation during the second term. I spent one and half days at the school every other week. I sat in the staff common room during breaks, accompanied the teachers in the playgrounds and spent significant amounts of time in deputy heads' offices. At the beginning, no one was curious about my research, but they were eager to get to know me as a person and a colleague. Only after two months, teachers and deputy heads started to listen to me carefully. I candidly explained what my research was about once more and my intention to visit the school until the end of the school year. Gradually most of the teachers welcomed me to their classrooms. I did ten unstructured classroom observations and in all of them I gained the name *abla* (elder sister).

One of the greatest challenges in Talip was the existence of factionalism (along political and ethnic lines) among the teachers, which I explain more fully in Chapter 3. This meant that I had to be careful not to become identified as a 'member' of any group or faction of teachers in the school. Although they started to perceive me as a colleague and knew that I was employed as a teacher in another school in the district, I tried to remain neutral. This was like walking a tightrope, though my visiting relationship with Talip made the task easier. Nevertheless, I could not enter the social circle of young teachers because I was from 'outside' the school. In Zinnur, the advantages of being a teacher were having full access to almost all the networks within and outside the school while in Talip I had the opposite problem of having to keep my distance in the relationships I established.

Although my initial intention was to focus micro-level school ethnographies, I found myself compelled to work on four intimately interrelated levels simultaneously. At the micro-level, I immersed myself in everyday schooling, teaching, performing other duties, observing classes and participating in the life of the school community. At the next level, forming the backdrop to the schools was the complex set of formal and informal relationships orchestrated by the municipality of Bahçelik at the local level. These had, as alluded to earlier, a significant impact on the lives and fortunes of the schools. The third layer of influence had to do with the changing educational discourses at the national level and the debates and constant policy changes these generated. Finally, I could see the effects on the schools of the educational standard setting instruments developed by global governance institutions, such as the United Nations (UN) and its specialist agencies and the European Union (EU), and how their adoption by national governments gave rise to initiatives that impacted schools. In fact, pedagogy at the school level reflected a complex sedimentation of influences emanating from all four levels, often clashing and colliding in contradictory ways, and sometimes creating unintended consequences.

Alongside participant observation and my daily immersion in the activities of the schools, I recorded thirty-nine interviews with teachers, twenty of which were at Zinnur and nineteen at Talip. Ten teachers (six in Zinnur and four in Talip) did not want me to record the interviews; instead, they asked me to take notes, which I did (For the full list of interviews see Appendix I). These took the form of conversations structured around certain main themes, touching on education in general and the school in particular, with enough flexibility to pursue topics introduced by the respondents. Although at the start I put great store in what the teachers said, I found that my observations served as a means of checking and triangulation. I used all the diverse occasions available to me: I attended marriage ceremonies, *mevlid* (veneration of the Prophet Muhammad), *kına gecesi* (henna night), dinners, picnics, shopping trips, funerals, brunches and dinners with teachers.[5] So, whether belly dancing, laughing, crying, praying, singing or joking I took part in many events that punctuated the collective life of Zinnur School. Socializing with young single female teachers and male teachers in the municipal park became a weekly routine without which many of my in-depth interviews would not have been possible. I conducted two focus group interviews in Zinnur and two focus group interviews in Talip with Year Eight pupils to get a feel for their aspirations and concerns. I also attended parent-teacher meetings predominantly attended by mothers at both schools and conducted two focus group discussions with the parents at each location.

Moreover, I made extensive use of archives, official documents and the internet. Some of my micro-level findings only became fully intelligible after rigorous research on secondary sources, which fleshed out the macro-context of educational policies. Last but not least, I conducted key informant interviews with a range of experts in the field of education as well as organizations centrally involved in policymaking (see Appendix I). Having access to the two distinct school microcosms technically belonging to the category of 'state school' gave me a better grasp of the effects of nationwide educational policies and how these are mediated by district-level and school-level managers.

Finally, I expanded the scope of my research to include 'adjunct institutions', such as libraries, education and culture centres run by the Bahçelik municipality, and a dormitory where some of the pupils lived, when I discovered their decisive impact not just on access to educational services but to processes of gender socialization. I attended almost all the major cultural events of the municipality that targeted either primary school pupils or their mothers and the events held by Islamic communities including an old Islamic *tariqa* order in Turkey, that I name the Hidayet community (a pseudonym), celebration of the International Turkish Language Olympics (*Uluslararası Türkçe Olimpiyatları*) of Gülen community and various other commemorations.

I present my finding in the five chapters to follow. Chapter 2 provides the background to my empirical chapters by analysing key turning points in the history of education in Turkey from the republic to the AKP period, with special reference to primary education. My periodization starts with the early republic's educational policies and traces transformations that culminate in the structural adjustment policies adopted after the 1980 military coup, leading to educational deregulation and privatization. The final section on the AKP period distinguishes between three stages with significantly different orientations, culminating in the shift to the '4+4+4' education system and the eventual eviction of the Gülen community from their prominent position as educational providers after their breakup with the AKP.

Chapter 3 offers an analysis of neoliberal policies in the education sector and their effects on state primary education. Although neoliberal reforms in the education sector are global in nature, marking a shift to SBM systems across the world, I concentrate on the specific ways in which these changes play out in Turkey and in the specific contexts of Zinnur and Talip Schools and the idiosyncratic local implementation of the SBM system. My findings concur with the literature on primary school finance that shows that endemic budgetary shortfalls are mainly compensated by the parents and the Parent Teacher Associations (*Okul Aile Birliği*, OAB), and that these further increase inequality in education since they reflect disparities in the wealth and social capital of the parents. However, unlike most studies that put the OABs at the centre of their analysis, I trace the education market through Zinnur and Talip. I illustrate how Bahçelik municipality intervenes as a provider of resources and examine closely how everyday school life is dominated by budgetary concerns. Formal and informal actors in education that claim to level inequalities by offering free educational services such as the *bilgi evi* (house of knowledge) of Bahçelik municipality and the dormitory of the Hidayet community are also featured in this chapter.

Chapter 4 provides a window to the 'culture wars' that have been raging in the domain of education. In this chapter I selectively take two school commemorations: First, I focus on the Day of Commemoration of the Adoption of the National Anthem and Mehmet Akif Ersoy which observes the day when *İstiklal Marşı* ('March of Independence') was officially adapted as Turkey's national anthem to honour its writer Mehmet Akif Ersoy. Then I examine the week during which the Prophet Muhammad was venerated in schools which was then named Holy Birth Week (*Kutlu Doğum Haftası*). These provide illustrations of the attempt to substitute a new foundational narrative of the nation, side-lining and superseding the official narrative of the republic. The focus shifts in Chapter 5 to the surveillance and control mechanisms that have been introduced into schools. I analyse the multiplicity of surveillance mechanisms, from closed-circuit television (CCTV) cameras to teachers being on 'guard duty'.

Although some of these measures originate in the 'secure school' framework, its applications in schools are selective and idiosyncratic – whether we look at the use of CCTV cameras or security practices involving 'visiting' police officers. Recent developments and debates on the dress code of teachers are also treated as part and parcel of control mechanisms, to the extent that they are related to the 'disciplining' of female teachers' attire and bodies.

Chapter 6 analyses the schools as gendered institutions and examines how diverse femininities and masculinities are constructed in everyday interactions. Male and female teachers, who describe their own practices with reference to familial ideologies and gender stereotypes of maternal nurturance vs paternal authority, contribute to constructing the gender regime of the school by acting out normative expectations of familial roles in the school context. The feminization of the parental role (where 'parent' and 'mother' become co-terminous) is further reinforced at the local level by the activities of the municipality and the AKP neighbourhood women's branch that promote a particular vision of motherhood. The school thus contributes to the entrenchment of idealized normative femininities and masculinities and marginalizes others considered as deviant.

I conclude that all the elements of the educational culture of the schools have a bearing on the pedagogy of gender differences. Taken together, these signal a radical departure from the republican drive towards gender equality. Although the diffusion of alternative norms of gender segregation and female modesty does not necessarily take pedagogically explicit forms, they are best captured through a capillary network of diverse influences bolstered by the day-to-day interactions of pupils, teachers, head teachers and deputy heads in schools.

The contested terrain: Education in Turkey from the republic to the AKP

In this chapter, I aim to offer a broad overview of the educational landscape in Turkey with particular reference to state primary education. My intention is not to rehash the 'official' details of almost a century-long history of state primary education, but rather to elucidate the socio-economic and cultural transformations that informed and motivated educational policies, as well as reforms to state primary education. It is hard to claim that the critical analysis of education in Turkey has led to a consolidated body of research. On the contrary, one can speak of diverse scholarly niches. One of these niches concerns the analysis of key turning points in education (Akyüz 2006; Berkes 1998; Fortna 2002; Kazamias 1966; Sakaoğlu 2003; Somel 2001). Another set of studies attempt the close examination of state ideologies, such as the Kemalist ideology and the Turkish-Islamic Synthesis (*Türk İslam Sentezi*) and their effects on curriculum content (Copeaux 2000; Ersanlı-Behar 1992; Kaplan 1999; Kaplan 2006).

In relation to state ideology, we also have in-depth studies of militarism as reflected in educational content (Altınay 2004b; Kancı 2007). The third niche of studies focuses on landmark institutions such as *imam-hatip* (prayer leader and preacher) schools (Aksit 1991; Gökaçtı 2005; Ozgur 2012), Girls' Institutes (*Kız Enstitüleri*) (Akşit 2005; Gök 2007a), Village Institutes (*Köy Enstitüleri*) (Kirby 2010; Makal 2008) and cultural centres such as People's Houses (*Halkevleri*) (Öztürkmen 1998). Finally, we have detailed studies on the educational endeavours of Islamic communities (Balcı 2005; Turam 2007). All these studies contribute to the understanding of the ways in which education in Turkey has evolved from the turn of the twentieth century to the present. I agree with Benjamin Fortna (2002) that periodization has significant implications and more often than not serves ideological purposes. However, given the scope of this study, I had to limit my focus. I have divided the temporal span of my overview into four main sections.

I start with the establishment of the republic and analyse the role of state education in the regime change from empire to nation state. The second section focuses on the years between 1950 and 1980, where I analyse the ways in which the mobilization of youth laid the foundations for various ideologies that shaped education in the following decades. More specifically, I focus on the 'birth' of the Turkish-Islamic Synthesis, which became the official ideology of the 1980s, and the 're-birth' of *imam-hatip* schools that were transformed from vocational institutions into mainstream schools during the AKP period. The third section provides an overview of the 1980s and 1990s, and the final section covers the AKP period from 2002 to 2016.

The early republic and the single-party period: The republican ideals

Imagining the everyday schooling of a male or a female pupil in state primary schools during the early 1920s when the Republic of Turkey was newly established is not that easy. This is partly because these were years that set the scene for colossal transitions for Turkey, as was the case for many newly established countries that were once a part of the Ottoman Empire. The difference with Turkey was that it had inherited its Ottoman past, yet the reformers of the time – led by Mustafa Kemal Atatürk (1881–1938) – decided to renounce the remnants of this past like many revolutionaries before them. Therefore, particularly during the first decade of the republic, society witnessed both miniscule changes and major reforms in almost all institutions. At least for a period, this created Janus-faced institutions: looking to the future as envisioned by the revolutionaries and looking to the remnants of the Ottoman Empire which were transformed into a past to be forgotten (Berkes 1998). Those readers who have been exposed to the simplifying master narrative of republicanism in Turkey would find this amorphous state of affairs puzzling, for textbooks in state schools at all levels – including universities – still narrate Atatürk's reforms as if they happened overnight. There were, indeed, reforms such as the change of the alphabet (Fortna 2011); however, particularly in education, reforms have short-term, long-term, expected and unexpected outcomes, implications and repercussions. There is always a hiatus between the ideal and actual practice. For instance, had the sultans of the Ottoman Empire – particularly those who introduced educational reforms before the establishment of the republic – foreseen that these modernization endeavours would pave the way for a revolution against the Ottoman state, they might have acted differently.

Public primary education was, in fact, quite diverse during these transition years in Turkey. One of the main reasons for this was the opposition from both the Sunni Muslim clergy (*ulema*) and religious and ethnic minorities: these groups considered state interference in primary education to be a threat to their religious autonomy (Berkes 1998; Kazamias 1966). During the Hamidian Era, a significant effort was made to establish modern institutions for the public good, with political, cultural and economic motives (Deringil 2011; Fortna 2002; Somel 2001). These modern institutions, which, by and large, were adapted to the needs of the Empire, functioned side by side with the traditional institutions, namely the *medrese* (religious school) system (Berkes 1998; Fortna 2002). However, primary education lagged behind the developments that took place at the secondary- and higher-education levels (Berkes 1998; Kazamias 1966).

The vernacular schools and the diverse religiously based systems were abolished, and all the educational institutions started to be controlled by the state after the introduction of the Law on the Unification of Education (*Tevhid-i Tedrisat Kanunu*) in 1924 (Berkes 1998), introducing a unified universal education system regardless of ethnic, religious and gender differences. The education of girls was seen as a significant marker of progress in a secular, modern Turkey (Acar & Ayata 2002; Akşit 2005; Arat 1997; Gök 1995; Helvacıoğlu 1996; Kağıtçıbaşı 2010; Kandiyoti 1987, 1989, 1992; Navaro-Yashin 2002a; Özyürek 2006; Tan 1994). Thus, the republic's modernization process not only improved women's status in society with the new civil code and universal suffrage, but it also legitimized women's public presence and mobility through education (Acar & Ayata 2002; Arat 1997; Kandiyoti 1987). However, initially, the periphery remained mostly untouched by the changes that were emerging at the centre (Kandiyoti 1991: 11).

The establishment of the Girls' Institutes in 1928, the People's Houses in 1932 and the Village Institutes in 1937 played a significant role in the extension of educational provision (Gök 2007b). Girls' Institutes were secondary vocational schools for training girls with the aim of 'modernizing' the household (Akşit 2005; Gök 2007a; Navaro-Yashin 2002a), which offers deep insights into the gender regime of the Kemalist modernization project. Although the curriculum of these institutions was identical across the country, in many ways there were significant differences between the institutions in the western and eastern provinces. For example, Girls' Institutes which were opened in cities with a high Kurdish population served the goal of assimilation.[1] People's Houses, which were run by the Republican People's Party (*Cumhuriyet Halk Partisi*, CHP), were centres disseminating the republican ideology through cultural activities.[2] Village Institutes explicitly aimed to reach the rural periphery, a rupture in policy having the same weight as the unification of education.[3]

In a nutshell, Village Institutes were designed to prepare the would-be-teacher, who was the daughter/son of peasants, for the hardships of rural society and to enhance her/his skills to develop lives in the villages (Kirby 2010). Imagine a teacher who is almost perfect in his/her subject areas, who can play Mozart on a violin or can play Turkish folk music with *saz*, a bookworm with practical knowledge on animal breeding, including fish breeding or beekeeping, agriculture, tailoring or building.[4] However this depiction should not mislead one since distinguishing feature of these institutions was not only their curriculum but also their pedagogy. İsmail Hakkı Tonguç (1893–1960), for example, one of the founding fathers of these institutes, saw the purpose of education as developing action, raising consciousness, and at the same time gaining knowledge and applying that knowledge to diagnose and solve problems (Özsoy 2004). Having said that, the main aim of these institutes was the capillary dissemination of modern/secular values throughout Turkish society. From 1937 to 1954, over almost three decades, the graduates of these institutions who were predominantly male (Gök 2007a) touched the lives of the villages and acted as 'organic intellectuals' in the Gramscian sense.

Illiteracy was one of the biggest challenges, and Village Institutes were not the only ones working to eradicate it. Literacy campaigns, particularly those targeting adult literacy, from the early years of the republic had a great impact on the lives of people in rural and urban areas as well (Sayılan & Yıldız 2009; Taşçı-Günlü 2008). Especially, compulsory military service played a significant role in increasing the literacy rates of men compared to women.[5] When it comes to state primary schools there were 341,941 registered pupils during the 1923–4 school year (TÜİK 2009: 68). And again, there was a huge gender disparity; while there were 273,107 male pupils, the number of female pupils was 62,954 (TÜİK 2009: 68). It is significant to mention that these numbers cover the period before the change of the alphabet from Arabo-Persian to Latin, which had long-term repercussions, such as breaking the link between the older generations and those who were born after the late 1920s (Fortna 2011; Parla 2008).

In addition, while some European states adopted textbook revisions in the aftermath of the Second World War as a part of the post-war reconciliation process (Pingel 2010), Turkey's 'Turkification' policies, which started right after the constitutional period of 1908, were reinvigorated with the nationalist

Turkish History Thesis (*Türk Tarih Tezi*) and the Sun Language Theory (*Güneş Dil Teorisi*). Anthropology was used as a truth claim for the history writing process (Hanioğlu 2011). This discourse also privileged Turkishness, tracing its roots to Central Asia (Hanioğlu 2011). Şükrü Hanioğlu (2011: 165) explains the motives of Mustafa Kemal in introducing a 'revisionist interpretation of human history', as follows:

> To validate the new regime Mustafa Kemal wished to erase any traces of Ottoman history. The best way to accomplish this goal was to present the Ottoman experience as no more than a modest footnote to a long and glorious past, and in the process subvert the role of Islam entirely, transforming it from the cement of Ottoman power to the principal cause of Turkic decline.

It was accepted, for example, that the Turkish 'race' is above all a distinct 'race' with its perceived essential characteristics (Copeaux 2000). According to Tuba Kancı, it was during the 1930s that textbooks started to be structured in line with the Turkish History Thesis, and this restructuring was not limited to history textbooks (2007: 110).[6]

Parallel to these developments, there were continuing debates over the ideology of the Kemalist regime, which were captured in the vernacular by Islamist journals and newspapers – such as re-emergence of banned pan-Islamist journal *Sırat-ı Müstakim* ('True Path') with a new name, *Sebülireşşad* ('Straight Path') during the last years of 1940s (Brockett 2011: 60–3). At the turn of the 1940s, the founding father of Nurcu movement in Turkey, a prominent Islamist Bediüzzaman Said Nursi (1878–1960), 'penetrated Anatolian society' with *Risale-i Nur* ('Epistels of Light') (Brockett 2011: 129). This is significant due to the fact that the current Nurcu movement represents a revival. Although *laicism* was described in the official narrative as the separation of the state from Islam, in response to the Ottoman state strategically 'injecting' Islam into the education system during the Hamidian era, in practice it meant state control of Islam (Fortna 2002). In this vein, in the name of 'rationalising religion' higher-education institutions such as the theology institutes and religious vocational schools, namely *imam-hatip* schools, were founded (Berkes 1998: 484–5). These religious vocational schools were designed to teach the knowledge needed to provide Islamic worship services inside the mosque.[7] Due to a gradual decrease in the number of pupils, they were later closed (Gökaçtı 2005); yet, the contemporary alumni believe that the Kemalist regime simply scrapped these schools (Ozgur 2012).

Mustafa Kemal Atatürk's project of modernity was 'a total project' (Keyder 1997: 37) that aimed to transform every sphere of life by overthrowing the

Sultanate, abolishing the institution of caliphate, adopting the Latin alphabet, introducing dress reform, enfranchising women and adopting a modern civil code (Abadan-Unat 1982; Arat 1997; Kandiyoti 1991; Tekeli 1982). This project was to encounter significant resistance after the transition to a multi-party democracy.

The transition to multi-party democracy, the Cold War and military coups

The austerity regime of the single-party period in the shadow of the Second World War ended with the transition to the multi-party period and the North Atlantic Treaty Organization (NATO) accession (Berkes 1998; Zürcher 2004). A barefoot, roadless, poor and illiterate country was persevering with statist policies under the guidance of the Kemalist elite (Ahmad 2002). The electoral victory of the Democrat Party (*Demokrat Parti*, DP) was the harbinger of change, which would have significant repercussions in the educational domain. One of the key changes was the gradual transition from state-led development to a market-led economy. The processes of commodification that were set in motion in the agricultural sector took their toll on rural Anatolia and triggered waves of migration from rural to urban areas (Keyder 1987). The acceptance of the United States' Marshall Plan, which aimed for the economic recovery of Europe in the immediate post-Second World War period, could be seen as the epitome of the political and economic shift introduced by the DP government (Ahmad 2002; Zürcher 2004). Another key change, in the words of Niyazi Berkes who was clearly a staunch secularist, was that 'the government of 1950s gave free reign to all sorts of obscurantism under the guise of restoring the freedom of religion and in the name of democracy' (Berkes 1998: 503). The tremors of those shifts could be felt in education.

A significant change was the sudden closure of the Village Institutes in 1954. These institutes, which were intended to consolidate the hegemony of the elites and 'enlighten' 'backward' Anatolia, morphed into the bedrock of a leftist student movement (Ahmad 2002; Altunya 2010; Kirby 2010). The teachers and students also rejected the status quo of the CHP (Karaömerlioğlu 1998). The DP government re-opened the *imam-hatip* schools. In line with these new developments, a wide range of religious journals increased their audience and the discussions over Muslim identity and the role of Islam in society started to gain state recognition with the official publication of *Risale-i*

Nur, 'which became the standard-bearer among publications concerned with emphasizing the importance of Islam to the Turkish nation' (Brockett 2011: 130). Yet approximately 80 per cent of the female population in the 1950s was illiterate, while only about 45 per cent of the male population was literate (TÜİK 2012: 19).

The left-wing, anti-imperialist intellectuals started criticizing the engagement of the DP government with the United States during the 1960s. For them it meant the acceptance of market liberalism, complying with the imperial endeavours of the United States and taking sides in the unfolding Cold War. Yet these ideas were limited to leftist circles, and the hegemonic discourse was that of anti-communism, which led the DP to take measures such as censorship of the national press (Örnek & Üngör 2013: 7–8). However, the popular DP government lost its appeal, particularly in the economic depression, which cast a shadow over the late 1950s. On 27 May 1960, the first military coup reshuffled politics; this is defined as the Second Republic by Erik J. Zürcher (2004). The prime minister and two ministers were hanged after long and humiliating trials. With the new constitution ratified in 1961, which is reputed to be the most progressive constitution in Turkey,[8] diverse student movements and unionization attempts found fertile ground (Ahmad 2002; Zürcher 2004).

Within a relatively short time the unions radicalized. One of the most high-profile organizations was the Turkish Teachers' Union (*Türkiye Öğretmenler Sendikası*, TÖS). Almost all the teachers working for the state were members of TÖS and their members became more critical of the government's growing relationship with the United States, or as left-wing teachers and students would put it 'capitalists and imperialists' (TÖS 1969). The Revolutionary Education Council (*Devrimci Eğitim Şûrası*) born out of TÖS was held as a reaction to the official National Education Council (*Milli Eğitim Şûrası*) that reviews and formulates educational policies almost every four or five years (TÖS 1969).[9] To mark the end of the meeting of the Revolutionary Education Council, all the attendees read the pledge – written by well-known left-wing poet Can Yücel who succinctly summarized the ideals of the teachers with his impeccable skill, paraphrasing the pledge to the nation:

> I'm a Turk, upright and revolutionary. My principle is to protect my country from internal and external foes and develop my homeland as soon as possible. My goal is to provide work to the worker, soil to the peasant, milk to the baby, bread and book to the child, and build a future for youth. May my being be a gift to national liberation and freedom.
>
> (TÖS 1969: 505)

While unions such as TÖS were looking for a radical transformation, the rise of the political left was brutally suppressed with the 12 March 1972 coup. State violence following the coup traumatized those who were active in the movement.[10] Nevertheless, the 1960s and 1970s were a period of global turbulence that witnessed youth protests across the world. Turkey was not insulated from these phenomena, although each student movement had its own context-specific characteristics. The Turkish movement might be divided into two broad camps with right-wing and left-wing tendencies; there were differences among the youth within these opposing camps as well (Saktanber & Beşpınar 2012: 274).

Right-wing students and intellectuals who had their own visions of the future were also developing new discourses and finding channels to disseminate their ideas. There were also newly emerging local reactions imbued with Islam as well as nationalism, such as the well-funded Association for Fighting Communism (*Komünizmle Mücadele Derneği*), which coincided with the anti-communist discourses that gained greater currency during the Cold War (Kenar & Gürpınar 2013: 22–5; Taşkın 2002). There was a wide range of right-wing youth groups with leanings towards Turkish nationalism or a blend of Islam with Turkish nationalism. The National Turkish Students Union (*Milli Türk Talebe Birliği*) is one such example. Although initially this association was the ideological voice of the CHP during the single party period, it evolved towards two tendencies: one was 'conservative Muslim' (*milliyetçi-mukaddesatçı*) and another line was 'ultra-nationalist' (*ülkücü*). The Turkish-Islamic Synthesis promoted by the Hearth of the Enlightened (*Aydınlar Ocağı*), founded in 1970, merged two ideologies into a new hybrid that amalgamated Turkishness with Sunni Islam.

Islamist youth could also gravitate towards the National Salvation Party (*Milli Selamet Partisi*, MSP) with ideological roots in National Outlook (*Milli Görüş*) as proposed by Necmettin Erbakan in 1969, aiming to reform society in accordance with Islamic principles (Toprak 1988). This party initiated the quasi-official emergence of *tariqa* (Muslim brotherhoods) and *cemaat* (communities) in the public sphere, which were officially abolished during the early years of the republic (Toprak 1988).[11] They were perceived as the voice of 'conservative Muslims' (*mukadessatçı*). They argued that the national values, beliefs and traditions of society were abandoned by the Kemalist state years ago and that the left-wing students, teachers and workers abandoned these values during the 1960s. In addition, Necmettin Erbakan considered *imam-hatip* schools as the backbone of 'Great Turkey' (Mardin 2006: 277). By the time the CHP entered into a coalition with the Islamist MSP in 1973, the stance towards religious education had become more flexible. This was clearly reflected in the educational policies of the 1970s. In particular, the number of lower and upper secondary *imam-hatip* schools, which doubled within a decade, was increased (Aksit 1991: 146–7). Moreover, in the second half of the 1960s, about 40,000 students were enrolled in these schools, and by the end of the 1970s this number had risen to over 100,000 (Aksit 1991: 146–7).

The growing numbers of clashes between rival youth groups on the left and right were followed by another *coup d'état* in 1980. Further massive changes were ushered in, marking key turning points in the domain of education. After the military coup, the Turkish-Islamic Synthesis was adopted as the state ideology at a point when the revival of Islam was used as a means of combatting both communism (in the broader context of the Cold War) and the fear of Kurdish separatism.

Decades of turmoil: 1980s and 1990s

The 1980s and 1990s were key turning points in the history of Turkey. Broadly speaking, direct and indirect military interventions, economic liberalization, increasing globalization, the revival of civil society and alternative identity politics (including the rise of political Islam and Kurdish ethno-nationalism) have marked these two decades (Kandiyoti 2012; Kasaba 1997; Keyder 1997; Zürcher 2004). There was a struggle, that 'seem[ed] to be between the old authoritarian-modernizations, paternalistic state, with its crumbling nationalist and populist legitimation, and a modernist conception of political liberalism and citizenship' (Keyder 1997: 48). These transformations challenged the values and ideals of the Kemalist modernization project, reflected in a wide variety of institutions (Keyder 1997). While education was a tool for social mobility and the levelling of gender differences in the early years of the republic, Islamization policies coupled with the liberalization of the economy after the 1980 military coup would have significant repercussions on education.

After the dissolution of parliament by the September 1980 *coup d'état*, the legal framework of the education system – at both primary and secondary levels – changed dramatically under the 1982 Constitution. First, a compulsory course named Atatürk's Principles and Reforms was included in the curriculum of all formal educational institutions (Kaplan 1999). Second, the restrictions that prevented graduates of the *imam-hatip* school from studying in faculties other than theology faculties were lifted. As a result, the *imam-hatip* schools became an alternative route to mobility and a cradle for the growth of Islamic constituencies (Ozgur 2012). For example, while there were 101 lower and upper secondary *imam-hatip* schools between 1969 and 1970, by the 1987–8 school year there were more than 700 with about 240,000 students (Aksit 1991: 146–7). The increasing proportion of girls was also striking, reaching 50 per cent in the late 1990s (Bozan 2007: 26).

Third, the religious culture and moral knowledge (*Din Kültürü ve Ahlak Bilgisi*) course, which teaches Sunni Islam, was made compulsory in both primary and secondary schools (Kaplan 1999). Therefore, the combination of Kemalism with Islam, known as the Turkish-Islamic Synthesis, became the official ideology of the education system (Kaplan 2002; Zürcher 2004). Sam Kaplan argues that 'Islamic heritage' was used 'to foster national unity' with a highly militaristic tone, to such an extent that primary-school textbooks glorified dying to protect the nation by drawing on an Islamic understanding of martyrdom (2002: 114–15). By injecting Islam into the national curriculum and supporting the expansion of religious education, the military engaged in a paradoxical enterprise. On the one hand, the military claimed to 'restore "true Kemalism"' (Ahmad 199: 18), while on the other hand it aimed to use Islam as a panacea against the 'communist menace' (Sakallioglu 1996: 246). This intervention was an attempt not only to shape the immediate indoctrination of the students, but also to socialize subsequent generations. Moreover, the liberalization of the economy was followed by cuts in the public sector, and the structural adjustment policies imposed by the International Monetary Fund (IMF) had a detrimental effect on state education. Thus, the sharp decline in the funds allocated to state education began in the 1980s (Gök 1995, 2005). These changes also led to increasing privatization and deregulation of education provision, although the demand for state education increased (Ercan & Uzunyayla 2009; Gök 2002; Gök & Ilgaz 2007; Rutz & Balkan 2009).

In broader terms, the 1990s were marked by both Kurdish conflict, which led to the largest internal migration in the country's history, and the 28 February 1997 process, which has often been likened to a postmodern *coup d'état*. First, escalation of the conflict between the Kurdish separatists and the Turkish Armed Forces (*Türk Silahlı Kuvvetleri,* TSK) had detrimental impact on education, following the largest demographic shift in the country's history from rural to urban areas with the displacement of Kurdish villages in the eastern and south-eastern regions (Yörük 2012). Various effects of such shift hindered access to education (Cemalcilar & Gökşen 2012). Significant changes included the closure of village schools, which also led to overcrowding in primary schools in big cities and further exacerbated regional disparities in education across the country (Şaşmaz 2015). Second, unlike the military coup of 1980, which dissolved parliament, the 28 February military intervention 'restricted itself to making "recommendations" to the coalition government' (Tuğal 2009: 46). This intervention, which Zürcher calls 'Kemalist restoration', forced the government to restrict religious education (2004: 300). This was a reaction to growing Islamization, which was perceived by the military as a threat to the secular state (Tuğal 2009; Zürcher 2004). There were three major repercussions in the field of education: reforming primary education, limiting the expansion of religious schools and restricting the function of the Qur'an schools (Tuğal 2009). By demanding eight years of primary education, the military had in fact been aiming to eliminate the lower secondary schools (Year Six, Year Seven and Year Eight) of the *imam-hatip* system (Gökaçtı 2005).[12] The reason for this was that the 'military reclaimed the image' of *imam-hatip* schools as a breeding ground for training Islamists, and therefore the early-age intake of *imam-hatip* schools was interrupted by the introduction of the eight-year basic education (Mardin 2006: 277). On 16 July 1997, a new law 1997 Basic Education Reform was passed that made eight-year basic education compulsory for all pupils between the ages of seven and fourteen. A decree established the age of twelve (Year Six) as the minimum age for attendance at Qur'an courses under the supervision of the MEB, which were previously under the supervision of the Presidency of Religious Affairs (*Diyanet İşleri Başkanlığı*, DİB). For graduates of *imam-hatip* school, access to higher education was again restricted, except in the case of theology faculties.[13] As we shall see in what follows, the educational policies under the AKP between 2002 and 2016 resulted in a total reversal and dismantling of the changes introduced by the 28 February intervention. What disappeared in the shadow of the power struggle, however, was the introduction of the 1997 basic education reform, one of the most comprehensive plans to expand access to education (Dülger 2004). The Marmara earthquake in August 1999 and the economic crisis of 2001 further worsened the situation in education, but the AKP ignited hope when it first came to power in 2002.

The AKP period: From 2002 until the 15 July 2016

The AKP period could be divided into four sub-periods: The first period covers the first six years between 2002 and 2007 during which educational reforms were carried out as part of the European Union (EU) accession process, at a point when the government presented itself as 'conservative liberal democrats'. 'We took off our National Outlook shirts', said Recep Tayyip Erdoğan – renouncing the links between his newly formed party and its predecessor, the Welfare Party (*Refah Partisi*, RP). During this initial period, there was an effort at harmonization with international standard-setting instruments in the domain of education (as in other sectors). Within the second period (2007–11) the alliance between AKP and Gülen community became visible, and they both reconfigured the civil society and introduced new legal frameworks. In the third period (2012–16) the government started to introduce its own educational policies more forcefully and initiated new waves of reforms. These included the reversal of the eight-year compulsory primary schooling and the shift to the 4+4+4 education system which was followed by the visible breakup between the Gülen community and the AKP that came to a head during the allegations of corruption levelled at the government in November 2013. After the failed coup of 15 July, which is still unfolding, Gülen community was labelled as a Fethullahist Terrorist Organization (*Fethullahçı Terör Örgütü*, FETÖ). Extensive purges of members of the police, judiciary, bureaucracy, Gülen-affiliated corporations, the media and education followed and are still taking place. This rift had significant repercussions in the educational domain. However, I do not cover this period. In what follows I start with the first period.

Igniting hope: 'Reformist conservative democrats' (2002–7)

Although privatization, decentralization and the expansion of vocational education were on the AKP's official party documents in 2002–3 (Şaşmaz 2015: 9), they were initially less clear about what shape the education system should take. The very first AKP education minister Erkan Mumcu, who had been in office for less than a year, candidly said that the government did not have a 'comprehensive' plan for education (Somel & Nohl 2014: 133). This changed with the appointment of Hüseyin Çelik as Minister of Education in 2003, a post he held until 2009. In the meantime, the agenda of 'global education reform' manifested in the Education for All (EFA) framework continued to determine education policy (Aydagül 2007; Dülger 2004; Şaşmaz 2015).[14] The 'eight-year and uninterrupted' (formerly: five-year) compulsory primary education programme of 1997 epitomized this 'reform' attempt to bring education in line with international standards. The AKP government adopted these long-term 'reform' efforts in education, following the lead of global institutions such as United Nation's Children Fund (UNICEF) and the World Bank (WB), while at the same time having to comply with IMF conditionalities that mandated austerity measures in the public sector (Aydagül 2007). The EU also gained further influence in policymaking in Turkey. The AKP government was eager to meet the EU targets set at the Copenhagen Summit in 2002, which paved the way for Turkey's accession negotiations in 2005 (Öniş 2009). This laid the foundation for numerous reforms in the public sector that had a significant impact on education. Moreover, in the first six years of its rule, the AKP gave the first signs of reshaping civil society and yet, in contrast to the previous decade, the field of education was relatively colourful. In this context, the AKP set three priorities in primary education: (i) further expansion of primary education; (ii) increasing privatization; (iii) curriculum reform and revision of textbook content. A brief summary of these areas is in order.

Further expansion of education and the 'Hey Girls, Let's Go to School!' campaign

Priority was given to increasing access to primary education through the enhancing of existing policies and programmes. In this regard, AKP expanded the pupil transport programme (known as bus transport for pupils in small settlements), increased the number of boarding primary schools in rural settlements – known as regional boarding primary schools (*Yatılı İl Bölge Okulları*, YİBO) – and continued to invest in the construction of new classrooms in order to reduce number of double-shift schools (one group of pupils taught in the morning and another in the afternoon), which were widespread in these years both in big cities like Istanbul and in the south-eastern and eastern provinces (Aydagül 2007; Şaşmaz 2015). Further steps were taken in 2003 with the implementation of the Hey Girls, Let's Go to School (*Haydi Kızlar Okula*, HKO) campaign, which aimed to eliminate gender disparity in access to schooling. Measures to promote access to education also included the distribution of free textbooks in 2004 (Özmen 2012; Yolcu 2014) and the expansion of the conditional education assistance programme, which targeted predominantly Kurdish parents (Beleli 2012; Yörük 2012). It is not possible to go into each policy individually as they are quite complex. However, a brief summary of the HKO, which was initiated by the MEB with UNICEF as part of a global campaign to achieve universal schooling for girls, is necessary as the HKO has contributed to the elimination of gender disparity nationwide, informed future policies and exposed significant inequalities.

The HKO was launched in 2003 after the then Minister of Education, Hüseyin Çelik, made girls' education one of the MEB's top priorities. This was in response to the UNICEF report, which estimated that about 800,000 children (aged six to fourteen) in the country were not in school (Şaşmaz 2015: 9–10). Girls' access to school, if not the expansion of education, was on the AKP's political agenda before it came to power (Şaşmaz 2015: 9–10). However, HKO offered an opportunity for the newly elected AKP to show its commitment to global governance institutions in its first term. The campaign had three phases: (i) conception and preparation (2002–3); (ii) development and social mobilization 2004–6; (iii) institutionalization (from 2007 onwards) (Şaşmaz 2015; YADA 2011). In the first phase of the campaign, ten provinces were selected that had the lowest literacy rate in the country (Şaşmaz 2015; YADA 2011). This phase was the most difficult and only successful because HKO was sensitive to the context of each province (Çameli 2008). The second phase involved working at both the local and national levels. At the local level, this meant working with local bureaucrats from ministries such as the Ministry of Interior and institutions such as the DİB, cooperating with local civil society actors, using the technical support of UNICEF, and getting teachers and local bureaucrats to visit parents (Çameli 2008; Şaşmaz 2015; YADA 2011). At the national level, it was possible to mobilize public, private and civil society actors (Aydagül 2007). In the meantime, HKO was already extended to all eighty-one provinces in 2006. In the third phase, MEB developed new strategies and projects and revised the existing ones to institutionalize what HKO had started. Overall, HKO brought up to 350,000 more children into primary school (Beleli 2012: 65). According to Batuhan Aydagül (2007) the campaign led to a 'paradigm shift' in education policymaking in the sense that the voice of civil society actors was heard, as were the stakeholder consultations and the need for evidence-based policymaking was recognized. The pitfall of the HKO was giving too much attention to gender parity rather than gender equity although throughout the three phases of the HKO what became visible was that the categories of social class, ethnicity, disability, faith and gender simultaneously play roles in girls' access to school. In the following years, the focus gradually shifted to secondary education. The literature on the HKO suggests that MEB tried to address almost all the findings within its limits including but not limited to child labour. However, two important findings during the HKO campaign were not taken into account: one was the language barriers faced by girls whose mother tongue is Kurdish, and another one was religious values (YADA 2011).

Neoliberal policies: Privatization in many forms and selective decentralization

From the perspective of primary education, one of the biggest challenges in the first six years of the AKP was to find solutions to low public funding. During these years, we witnessed a steady transformation of education through neoliberal education policies (Gök 2007b; İnal & Akkaymak 2012; Okçabol 2009; Yolcu 2014). To start with privatization, first of all, there was a visible expansion of public-private partnerships that reinforced privatization. This includes the well-known 100% Support for Education campaign of 2003, which aimed to encourage the private sector to invest in education infrastructure through subsidies in the form of a 100 per cent tax deduction (Yolcu 2007: 127–8). Second, as part of the drive to transform schools into partially self-funding entities, the School-Based Management (SBM) system was introduced in 2005 (Yolcu 2007) which I discuss in more detail in Chapter 3.

Third, privatization was promoted through incentives for private institutions (Ercan & Uzunyayla 2009; Gök & Ilgaz 2007). Moreover, it is important to note that the AKP made two failed attempts to increase the number of private schools by introducing a voucher system for the state education system (Kurul 2012). The basic logic of this system was to offer vouchers to academically outperforming children from low-income families to attend to private schools. This is simply a redistribution of the budget allocated to state education to private schools, thereby reducing the resources of the state schools. The then President Ahmet Necdet Sezer vetoed this attempt (Yelken & Büyükcan 2015). The ministry again proposed the same education voucher system with minor changes; the second attempt also failed because of a veto. It had to wait until Abdullah Gül became president in 2007. Another very striking example of private sector support and privatization concerned the modalities of providing free textbooks. The MEB started to buy textbooks from the private sector that it had previously published in its own publishing houses (Yolcu 2014: 61). And these developments creating a market for textbooks invited entrepreneurs without a publishing background into this market (Özmen 2012: 51).

The early years of AKP also witnessed selective decentralization attempts in education. It would be fair to claim that the introduction of the SBM, in line with the drive to turn schools into partially self-funding entities, was one of the most significant changes in state primary education in this regard.

In addition, the new Municipality Law (2005), which meant devolution of significant power to the municipalities, had significant impact on the educational landscape (Official Gazette 2005a).[15]

Curriculum reform and clashing pedagogical approaches

The curriculum development project led by Professor Ziya Selçuk, who was then president of Board of Education and Discipline (*Talim Terbiye Kurulu Başkanlığı*, TTKB) – an influential department of the MEB with decision-making powers in curriculum design, educational assessment and content selection. Selçuk, who also became Minister of Education in 2018 and held the post until 2021, recommended a constructivist approach that emphasizes building knowledge through collaboration and cooperation between teachers and pupils, and takes into account pupil's different talents (Özmen 2012; Somel & Nohl 2014). However, the curriculum reform did not fit well into the existing structure of the education system (İnal & Akkaymak 2012). First, of course, it meant a change in pedagogy. However, the in-service training received by thousands of teachers who were not familiar with this new pedagogy was not enough to change their pedagogical perspectives. Moreover, these changes increased the need for materials, tools, resources and technology (such as the internet, books, etc.), which meant additional expenses for parents and teachers (see Chapter 3). Secondly, the necessary link between curriculum, pedagogy and assessment was not well established. The new curriculum had torn apart the structure of education, left teachers unprepared and led to inconsistencies and contradictions between the systems of teaching, assessment and testing (Koşar-Altınyelken & Akkaymak 2012).

In the meantime, new textbooks were written. Both curriculum and the textbooks were assessed with the project of Promoting Human Rights in Primary and Secondary School Textbooks by History Foundation in cooperation with Academy of Science and Human Rights Foundation known as the 'Human Rights in Textbooks' (Aydagül 2007). This led many civil society actors to direct their attention to the actual content of textbooks. Leading scholars and intellectuals in Turkey participated in the project by critically analysing the findings of this research, which offered an in-depth understanding of the content of textbooks.[16] Yet these initiatives had a relative impact on the content of textbooks, which was revised during the curriculum reform process (Tüzün 2009).

In 2005, MEB compiled a compulsory literature canon known as 100 Essential Works (*100 Temel Eser*). Turkey's lowest ranking among Organization for Economic Co-operation and Development (OECD) countries in terms of pupils' reading skills (MEB 2005: 120) may have been one of the reasons that led to such a compilation. However, this compulsory list met with criticism from the beginning, as it was claimed that this 'canon' would not capture the diversity of voices in society (ÇV 2009). Finally, the increasing incorporation of Islamic content into the curriculum was initially done haphazardly and therefore went unnoticed. One of the reasons for this oversight might be the widespread perception that the curriculum consists solely of the content of textbooks or selected books. For example, the revision of the list of dates for school celebrations called Significant Days and Weeks (*Belirli Gün ve Haftalar*) in 2005 (TD 2005: 637) was ignored because this list appears under the heading of 'social activities' or extra-curricular activities. Islamization would gain momentum in this ignored area of education and entrench itself through changes in extra-curricular school activities, which I discuss in Chapter 4. Another significant development was the revision of religious culture and moral knowledge (*Din Kültürü ve Ahlak Bilgisi*) courses in primary and secondary schools, which became compulsory with the 1982 Constitution, in 2005–6 (Kaymakcan 2007). Education Reform Initiative (*Eğitim Reform Girişimi*, ERG), which is one of the prominent civil society actors in education, opened the discussion on compulsory religious education in terms of content and pedagogy. This was significant in a context where this course was compulsory for Alevi pupils as well. However, the revision process had not changed the fact that core of the course stayed Sunni Islam (Kaymakcan 2007: 6).

***

Other attempts by the AKP are worth noting. Firstly, the attempt by the AKP to expand access to Qur'an courses in 2003 could be read as abolishing some of the limits imposed in the previous decade. A strong opposition to this attempt emerged and this revision was aborted. Nonetheless, the number of enrolled students (adults and children) was 90, 353 in more than 3000 Qur'an courses in the 2000–1 school year, and the number of these courses increased to 8,696 in the 2009–10 school year, a threefold increase within a decade (Yıldız 2012: 253). Secondly, the AKP gave strong support to *imam-hatip* schools. This was achieved by means of a regulation to integrate *imam-hatip* school graduates into university education – as mentioned previously, these students were restricted to the theology faculties prior to this.[17] In summary, the changes in state primary education during the first six years of the AKP reflected an amalgamation of global educational targets, reforms inspired by the EU accession process, and the influence of a dynamic and varied civil society.

***

AKP-Gülen Alliance (2007–11)

The AKP gained more confidence after its victories in the presidential and parliamentary elections and made its alliance with the Gülen community visible. These Islamist actors neither shared the same worldview nor had the same experience and knowledge in the field of education of the early 2010s. While the Gülen community had claimed to be a civil society actor with extensive organizations promoting *ılımlı* (moderate) Islam in Turkey and abroad (Balcı 2005; Bekim 2003; Turam 2007; Yavuz 2003), the AKP had its roots in the Islamic politics of National Outlook proposed by Necmettin Erbakan during the late 1960s that emphasizes *ummah* (the Muslim community) (Tuğal 2009). Moreover, the Gülen community had sustained involvement and expertise – from pedagogy to curriculum development through to teachers – in both the private and state education sectors, with its fervent members participating in the teaching profession and in educational markets that I summarize below. In contrast, the AKP embraced *imam-hatip* schools as its niche and continued to view the entire education system through the prism of these schools. By entwining Islamic ideology with the market, these two actors followed their respective interests within the boundaries that they both constructed between 2007 and 2011. Within this period both actors aimed to redesign civil society which had colossal impact on education.

Reconfiguring civil society and revising the legal framework

On 27 April 2007, the TSK published a statement on its website (known as the e-memorandum due to its being exclusively online) (Atasoy 2009). In the meantime, the parliamentary election, which was on 7 June, was also approaching. Briefly, the statement criticized the government for attacking the very foundation of the republic and for attempting to reconstruct its foundational values (Atasoy

2009). The statement was explicitly giving reference to the celebration in schools of the Holy Birth Week (*Kutlu Doğum Haftası*) (venerating the birth of the Prophet Muhammad) that had been observed since 1989 under the auspices of the DİB. Following the statement from the TSK, the proponents of secularism – and particularly those non-governmental organizations (NGOs) that perceived themselves to be the protectors of republican secular ideals – took to the streets in public demonstrations, which are known as the Republican rallies (*Cumhuriyet mitingleri*) (Kuzmanovic 2013). The large majority of protestors were uncomfortable with both the AKP's push to soften Islam's separation from public life and extreme secularists' push for the military to remove the AKP from power. Yet the most puzzling development to leave its mark on society was the onset of the messy and extensive *Ergenekon* investigation, a judicial investigation that started in June 2007 with 'the discovery of a crate of grenades in Istanbul shanty town' (Jenkins 2009: 9) and ended with the dismissal of all charges in 2015 after the accused served lengthy jail sentences. What started out as an attempt to prosecute TSK officers – almost from all ranks of the military hierarchy – who were alleged to have plotted a coup to overthrow the government, soon broadened out to target numerous opponents of the regime (Jenkins 2009: 9). Within a short period of time the *Ergenekon* trials were expanded to include civilians such as professors, journalists, prominent figures in civil society, union members, leaders of NGOs and others.

I am not interested in the competing theories on this plot; yet, it obviously led to a common understanding that the rule of law could easily be discarded. My primary interest is in the repercussions of this controversial trial on the educational landscape. One of the most significant outcomes was the attempt to silence and marginalize the Kemalist nationalist civil society and its organizations, such as Association for the Support of Modern Life (*Çağdaş Yaşamı Destekleme Derneği*, ÇYDD) and Atatürkist Thought Association (*Atatürkçü Düşünce Derneği*, ADD), which had been the main opponents to the educational initiatives of the Gülen community (Kuzmanovic 2013; Turam 2007: 71–3). The prominent figures and the leaders of the nationalist/ Kemalist NGOs who took part in a wide range of demonstrations to defend the republic and its ideals were prosecuted, arrested and 'humiliated' – as in the case of Türkan Saylan (1935–2009), the head and one of the founders of ÇYDD (Kuzmanovic 2013). Saylan was known for her secular Kemalist outlook, and she had developed projects to support the education of those who were in disadvantaged positions in Anatolia.[18] Until the *Ergenekon* trials, the educational landscape particularly in low-income areas – in both Anatolia and big cities – had become the 'playground' for these competing players and ideologies. The AKP had not fully realized at that point what it would mean to cede this 'playground' to the fraternal Gülen community.

Starting from 2008, which coincides with the *Ergenekon* trials, the AKP also transformed the basic premises of republican education and attempted to revise, replace or eliminate republican symbols. The first attempt was to hollow out existing state symbols that refer to Atatürk and republican ideals. These attempts started with the revision of the regulations on Atatürk Corners in private schools in 2008 and stretched to the elimination of republican ideals from education as manifested in the Decree Law on the Organization and Function of the Ministry of Education 652 (Official Gazette 2011). One of the fundamental principles of Turkish national education, namely 'Atatürk's Reforms and Principles and Atatürk's Nationalism', was eliminated from the aims of the MEB.

The composition of civil society and the composition of the key decision-making bodies in education were reconfigured as well. The composition of *Milli Eğitim Şurası* (the Council of Education) that informs educational policies by means of making recommendations was changed (Şaşmaz 2012). Therefore, it would fair to claim that these measures taken to ensure political control of decision-making processes.[19] Another very significant change concerned the role of *Talim Terbiye Kurulu* (the Board of Education and Discipline), which had been one of the most influential departments of the MEB with its decision-making powers in designing the curriculum and assessing educational content, including textbooks (Şaşmaz 2012).

Moreover, membership composition of teachers' trade unions changed dramatically. The AKP-led Union of Educators' Association (*Eğitim Birliği Sendikası*, Eğitim-Bir-Sen), which is affiliated to Civil Servants' Union Confederation (*Memurlar Sendikası*, Memur-Sen), became the leading teachers' union within a short period. Within a decade membership rocketed from 18,000 to approximately 195,000 in 2011 (Göktürk et al. 2012: 110). In parallel, the proportion of Memur-Sen members also increased significantly between 2002 and 2011, from about 6 per cent to 43 per cent of all members (Göktürk et al. 2012: 113). Again, this was a partial result of the *Ergenekon* trials that, just like the Kemalist NGOs, also targeted other teachers' trade unions in particular the Union of Education, Science, and Culture Workers (*Eğitim Bilim ve Kültür Emekçileri Sendikası*, Eğitim-Sen), a secular union on the political left. Being the leading union depends on the number of members, and Eğitim-Bir-Sen became one of the powerful apparatuses of the AKP.

Lastly, both the AKP and the Gülen community sought the consent and loyalty of their followers by providing education, social services, material support and particularly work opportunities. There was a widespread perception in society of clientelistic ties and preferential treatment in the allocation of jobs and positions. The swelling numbers of Eğitim-Bir-Sen members appear to also be related to the preferential treatment afforded to followers of the ruling party (and, at the time, the Gülen community). I suggest that the emergence of ongoing debates about the validity of almost all central examinations in the educational system during these years was due to perceptions of nepotism and cronyism. The growth of unrest in society on the question of the fairness and validity of the central tests indicated a loss of confidence in a system that was meant to be competitive and meritocratic.

The Gülen community: An 'invisible' major player in education

For the AKP government, the Gülen community[20] was the source for a skilled, bright and well-educated workforce whose skills surpassed those of graduates from *imam-hatip* schools who formed the core of National Outlook cadres. The blueprint of this influence may be found in the concept of the *Altın Nesil* (Golden Generation), which refers to a new generation whose worldview is based on piety and who combine Islam, Turkish nationalism and a positivistic outlook with community orientation, active commitment and high educational achievement (Balcı 2005; Bekim 2003; Turam 2007; Yavuz 2003). A very significant change in the strategy of the Gülen movement during the AKP's second term was that they decided to target children's education fervently, and education policies that were implemented during these years paved the way of the community to become a major player. Yet exact share of the community in education was not possible to estimate. Firstly, the community was a significant actor in private education both with its followers' for-profit private schools dubbed as Gülen schools and the private *dershanes* (tutorial college), which offered education services to pupils preparing for common entrance exams. Secondly, educational publishing companies were in the portfolio of the community. These publishing companies could be divided into three main groups. One group produced multiple choice packs, test papers and mock exam papers covering all the key subject areas that are tested in the central exams. The second group of publishing houses produced the textbooks that the MEB distributed for free. The third group published works of fiction and non-fiction targeting children.

Thirdly, the community added children's television to its media portfolio by being the first to establish a children's channel, Yumurcak TV. Under the

Samanyolu TV Group, Yumurcak TV was established in 2007 and became
one of the top ten television channels in 2009, ranking eighth in 2010 (Tuğla
2012: 162, 174). Lastly, music and audio-visual materials might be added to the
'publishing' portfolio of the community. I engage with the questions of how
and to what extent music albums were also transformed into a resource for the
community to influence children in Chapter 4. The community also introduced
an international festival, which served as a symbolic marker of its degree of
power and confident visibility. The International Turkish Language Olympics
(*Uluslararası Türkçe Olimpiyatları*), which had become an international Turkish
language festival featuring the language skills of thousands Turkish language
learners from around the world, was among the innovations of the community
since 2003. To conclude, the Gülen community's power to influence children
regardless of their backgrounds was expanded systematically, However, their
share in the entire education sector was invisible. Yet it is possible to claim
that Gülen community was among the private providers of education to profit
from many education policies that was introduced since AKP came to power.
For instance, in between 2007 and 2011 such policy was introduction of
common exams to Year Six, Year Seven and Year Eight pupils known as Level
Determination Exams (*Seviye Belirleme Sınavı*, SBS) which encouraged primary
school pupils to go to *dershanes*.[21]

'Pious generation' (2012–16)

While articulating his 'pious generation' ideal, Recep Tayyip Erdoğan was
starting the golden age of the *imam-hatip* schools. This was the first time in the
history of the republic that a government aimed to marginalize state education
and state primary schools. A brief touch on the historic 4+4+4 'reform' should
clarify what I mean. A new school reform bill was introduced in February
2012 and passed at the end of March 2012, with no time or space allowed for
public debate. The reform took effect in the 2012–13 school year. At the outset,
it specifically transformed eight-year compulsory education into a 4+4+4
system of 'interrupted' education (four years of primary education, four years
of lower secondary education and four years of upper secondary education)
(Official Gazette 2012b). The key point of the reform was that lower secondary
vocational schools, including *imam-hatip* schools, which were closed during
the 28 February process, were re-opened. Moreover, 4+4+4 also introduced
new curriculum content for primary schools, such as the Qur'an and the

Life of Muhammad, the Prophet as elective courses. Proponents of the law such as Foundation of Volunteer Organizations of Turkey (*Türkiye Gönüllü Teşekküller Vakfı*) comprising pro-Islamic NGOs including but not limited to Association of Independent Industrialists' and Businessmen's (*Müstakil Sanayici ve İş Adamları Derneği*, MÜSİAD) – favoured these aspects of the law (Memurlarnet 2012).

Opponents of the law highlighted features that could have deleterious effects on the education system. First, there was a critique of the early age of intake – five years old for primary school, and nine years old for vocational schools. Many universities, NGOs, trade unions and the opposition CHP criticized the school reform law by claiming that such an early intake could harm the early development of children (BOUN 2012; ERG 2012; METU 2012). As a result of this opposition, the age was raised to six for primary schools and ten for vocational schools. Moreover, in response to the growing opposition to the reform, then-Prime Minister Recep Tayyip Erdoğan defended the law with the statement that the AKP wanted to 'raise a pious generation'. This statement gave rise to two main questions from the public: whether this school reform was a 'social engineering' project, and whether it was an act of revenge for the 28 February process, since the Prime Minister explained this initiative by saying 'Fascist pressures have been corrected through democracy' (BBC 2012). Second, there was widespread concern that this education reform could have severe gendered effects. The endeavours of the MEB and civil society to increase girls' educational enrolment since 2003 that I discussed above constitute the backdrop to these concerns. The eight-year compulsory primary education introduced in 1997 also had an impact on the schooling process, since it provided a long, uninterrupted basic education to children (Kağıtçıbaşı 2010).

Break of alliance

The alliance between the Gülen community and the AKP was not popular; on the contrary, it created an atmosphere of unease and uncertainty that permeated society. Although I engage with the ways in which this mood also impacted upon everyday schooling in Chapter 5, I would like to offer brief reflections on this rapidly changing context. The power struggle between the Gülen community and the AKP, which started to become visible with the 'National Intelligence Service (*Milli İstihbarat Teşkilatı*, MİT) crisis', was transformed into a kind of 'war' after the 17 December corruption scandal referred to above (Tremblay 2014).[22] In the aftermath, the AKP government started to take retaliatory measures to the extent that the Gülen community was officially declared a terrorist organization referred to as FETÖ that allegedly aimed to 'infiltrate' the state through its 'parallel' organizational structure in alliance with 'foreign' powers.

This tug of war between these former allies reshaped the educational landscape. More precisely, the AKP government attacked all the Gülen-affiliated institutions, networks and businesses both in and outside the country. Following the November 2013 MİT crisis, the AKP government started to articulate their plan to close the *dershanes*, which offered education services to pupils preparing for common entrance exams. The government argued that the *dershanes* exacerbated inequalities in education. This plan, and the claim behind it, was not in line with the educational policies of the government that had, so far, been eager to foster privatization. As I mentioned above the Gülen community held a big market share in this sector. The headline of the *Zaman* newspaper following the launch of the plan called it a 'night raid' (*gece baskını*) (Hürriyet 2013). The answer to this headline was given by President Recep Tayyip Erdoğan on a television channel where he claimed that *dershanes* marginalize the children of the poor (Hürriyet 2013). Nevertheless, it was only after they had weathered the storm created by the corruption scandal of 17 December that the AKP felt confident enough to act, unleashing a veritable onslaught on the educational domain. The AKP government started to redesign, reconfigure and reshape every aspect of education that was touched by the Gülen community. One of the striking developments, among the others, was the rapid expansion of the Turkish Youth and Education Foundation (*Türkiye Gençlik ve Eğitime Hizmet Vakfı*, TÜRGEV), the Ensar Foundation and Association for Dissemination of Science (*İlim Yayma Cemiyeti*) and their growing influence on the field of education (Lord 2018: 193). TÜRGEV, which is managed by Erdoğan's son, has various privileges in the realm of education, such as briefing head teachers on the foundation's educational concerns, outlining the foundation's new ideal generation, and having access to land for building dormitories and educational institutions. With a relatively recent study on these civil society organizations Bilge Yabanci states that 'from the secular and Kemalist state that had dominated the youth policy until the early 2000s, the AKP relies heavily on civil society actors, government-oriented youth organizations, in its quest for a new nationalist project of establishing an alternative cultural hegemony' (2019: 493).

To conclude, what I have explained so far however radically changed aftermath of the failed military coup of 15 July 2016 which 'was a dramatic watershed providing Erdoğan (in his own words) with a "God sent" opportunity not only to liquidate all influences of Gülen community in the public sector, business, and the media but to utilize the state of emergency to rule by decree and eradicate all possible foci of opposition' (Kandiyoti & Emanet 2017: 873). Notwithstanding, the domain of education in Turkey has been highly contested since the foundation of the republic. It has been buffeted by constant policy changes that reflect power struggles as well as the effects of changes at the global level with, on the one hand, attempts to meet internationally set educational standards and, on the other, the adoption of neoliberal policies leading to deregulation and privatization in the education sector. It is nearly impossible to fully grasp the dynamics operating at the micro-level, which I tried to capture in my ethnography of two schools.

Politics of marketing education

The aim of this chapter is to provide insights into the ways in which global neoliberal changes in education – particularly in the field of public primary education – have been adopted and modified in Turkey in line with the AKP's policy priorities. Since the AKP came to power in 2002, education has been changing steadily through comprehensive neoliberal education reforms and policies. Some scholars of education in Turkey have also engaged in debates about the impact of neoliberalism (Harvey 2005) on state education, and especially those who focused on the period of the AKP government argued that the impact became dramatic after the AKP came to power (Gök 2007b; İnal & Akkaymak 2012; Yolcu 2014). What began with the IMF's structural adjustment policies in Turkey in the 1980s have been consolidated through marketization, commercialization and deregulation that transformed a highly centralized state education system (İnal & Akkaymak 2012; Yolcu 2014). As I mentioned in the previous chapter, even though the AKP theoretically adopted the templates that all states implementing neoliberal reforms (prescribed by international actors such as the WB, the OECD or the EU) were expected follow, what we rarely hear about is how these reforms and policies were used as tools to reshape state education in a manner reflecting the ruling party's ideological priorities. In other words, under the surface of compliance with international neoliberal prescriptions the AKP was implementing policies that reflected their domestic agenda and priorities.

In an attempt to explain my argument in this chapter I focus on School-Based Management (SBM) policy from the vantage point of Talip and Zinnur Schools. SBM has been among the trendy education policies throughout the world. Giving heed to the discussions in comparative education provide significant insights into making sense of this policy. Here I refer to the rich debate between scholars who see uniformity with the neo-institutionalist approach (Boli et al. 1985) and those who focus on local contexts (Anderson-Levitt 2003) as well as those who pay attention to the 'socio-logical' (Schriewer & Martinez 2004) aspects of transnational policy borrowings. And I agree with Gita Steiner-Khamsi and Ines Stolpe in the sense that there is '[...] a convergence of educational reforms, but perhaps it is only at the level of brand names, that is, in the language of reform. Once a discourse is transplanted from one context to another and subsequently enacted in practice, it changes meaning' (2006: 7–8). I am interested in understanding the 'meaning' and consequences of SBM in the Turkish context. In addition, my intention is not limited to support the prevailing arguments about SBM in Turkey, such that SBM has turned schools into 'quasi-private' (Candaş et al. 2011) or not fully 'public' enterprises (Yolcu and Kurul 2009), increased inequality (Köse and Şaşmaz 2014), or created a market, thus turning public good into a commodity. My aim is also to illustrate political aspect of SBM that clarifies the extent to which alliance between AKP and Islamist civil society actors, the penetration of Gülen community and other Islamist communities such as Hidayet community into the schools and their connections to parents and pupils were playing decisive role in Islamization of everyday schooling.

In what follows I examine the local education market in Bahçelik and trace political aspect of SBM by examining the so-called 'fundraising activities' of Zinnur and Talip Schools, which received no budget from the MEB. In the first main section of the chapter, I begin with a rather short explanation of the legal framework of SBM and engage with the literature that deals exclusively with this educational policy in the country. Comparatively, I look at the important role played by teachers and mothers in fundraising and financing both school contexts. In the second section, I continue to trace education market by offering a rich analysis of the role of for-profit Hidayet Dormitory in which some of the Zinnur School pupils stayed. Finally, I touch on *bilgi evi* (house of knowledge) in the district.

SBM in Turkey

In keeping with global neoliberal restructuring and its effects on education, Turkey's transition to SBM could be claimed as major shift, a move that is not peculiar to the context of the country. For more than three decades, SBM – a key form of decentralization – has been transforming state-funded education globally (Abu-Duhou 1999; Gamage & Zajda 2009; Grauwe 2005). Brian J. Caldwell, who is one of the leading scholars on SBM, describes it as 'the systematic and consistent decentralization to the school level of authority and responsibility to make decisions on significant matters related to school operations within a centrally determined framework of goals, policies, curriculum, standards, and accountability' (2009: 55). The simplicity of this definition should not mislead one, as SBM is a complex phenomenon with different implications with respect to 'what is decentralized' (Abu-Duhou 1999: 30) and 'who, at the school level, receives authority?' (Grauwe 2004: 2). Various names have been given to SBM systems, such as site-based management, school-based governance and self-managing schools, which is not surprising given this trend's diversity in rhetoric and practice within each context across the globe (Abu-Duhou 1999; Caldwell 2009; Gamage & Zajda 2009).

SBM was introduced in Turkey in 2005 under the name of the governing body, the Parent Teacher Association (*Okul Aile Birliği*, OAB) (Official Gazette 2005b).[1] One of the distinctive features of OAB in the country is that it radically changed provision of public education (Candaş et al. 2011: 59–61; Köse & Şaşmaz 2014; Yolcu & Kurul 2009: 40–1). At the outset, OAB could be easily clustered as finance-based SBM, which broadly refers to school systems in which the decision-making power over the budget allocated by the centre is transferred to the schools. However, such definition does not make sense in a context where not all schools receive a lump sum budget from the centre, as some studies illustrate (Candaş et al. 2011: 48; Köse & Şaşmaz 2014: 42–5; Yolcu 2007: 232–8).[2]

In addition, the regulation on OABs, especially in the section that specifies the responsibilities of the governing body in relation to fundraising, also suggests that the basic premise of SBM in the country is prescribing schools how to fundraise. According to the latest version of the regulation during my fieldwork, OABs (i) may receive or solicit conditional/unconditional grants and donations in cash and kind; (ii) may run or sublease the canteen; (iii) may generate income through social, cultural and sporting activities, courses, projects, campaigns and the like; (iv) may engage in 'other' income-generating activities, albeit without 'forcing' parents to donate to schools (Official Gazette 2012a).[3] Even more noteworthy is the section on the use of income generated by OABs, which states that 20 per cent of the income generated by OABs through running or sub-letting of canteens must be transferred to bank accounts of local authorities (provincial and district directorates) and 1 per cent to the Treasury (Official Gazette 2012a). In rhetoric, it is claimed that the intention is to distribute these amounts of money earned at schools to those schools that are not able to generate sufficient revenue. In practice, however, there is no transparency in how local authorities distribute or spend these sums, as some studies found out (Köse & Şaşmaz 2014: 91–3). What is more, to regulate this process MEB also established an online information system called Information Management System of Education Financing and Education Expenses (*Türkiye'de Eğitimin Finansmanı ve Eğitim Harcamaları Bilgi Yönetim Sistemi*, TEFBİS) in 2011.[4]

The literature on OAB in Turkey illustrates the extent of inequalities between schools created by the introduction of SBM policy (Altuntaş 2005; Köse & Şaşmaz 2014; Özdemir 2011; Yolcu 2007). It is clear from this literature that there are 'low-income' schools and those that are 'rich'. Then I think the crucial question is not what a 'low-income school' is, because it is obvious that these are schools that do not receive funding from the state. So the crucial question is what constitutes a 'rich' school. In seeking an answer to this question, I have drawn much inspiration from the analysis of the 'education market', more specifically from the approaches developed by scholars known as new class cultural theorists, who 'explore how class is made and given value through culture, examining how different classes are differentially attributed with value' (Reay 2006: 290). They trace market ideology beyond 'the consumption orientations and behaviour of parents' and 'the marketing activities of schools' (Bowe et al. 1994: 41). Very broadly, their approach suggests looking at schools from a 'marketing perspective' and asking questions such as: What are the marketing strategies of schools, what is of value in an educational market, who exploits this market, what role does gender play and more. Stephen Ball argues that 'a system of exclusion and differentiation is created which reasserts and ramifies relative advantages of the middle and upper classes within State education' (1993: 13). Although Stephen Ball refers to context-based tensions played out in education sector, particularly in the context of UK, the emerging issues are not irrelevant to many contexts, thanks to the neoliberal education policies that tainted the education systems across the globe. I am also concerned with understanding 'exclusion' as well as 'differentiation' in this market. Having said that a brief comparison of two schools in terms of their income generation activities is in order.

Zinnur and Talip Schools

I will start this section by comparing the two schools in terms of their budgets and income generation activities. Zinnur did not receive a lump sum budget from the centre – not a single penny – yet, the electricity and water bills were covered by local authorities. Throughout the school year I discovered that the school had variegated income generation activities which included but not limited to (i) subleasing the school canteen; outsourcing transportation services; (ii) co-curricular activities such as tutoring provided by the teachers at the weekends or extra-curricular activities such as outsourced courses; (iii) offering advertising opportunities to private education service providers within the school[5]; (iv) persuading parents to donate. Among all, head teacher İsmail told me that donations made by parents constitute the biggest share. It was because in the school parents made consistent donations. The amount of donation that the OAB imposed was 100 liras (approximately 6 pounds sterling as of 2022)[6] for a school year, which was divided into two equal instalments. As I described in Chapter 1, Zinnur had a reputation in the district which had attracted lower-middle-class parents to the school as well; however, most pupils came from low-income households.

Talip like Zinnur was reliant on income generation activities. The number of pupils at Talip was almost three times more than Zinnur and therefore, in theory, Talip's budget could be higher even though OAB fixed the donation amount to 40 liras (approximately 2 sterling) per school year – less than half the amount that the OAB of Zinnur proposed. However, it was a challenge to make parents donate, as will be illustrated in the coming subsections. Moreover, Talip also generated income from the subleased canteen, and from the extra-curricular and co-curricular activities it offered. These attempts did not create a substantial income or profit either. Nonetheless, when looking for similarities as well as differences between Talip and Zinnur in terms of income generation activities, what I found striking was that teachers played a significant role in what I call persuading parents to donate or more accurately marketing the schools. In what follows, I focus on the teachers who taught Year Five through Eight and their marketing strategies.

Marketing in Zinnur: 'Eating "the soup" of Islamic communities'

Among the various reasons given by the teachers for receiving regular parental contributions were the comparatively better infrastructure of the Zinnur, the less overcrowded classes (about thirty-eight pupils) and the close relations with the Islamic communities, and Bahçelik municipality – forms and benefits of such relationships are discussed below. The teachers also mentioned the 'good reputation' (as they put it) of the school in the district, which was enhanced by the academic performance of the pupils. In doing so, however, they neglected their own role. More specifically, they took it for granted that teachers (working Year Five through Eight) played a key role in getting parents to donate to the school, even though these donations were a large part of the revenue sources of the school. More than that, there was a kind of 'tacit marketing system' in the school whereby these teachers had to act as fundraisers in the classes where they were assigned as 'classroom teacher'.[7] And I observed how successful they were in their roles. I had a lot of questions, like what was behind their 'success'? What were their reasons? How did they get the parents to agree to donate? Or, to be more specific, how did they market Zinnur?

As my fieldwork progressed, it became clear to me that there was a sense of solidarity among these teachers and a shared understanding of the country's education system. The young male teacher Yakup summarized this understanding, which could also be described as a kind of agreement, succinctly during our in-depth interview. Yakup posed a rhetorical question, he said, 'is there anyone who had not eaten the soup of Islamic communities [*cemaatlerin çorbasını içmeyen mi var?*]'? The expression he used 'eat the soup' has a double meaning. Literally, he meant his habit of visiting Menzil, a village in Adıyaman province, and eating the soup served by the Menzil community (*cemaat*), an offshoot of the Naqshbandi *tariqa* order, which bears the name of the village. Yakup also meant that access to 'so-called free education' (as he called it) is not an option for the majority unless it is supported in some way by the Islamic communities. In other words, he emphasized the importance of the role of Islamic communities not only in ensuring social mobility but also in attainment. This view was a common thread throughout many of the interviews with the Zinnur teachers. Ten out of sixteen teachers who taught in Year Five to Year Eight classes told me that they owed their teaching careers to one of the influential Islamic communities in the country namely various offshoots of Naqshbandi *tariqa* orders, and offshoot of Kadiri *tariqa* order and Nurcus.[8] They also expressed that they received Islamic education and tacit knowledge in line with the community that supported them, and these communities still gave them a sense of belonging. Among these teachers, there were even some who had spent their entire school life – from primary school to university – in some kind of single-sex dormitories run or managed by the Islamic communities. In these dormitories, so-called *abis* (elder brothers) or *ablas* (elder sisters) had acted in *loco parentis* (in place of the parents). Their educational past as well as their view of education shaped their role in marketing the school, which I will explain below with two examples.

'*Hizmet*' (service)[9] within Zinnur

Aybike, who was a female teacher in her mid-twenties, was succeeding in fundraising for the school. The working-class pious mothers often commented that they found her credible despite her relatively young age and rather limited teaching experience. Aybike worked well with the mothers but not with the fathers of the pupils which was an advantage in a school where fathers hardly involved in education of their children. She expressed this very clearly in one of our daily conversations with the teachers in the staff common room during a break. She said that she would not 'talk to the fathers without the presence of a third person'. Aybike was by no means alone in this, as she was one of the teachers who defined themselves through their commitment to the now-criminalized Gülen community.[10] However, the others at the school, namely Fatih, Gülşen and Hüsnügül – male and female – did not express this as boldly as she did.

Aybike worked hard, and she told me that she had selected a group of 'smart' pupils (both male and female) based on their academic success from the classes she taught, asked their mothers to provide her with tutoring space in their homes, held free tutoring meetings, and gave regular feedback to the mothers. Throughout the year, a meeting was held every fortnight in one of the pupils' homes. She also told me that she selected reading materials and regularly helped pupils with their homework. What the entire teaching staff, including me, knew – not from the Aybike's own account but from disclosures of pupils and their mothers – was that she enforced some rules; for example, she discouraged boys and girls from socializing with each other. She also offered Islamic teaching, although her area of study was not Islam, or more specifically she was not responsible for religious culture and moral knowledge classes. All the teachers and I saw her making pupils recite verses of the Qur'an during class intervals and breaks throughout the school year; however, she did not share the content of this teaching with me or other teachers.

Other teachers who were also followers of Gülen community, like Aybike, carried out the same activities and they referred to service to God, namely *hizmet* (service). From our conversations with female teachers Gülşen, Aybike and Hüsnügül throughout the school year in school, in dormitories subsidized by the Gülen community, known as *ışık evis* (house of light), I learned that they were supported by the Gülen community from secondary school or primary school to university and even in finding a job as a teacher in MEB. They did not mention the name of the preacher Fethullah Gülen nor did they explain the ideal of *Altın Nesil* (Golden Generation), which was contrary to the findings of the literature on Gülen community, which focuses on the movement's activities in education. They told me that they consider teaching as the 'profession of the Prophet'[11] and are committed to *hizmet*.

I observed that all Gülen follower female teachers mostly acted on behalf of mothers and by doing this they were blurring the line between the school and the home, as well as between teacher and parent in the school. I also learned from the mothers' accounts that the educational knowledge, material resources such as books that these teachers provided were of great help to them. This was especially true for those working-class pious mothers who were illiterate, who lacked knowledge, who could not afford paid tuition and who were not politicized – therefore they did not have the political connections in Bahçelik to draw on that I engage with later. In this regard these teachers offered support to mothers. Nonetheless, even they favoured pupils with the most promising academic achievements, they all cajoled almost all the mothers in their classrooms (Year Six, Year Seven, Year Eight) to make donations to the school. In the context of Zinnur, this meant that all Gülen community teachers were involved in making donations of almost 16,000 liras (approximately 900 sterling) possible, a sum that was highly praised among teachers.

'Talk to people according to their level of understanding'

Yekta contributed another vivid account; the above quote is taken from his interview. He was among the successful fundraising teachers who were teaching through Year Five to Year Eight. In response to my question about his ability to communicate with all parents with predominantly working-class backgrounds in Year Six classroom where he was responsible to fundraise, Yekta told me that the hadith of the Prophet Muhammad, '*Kellimun nase ala kaderi ukulihim* [Talk to people according to their level of understanding]', captured the approach that he applied when talking to parents. In a didactic and rather stern tone he explained to me in detail how his past formal and informal educational experiences taught him to speak to people from all walks of life, and how he was inspired by ideas on *irşad* (Islamic guidance) and *tebliğ* (the Islamic duty of proclaiming God's orders and sanctions). He was a Kurdish teacher in his early fifties, a graduate of *imam-hatip* school and during our interview he gave examples of his past *tebliğ* attempts when he was a young student to explicate his point. I found many similarities between his account and the prominent members of *imam-hatip* school community that Iren Ozgur (2012) interviewed in her rich ethnographic work on these schools.

Yekta told me that the only forum to talk to parents was the well-attended parent-teacher meetings that were held in two terms. Like many of his colleagues, he meant the 'fathers' when he used the word 'parents' because the mothers were often at school while the fathers were hardly concerned about their children's education. In other words, these meetings were clearly about convincing the fathers to continue donating to the school – on the assumption that the fathers were the main decision-makers on household expenditure (see Chapter 6). In other words, parent-teacher meetings were intended to convey the message of what fathers need to know about important issues before they decide to donate and/or continue to donate. In the classroom, from which Yekta was responsible for soliciting the donations, only a few parents failed to donate on time despite the OAB offering termly instalment options, as I mentioned earlier. And the parents who had not donated on time personally informed Yekta of the reasons that prevented them from doing so and asked for further instalments. To sum up, Yekta persuaded all the parents to make donations which meant almost 4,000 liras (approximately 225 sterling).

As I mentioned above significant number of teachers teaching Year Five through Year Eight across the sample in Zinnur, regardless of gender, age, and political leanings or predispositions, reflected their sense of belonging to a broad spectrum of Islamic communities as well as Islamist constituencies. They were all involved in marketing Zinnur, and they all 'successfully' marketed the school. In other words, Yekta and Aybike, along with the other Gülen-affiliated teachers, were not alone in their success in convincing parents to donate in Zinnur. What distinguished them from the others was their distinct habitus.

***

Pierre Bourdieu's work, which he co-authored with Jean-Claude Passeron, on French higher education, deals in detail with the significance of having a particular *habitus* (Bourdieu & Passeron 1990). Bourdieu and Passeron (1990) explain this with the notion of *cultural capital* that refers to an amalgam of resources such as knowledge or particular skills that offer advantages. Furthermore, it is not only about having a certain kind of 'culture' as an asset but also gaining access to networks or having membership in groups or a community, which they refer to as *social capital* that explains such phenomena (Bourdieu 1986; Bourdieu & Passeron 1990). In the broadest sense, according to Bourdieu, *habitus* refers to taken-for-granted manners, perceptions, attitudes, behaviours, traits, reflexes, ideas, bodily movements, most of which are conditioned by dispositions that are broadly shaped by structures (Bourdieu 1996, 2010).

The relevant literature in Turkey that has dealt with education points to a distinct *habitus*. In this literature, the work of notable sociologist Nilüfer Göle (1996) is particularly worth mentioning. Working with focus group interviews with veiled Islamist female university students, Göle uses the concept of *habitus* in relation to the individual dispositions of these young girls, detailing the exclusion and disadvantage they face in the 'secular' education system because of their headscarf, and attempts to move from the dispositions of these girls to notions of a collective Islamist intellectual *habitus* that challenges the conceptualization of modernity in Turkey (1996). In a different direction, Iren Ozgur's (2012) meticulous ethnographic research on *imam-hatip* schools combines life stories of *imam-hatip* alumni (well-known political figures), curricula, hidden curricula – what Ozgur calls 'experience' – and interviews with *imam-hatip* students. Ozgur illustrates how *imam-hatip* schools imparted a distinct *habitus* (2012). Ozgur explains, 'The formal and informal curricula at İmam-Hatip schools transmit a habitus that facilitates strong ties to Islamic norms and practices. [...] They emulate the Prophet in religious practice, social interactions, and even personal hygiene' (2012: 102). Thus, while Göle (1996) sees a distinct *habitus* as part of the cultural struggle against the conceptualization of the 'modern' or 'civilized', Ozgur (2012) explains what entails similar dispositions and illustrates the formation and reproduction of a distinct *habitus*. My intention is neither broad conclusions on social groupings with regard to society in general nor studying an institutional *habitus*.

My intention is to give meaning to the empirical findings presented in this chapter, which focus on local education market and 'marketing practices' of teachers, mothers and other actors. Diane Reay's (1995, 1998, 2004, 2006, 2009) interpretation of *habitus* offers significant insights. In particular, I am interested in the way Reay utilizes *habitus* in her ethnographic account on mothers' involvement in primary schooling in UK, which suggests using *habitus* (i) as an approach to interpreting the actions of teachers, pupils, parents; (ii) to understand the present through the past or, as Reay puts it, to acknowledge the 'influences of the past'; (iii) to consider the wider context; (iv) to think about 'differences as well as commonalities among social groups, and in connection with the related notion of field' (1998: 32–3). The concept of the *field* is undoubtedly also key to understanding the *habitus* in Bourdieu's theoretical universe: 'social reality exists, so to speak, twice, in things and in minds, in fields and in habitus, outside and inside social agents. And when habitus encounters a social world of which it is the product, it is like a "fish in water": it does not feel the weight of the water and it takes the world about itself for granted' (Bourdieu & Wacquant 1992: 127).

If we return to the Zinnur School and the teachers who succeeded in marketing the school I have described above, it is clear in their actions that their past education, whether tacit knowledge acquired through their informal or formal Islamic education or socialization processes in formal and/or informal educational settings with the support of a wide range of Islamic communities and constituencies, shaped their *habitus*. Yet while I recognize their past education, I am equally concerned about their actions within the school. The influences of the past were evident in Gülen-affiliated teacher Aybike's actions, which she had learned during her socialization process in informal education settings including but not limited to *ışık evi*. She selected pupils, used their homes as a place to tutor, gave instructions on religion and acted in place of these pupils' mothers. In other words, she was committed to offer *hizmet* like other Gülen-affiliated teachers. Yekta, on the other hand, was a graduate of an *imam-hatip* school and what influenced him in his actions in persuading fathers to donate were the ideas about *irşad* (Islamic guidance) and *tebliğ* (the Islamic duty of proclaiming God's orders and sanctions) that he had learned at *imam-hatip* school. Distinct *habitus* of *imam-hatip* students and alumni that Iren Ozgur explains in her work that I mentioned above was visible in the presence of the school context in the actions of Yekta as well.

The point is that I am not arguing that Yekta, Aybike and other teachers felt a sense of belonging to other Islamic communities all had the same collective *habitus*. In other words, while there were visible common dispositions at the surface, the differences were clear. I will give heed to Diane Reay again, Reay explains, 'At times, Bourdieu seems to be suggesting a degree of uniformity. At other times, he recognizes differences and diversity between members of the same cultural grouping and writes in terms of the singularity of individual habitus. Habitus, within, as well as between, social groups, differs to the extent that the details of individuals' social trajectories diverge from one another' (2004: 434). In Zinnur although there seems to be 'degree of uniformity', details of 'individuals' social trajectories' suggest that these teachers are from different social groups. During the interviews they all espoused Islamic or counter-Kemalist and communitarian values rather than universalist values such as gender equality or secularism. Besides in their actions it was quite evident that they favoured (some enforced) gender-segregation, for instance, while Aybike did not want to talk to fathers alone, Yekta chose fathers to address in the parent-teacher meetings.

In other words, Islamic norms developed during their socialization process in the past and their present positions suffused to everyday interactions through the way they share space and avoid one another in the presence of the school day. Another significant commonality was their disbelief in 'free' education, a view the roots of which lie in their past education, that is, they owed their teaching careers to either an Islamic community or an Islamic constituency. Yakup above explained this succinctly with a rhetorical question, which was: 'Is there anyone who had not eaten the soup of Islamic communities?' However, I argue here that these teachers did not form a social grouping within the school. Rather, they formed an alliance of teachers who defined themselves with their affiliation to either an Islamic community or a constituency in order to market the school. And by marketing the school they simultaneously aimed to achieve the respective goals of different social groupings, such as Gülen community, or the Hidayet community or *imam-hatip* alumni who were ardent followers of AKP. In other words, there was not one distinct *habitus* but rather different individual *habituses*.

***

Marketing in Talip: Failing to persuade parents

The context of Talip was in contrast with the context of Zinnur where the significant number of teachers formed an alliance and dominated the marketing practices of the school. In Talip neither was there a common understanding of education nor a similar educational history of the teachers. Added to this was the obvious political and ethnic factionalism among the teachers. At the risk of caricaturizing, it is possible to distinguish four broad groups as: veiled and unveiled pious Muslim teachers who were either ardent followers of the AKP or affiliated to an Islamic community; left-wing secular and right-wing unveiled Kemalist teachers; young teachers; and middle-aged male teachers. The strong commitments to the different identities of the cliques of teachers were transforming everyday schooling into an arena of conflict. The protests on the dress code, the role of Islamic communities in education and reactions to a wide range of educational policies including 4+4+4 education reform fuelled these conflicts during the school year (see, for instance, Chapter 5). All these had dire consequences for the marketing of the school.

Moreover, there were also clashes between the teachers and the parents (more precisely mothers). In school there were a lot of mothers who made official complaints about some of the teachers via ALO 147, a call centre that was set up, in principle, to provide services to parents, teachers and pupils. However, in practice this service became popular among those mothers who wanted to voice their negative evaluation of teachers' practices in the school. This made the teachers more defensive and further fuelled the cleavages among them, to the detriment of joint income generation activities. I discuss some of these conflicts in more detail in Chapter 5, but here it is important to understand the impact of the lack of solidarity which in turn had profound negative consequences – that is, they could not persuade most parents to donate. In other words, the teachers could not market the school and, as a result, the school suffered from budget deficits that were far from sufficient to fund basic classroom supplies. This became even clearer to me when I began to conduct classroom observations, and only then did I discover quite 'creative' solutions 'created' by the teachers, who had a distinct *habitus*, which I will explain below.

'Pay-as-you-go' method in visual art classes of Kevser

In Talip, I observed that what I call 'pay-as-you-go' method, meaning that pupils had to give money to teachers for a variety of materials and items before and/or after and/or during class time, was widespread. It is possible to divide classroom spending into two broad groups. The school did not offer a free copying or printing service, so one group of classroom materials consisted of printable exercises, worksheets and exam papers. The second group consisted of teachers' 'shopping lists', with some of the most common materials being whiteboard markers, soap, tissues and cologne for pupils. Asking for money, or in their words 'collecting money [*para toplamak*]', had become so routine for the teachers in Talip that none of them commented on it during the interviews, and if I did, they quickly changed the subject. The veiled pious teacher Kevser, in her early forties, was an exception. Her account of her version of the 'pay-as-you-go' method came out clearly in our interview:

Kevser: I taught pupils *ebru* [marbling].
Zühre: How did you do that?
Kevser: It was very difficult.
Zühre: Are you referring to the paint?

> **Kevser:** I bought the paint. It is cheaper if you make a lump sum purchase for all the pupils. It is expensive if pupils buy it per unit. I bought all the supplies. Besides pupils could not find the supplies, it was even difficult for me. Instead of making them buy the paints, I asked for 1 lira from each pupil and so this made it possible for almost all the pupils to try their hand at paper marbling. [...]
>
> **Zühre:** What do you do in general [in your classes]? Art supplies are necessary in art classes ...
>
> **Kevser:** Well in general in rural areas [she refers to Bahçelik] there is always a lack of educational tools. A father gives two liras [approximately 0.10 sterling] to his child as pocket money. Pupils would like to use that money to buy something from the canteen rather than buying colours. Besides, supplies for art classes and paint colours are expensive things. Pupils seldom bring such items to the classroom. That's why I collect money say between two and three liras. I know collecting money from the pupils is not the right thing to do, but I do it. I am supposed to do it. I am forced to do it this way. [...] A paper-marbling package is sixty liras [approximately three sterling]. None of the pupils can afford it. [...] I made them paint the walls of the playground as well with acrylic in the same way. Again, I bought the acrylic paint.

Asking pupils to hand over cash is not a new phenomenon. The studies from the late 1990s show the extent to which this approach gave way to a more systematic method of obtaining money from parents (Kavak et al. 1997). This was at a time when the severe inequalities in state education were becoming apparent following the introduction of the IMF and WB's draconian structural adjustment policies in the 1980s. To describe the stark inequalities in the wake of increasing privatization, Fatma Gök coined the term 'learn as much as you pay [*paran kadar oku*]' (2002: 101). What distinguishes the 1990s and early 2000s from the 2010s is the marketization of education through the introduction of quasi-privatization with SBM, as I explained above. The term 'learn as much as you pay' proposed by Gök (2002) became a reality in state education and even transformed into 'pay as you go'.

Returning to Kevser's account above, it is clear that her visual art classes, which require relatively expensive materials, would not have been possible without her efforts and the pupils' contribution. In classroom observations I conducted in Talip, I found that the teachers overwhelmingly preferred the talk and chalk method, which was cheaper but not completely 'free'. Kevser, however, did not shy away from investing more time in finding discounts and encouraging pupils to spend their pocket money on what she calls a 'joyful activity' (rather than having pupils buy, for example, the most popular snack in the school canteen – bread stuffed with French fries). And in this way, Kevser turned the pupils into 'customers'.

Throughout our interview, Kevser repeatedly referred to what she saw as the positive role of a broad spectrum of Islamic communities in education and openly stated that she had never accepted the 'secular' character of education. The nature of the socialization processes she recalled later in the interview in relation to her youth and/or childhood experiences was similar to the teachers in Zinnur who made an alliance to market the school. Nevertheless, it was not only her repeated praise of the Gülen community, but also her sense of responsibility for what she called 'rural areas', as seen in her account above, and her willingness or 'courage' to create solutions with her interpretation of the 'pay as you go' method that aroused my suspicion. However, I was not sure whether she was a disguised ardent follower or a mere sympathizer of the community, imitating its followers.

In the following subsections, I turn to the marketing practices of Year One, Year Two, Year Three and Year Four teachers, referred to as the *sınıf annesi* (classroom mother).

'Classroom mothers': Pressing mothers into service in Zinnur and Talip

As I already mentioned in several subsections above, the word 'mother' was used interchangeably with the word 'parent' in the everyday schooling of Talip and Zinnur. This was simply because the fathers of the pupils in both schools were hardly involved in the education of the pupils on a day-to-day basis. This was even more evident in Years One to Four. Much attention is paid to parental involvement in the relevant literature, but the role of mothers in school or the absence of fathers is hardly acknowledged – the work of Meral Apak Kaya (2014) and Hüseyin Yolcu (2007) can be considered notable exceptions.

In her inspiring ethnographic account of mothers' involvement in their children's education in the UK context, Diane Reay (1998) offers rich insights, arguing that the failure to clearly define the place of gender in home-school relations obscures a number of critical issues. Reay (1998: 10) explains:

> First, it serves to hide from the reader's view inequalities operating within
> parenting relationships. Secondly, it results in a privileging of 'the male' in the
> text. Usage of the term 'parent', without any qualification as to *which* parent,

acts as an invitation; it leaves open the possibility of paternal involvement. Its consequences are the inclusion of fathers in an area which, in reality, many have left to their children's mother. [...] This 'genderless' parent operates discursively to deny women's work. However, this universalizing theme of the discourse not only renders invisible inequalities between the sexes but also those existing between mothers.

The assumption of a 'genderless parent' is, as Reay points out, particularly striking in a context where the voluntary work of mothers in schools has been conceptualized under the name *sınıf annesi* (classroom mother). This is the name given to an informal practice of mothers volunteering in the classroom that had become increasingly visible across the country and whose content, if not its scope, varies greatly from school to school – indeed from classroom to classroom (Kaya 2014; Yolcu 2007). For example, Kaya identifies the competencies assigned to mothers in the role of *sınıf annesi* by comparing them to the competencies assigned to twenty-five different occupations, such as secretary, laundress, payroll clerk, counsellor, cleaner and so on (2014: 200–6). It is interesting to see the variety and scope of work performed by mothers. Yolcu (2007: 201–10) has found that mothers in classrooms primarily act as 'buffers' between OAB and parents, helping to keep the flow of donations smooth by, for example, preventing possible confrontations between teachers and parents.

In both Zinnur and Talip, tasks of *sınıf annesis* changed greatly – as one would expect given the many differences between the two schools that I have explained so far. In Zinnur, *sınıf annesis* fostered a sense of community, handled communication between the teacher and the mothers, informed the mothers about the decisions of the OAB, coordinated events, and assisted the teacher in a variety of activities, such as extracurricular activities, persuading the mothers to donate in kind and soliciting donations that the OAB determined. In Talip, however, other duties were added, such as managing and cleaning the classrooms, shopping, cooking food for the class, and assisting during class, for example, by taking pupils to the toilets. Notwithstanding this, I propose to consider *sınıf annesi* as a classroom-based marketing practice (in the Year One, Year Two, Year Three and Year Four classrooms), but not just the tasks of a mother selected as a *sınıf annesi*. Such an approach offers a better understanding of the relationship between mothers and teachers and their role in marketing the school. In what follows, I will explain my point of view through two illustrative cases: while the first, Handan, shows a well-established system, the following case of Nigar illustrates the opposite.

Handan

Handan, a pious, experienced veiled female teacher in her early fifties, was among the 'celebrity' teachers in Zinnur. For the mothers of Year Three pupils, almost all of whom dropped out of school early and got married at a young age, Handan was not a mere *öğretmen* (teacher); she was perceived as an *abla* (elder sister) to be respected. Havva was *sınıf annesi* in Handan's classroom and Handan always referred to her 'my classroom mother [*benim sınıf annem*]'. However, the other young, veiled pious working-class mothers in their early and late twenties (I call them 'wannabe classroom mothers') would not let Havva step up and take the lead. I observed several of Handan's meetings, which often involved the following scene:

Jîn: Tell us, Handan *hanım* [Ms. Handan], what do you want from us?
Ayşe: Handan *abla* [elder sister], I prepared a cake for you!
Havva: Tell us, Handan *hocam* [my teacher], how much is this?
Dilber: Handan *öğretmenim* [my teacher], how we should treat the kids at home?

The communication between Handan and the young mothers gave the appearance of deference on the part of mothers, and yet behind this deference there was a relatively complex scene. There was reciprocity with respect to the amount of time and energy both parts invested. Handan devoted a significant amount of time talking to mothers after school and the subjects discussed were mainly the mothers' own problems, such as divorce or financial problems. Handan told me that she was available on the phone day or night. This was not surprising given that Handan had selected these mothers – if not the pupils. She explained how she applied a kind of tacit selection process:

They say, 'I want you teacher Handan. I want my daughter to be your pupil'. When a parent comes to me in this way, I say that I have rules. I tell them that I do extracurricular activities and I use resources. I tell them that I demand things. So, if a parent comes to me, she/he knows what I expect. Though, with the parents' help, we always protect and cover those who are coming from poor families. I also keep a place for the poor kids. And yet it is not easy to mingle the poor kids, whose families cannot contribute, with the rich kids... I know I am not easy [smiles] ...

It is clear in Handan's account that only those mothers who offer their time, put their energy and give their money for everyday schooling could enter her classroom. Mothers were expected to donate to the school (remember the amount of donation in Zinnur was 100 liras) and also contribute in-kind, in cash and in the form of service in facilitating Handan's classes.

I think it is necessary here also to explain the subtext of 'mingling poor kids'. As can be seen in her account above, she set up a system at classroom level to 'cover' 'poor' pupils, but this was not perceived as a kind of 'charity work'. The claim was to protect 'financial stability' at classroom level and to maintain the 'integrity [*bütünlük*]' in the class. The other teachers of the pupils in Year Two, Year Three and Year Four also referred to the same word 'integrity' with the same claim. However, I think the intention was also to protect the interests of the mothers who abided by the 'rules' set by Handan. Certainly, 'tacit selection' was not the only reason that made Handan a 'celebrity' teacher in the school. Handan knew how to play to the *habitus* of young mothers by showing compassion, sometimes being direct, and sometimes without being 'polite'. I will return to this point later below.

Nigar

While Nigar's experience was one of the most graphic among the cases in Talip, it is an illustrative of the ones where the classroom-based system – *sınıf annesi* – was not well established. Nigar was in her fifties and had been working for more than two decades and was feeling tired. She had lost her motivation, particularly after she felt vulnerable with having to teach Year One pupils (aged five, six, seven). It was not easy for her to take five-year-old pupils to the toilet, one of the tasks she found most demanding following the introduction of 4+4+4 education reform that I discussed in Chapter 2.[12] During the classroom observations, I saw that she did not have many classroom supplies, for instance, I noticed that her marker did not have ink most of the time and half of the sentences she wrote were invisible. There was no compassion in her voice; nor was there a smile on her face during the classes – almost the total opposite of Handan's manner. As well, she did not have the assistance of a *sınıf annesi*.

In the middle of the second term, Nigar was attacked by one of the mothers during the daily ceremony. Briefly, a young mother, who was formerly the *sınıf annesi*, attempted to pull her hair to demean her before the crowd; however, Nigar calmed her down. Surprisingly, or not surprisingly (knowing the clashes in Talip), none of her colleagues supported her during or after this incident.

In the following days, she became more direct, and she told me that she was 'giving instructions' to the children of 'the terrorists', 'AKP voters', 'followers of Islamic *tariqa* orders [*tarikatçılar*]' and 'radical Islamists'. She also told me that she said to mothers who covered their mouth with a *peçe* (a garment that veils the face and/or mouth), 'Open your mouth I cannot understand you.' What I gleaned from our informal chats (she spoke differently when the recorder was on, and she admitted it openly) that it was not about a comprehension problem, rather an attack on mothers' political inclinations that were reflected in their garments.

She described herself as a right-wing Kemalist and the '"true" owner of the republic' as she put it. I observed many of Nigar's meetings with mothers and it was clear to me that Nigar valued her own status to be upper than of the mothers. And this, of course, did not go unnoticed by the mothers whose *habitus* was different from hers (i.e., non-verbal communication, style of language, gestures, attire, political dispositions, social class among the others). One day, when the meeting was over, some of the young mothers in their early twenties started imitating Nigar with exaggerated facial expressions. 'You should study more with your children!' they repeated, to ridicule her. It was like pupils mimicking a teacher as soon as she/he turns her/his back on them. The relationship between Nigar and the mothers was clearly an unwelcome accord of obligation.

***

I give heed to Diane Reay once more to better analyse the difference between Handan and Nigar above. Her suggestion with regard to differences such as gender among the others offers a better grasp of *habitus*. Reay states,

> Habitus is a way of looking at data which renders the 'taken-for-granted' problematic. It suggests a whole range of questions not necessarily addressed in empirical research; How well adapted is the individual to the context they find themselves in? How does personal history shape their responses to the contemporary setting? What subjective vocations do they bring to the present and how are they manifested? Are structural effects visible within small scale interactions? What is the meaning of non-verbal behaviour as well as individuals' use of language? These questions clearly raise issues of gender and 'race' alongside those of social class.
>
> (1995: 369)

To return to the contexts of Talip and Zinnur, Nigar was definitely not 'well adapted' to the school context. In other words, she was not familiar with the *field*, and to use the simile of the 'fish in the water' that Bourdieu and Wacquant (1992: 127) used to explain the concept of the *field*, she was 'out of the water'. The mothers could not communicate with Nigar in the way she expected. And at the same time, Nigar did not understand why they were pulling her hair or imitating her. In other words, Nigar could not interpret the body language, facial expressions, gestures and style of language of the pious working-class mothers. Handan, on the other hand, played the role of the *abla* (elder sister). As we have seen above, the mothers addressed her with 'respect'. They were all willing to do what Handan asked.

Diane Reay argues that '[h]abitus demands a complex analysis which both recognizes diversity within social groupings and highlights the crucial importance of the context in which actions take place' (1998: 33). Certainly, the *field*, which in this context is the local education market in the district, is significant. Comparisons between the attitudes of mothers in the past and in the present were a consistent theme in many of the interviews I conducted with mothers, teachers from both schools and women working for Bahçelik municipality. They all consistently told me that in the past mothers rarely had permission from their husbands to enter public spaces, including schools, because they were worried about possible encounters with unrelated men – for example, male teachers or the head teacher. Teachers working in *bilgi evis* (house of knowledge), which I explain below, told me that the local policies developed by the municipality targeting pupils, mothers and mother-child dyads changed fathers' attitudes and reshaped their perceptions of the school. In the course of the fieldwork, I also realized how these policies defined the boundaries of mothers' participation through the notion of 'good mothering', which I discuss in Chapter 6. These developments not only legitimized the absence of fathers in their children's education but also encouraged those pious working-class mothers who had dropped out of school early, who lacked knowledge, who were not politicized (i.e., who had no political connections in the district) to involve in education of their children. To return to the comparison of the cases of Nigar and Handan's: While Handan supported these policies, Nigar was not aware of them. However, for a better understanding of the *field*, one needs to include an important 'actor' in this local education market, namely the Bahçelik municipality or the 'patron' of the local education market which defined the 'rules of the game'.

***

The Bahçelik municipality: The 'patron' of the education market in the district

The role of the municipality in the local education market or in the *field* was evident from the vantage point of both schools. The mayor and the higher echelons of the Bahçelik district bureaucracy were recognized by most of the teachers, head teachers, deputy heads and mothers as their 'patrons'. In other words, they acted as if the reciprocal benefits were the mayor's to bestow. For the municipality, performing the role of 'patron' was a significant component of the AKP's overall mission in the district. Added to this, Bahçelik municipality was buttressed by the AKP, received a wide range of donations and grants, not only from national and international organizations but also from Islamic civil society, businessmen and businesswomen. While some of the allocated donations were formal and visible, others were informal and 'invisible'. For instance, in Zinnur – not in Talip – I observed that one morning more than 400 brand new coats were brought to the school, which were donated by a businessman or businesswoman who wished to remain anonymous. These coats were distributed to the pupils who were in need and the rest of the coats were sent to the school next to Zinnur. The kind of reciprocity that was expected from such donations was never spelt out. Talip was not in the network like Zinnur; therefore, they did not receive – or even hear of – such donations at the beginning of the school year, though the pupils in Talip were more needy. Bahçelik municipality developed fundraising events and identified networks that might support schools by the provision of in-kind services. Presumably for pro-Islamist AKP businessmen it was profitable.[13] However a school had to be in the network in order to benefit from such services, and in order to be part of the network teachers working in the schools had to have particular *cultural capital*. In other words, the 'patron' of the education market values particular ways of thinking which will be discussed in great detail in the following chapter. Nevertheless, while Zinnur was in the network Talip struggled to enter, I will illustrate the key event that helped Talip to enter this network below which will also further reveal the logic of the *field*.

'Robin Hood' of Talip: Taking from the affluent Islamist network

As I mentioned in Chapter 1, the newly appointed deputy head of Talip, Ahmet, lamented the wide disparities between the schools in the district and he was anxious to make the school 'better'. Ahmet realized that he would only get the support of the Bahçelik municipality if the school showed commitment. To achieve this, he found creative ways. In the many hours I spent in his busy office, I was able to observe almost all the strategies he developed. However, the most vivid was the event he organized on the occasion of the Holy Birth Week (*Kutlu Doğum Haftası*), which marks the birth of the Prophet Muhammad. Very briefly, Ahmet organized a poster competition for the week, selected the posters, designed an exhibition (some of which you will find in Chapter 4) and asked higher echelons of district bureaucracy, including the mayor, to open the exhibition, although he was unable to reach the mayor. Among the many other commemorations, the choice of Holy Birth Week was a strategic move. This is because in the 2012–13 school year, the observance of the week was still controversial in schools across the country. In Bahçelik, however, it was one of the biggest commemorations as the week was on the cultural agenda of the municipality – the details of which will be explained in the next chapter.

Following the opening of the exhibition, rumours were spreading among the teachers in Talip. One of the most interesting ones was that Ahmet – and the other deputy heads – had removed the portrait of Atatürk from the wall on the day that the higher echelons of district bureaucracy had paid a visit to the school to open the exhibition. As I have already explained, there was factionalism (along political and ethnic lines) among the teachers in the school and this seemingly 'trivial' act of removing 'a portrait' from the wall was perceived as very simplified way of saying 'I am pro-AKP [*AKPciyim*]'. The point is, what Ahmet considered to be suitable was not considered appropriate in many teachers' eyes. Ahmet did not discuss why such a rumour emerged or whether the rumour was true or not. Maybe it was just too obvious. I interpreted this rumour as an indication of growing unrest among some of the teachers, if not all, about Ahmet's marketing approach. Perhaps the donation in the form of services to Talip that followed the exhibition was a gesture of recognition of the school by the AKP followers in the local bureaucracy as well as the AKP municipality. The school received an offer to refurbish one of the classrooms to be used as a music room. The school suddenly became 'visible' to the 'patrons', or more accurately, 'rewarded'.

Brunching with the mayor of Bahçelik

Zinnur, in contrast, was already visible to the 'patrons' of the local education market. This became clearer to me when a brunch was organized to find a solution to the narrowness of the playground. In short, although Zinnur had a very large playground compared to Talip, the space in front of the school was so narrow that it created hustle and bustle during daily ceremonies. In addition, the land next to Zinnur's playground was empty, but the school needed advice and support to expand the school grounds so that it could have a proper ceremonial area. For this reason, the mayor of Bahçelik was invited to a very well-organized brunch. Although such consultation is part of the official duties of the municipalities, the schools were expected to offer something in return. In Zinnur, the mayor was offered a 'captive audience', which was evident in the rather long speech the mayor gave after the brunch. The bulk of the speech focused on the topical issue of the time, Kurdish Opening.[14] It was clear to me that the intention was to support AKP's national policy at the local level, where a significant number of citizens of Kurdish-descent reside. After the brunch was over, one of the teachers encapsulated the essence of the brunch: 'You scratch my back and I'll scratch yours [*al gülüm ver gülüm*]'. Most teachers in Zinnur knew the 'rules of the game' that govern the marketing practices in the local education market.

Making up for educational shortfalls: Filling the gaps and shaping the minds

Mapping the political education market in and around Zinnur and Talip would be incomplete unless the role of other significant actors – namely the Hidayet Dormitory of Hidayet community and the *bilgi evi* (house of knowledge) of the AKP Bahçelik municipality – was examined. By analysing Hidayet Dormitory, I will shed light on the for-profit private providers of educational services, and I will elaborate on the marketing strategies of Zinnur. My brief mention on *bilgi evi*, on the other hand, will further explain the role of the AKP municipality in the education market.

Hidayet Dormitory: 'In place of the parents'

Hidayet was a faith-based for-profit male-only dormitory owned by an Islamic community known for its links to an old Islamic *tariqa* order in Turkey, that I name the 'Hidayet community' (a pseudonym). There was no official connection between the school and the dormitory. However, all the boys – aged between twelve and fourteen – staying in Hidayet were registered at Zinnur. This was simply because the dormitory was in the Zinnur's catchment area. On the day of our official interview, the dormitory deputy head Hüseyin and a group of male teachers – most of whom were university students in Istanbul in the role of *abi* (elder brother) – gave me a tour of the facilities. However, this was not the first time I encountered Hüseyin and some of the university students. They acted in place of the parents of the boys staying in the dormitory and they had paid frequent visits to Zinnur to receive regular feedback on their performance in the classes. In other words, we were accustomed to seeing each other and evaluating boys' progress. Halim who was a teacher at Zinnur and a Hidayet community follower accompanied us as well. After a small talk, Hüseyin and Halim started to speak enthusiastically about the academic performance of the most prominent boys, and made comparisons between boys within their peer groups. Halim was volunteering at the dormitory and offering free tutoring to those boarding at Hidayet in his spare time and that is why he knew all of them. I also weighed in, revealing my own knowledge of some of the boys in question. In the meantime, they all showed me the modest study rooms and communal areas, such as the light and spacious canteen area. While we were heading towards an office, Hüseyin shared his own understanding of education. In his account, 'education had two wings': one was 'education (*eğitim*)' by engaging with the key sources of Sunni Islam – the Qur'an, hadith and *sunna* (prophetic custom) – and the transmission of norms, values and beliefs in line with the Hidayet community. Another was 'instruction (*öğretim*)' that would help children to acquire contemporary knowledge.

Hidayet Dormitory was officially named to provide boarding facilities to Year Six, Year Seven and Year Eight pupils, however; what I learned from Hüseyin and from the disclosure of pupils and teachers in Zinnur that its functions went well beyond that of a simple dormitory which were: (i) to prepare Year Eight pupils for nationwide competitive exams with a structured tutoring programme; (ii) to closely monitor the academic progress of pupils at school by acting in place of the parents; (iii) to offer tutoring in mathematics, English and Turkish; (iv) to provide intensive religious instruction in line with an unofficial religious education curriculum reflecting the ethos of the Hidayet community. Hüseyin also told me during our interview that prospective pupils were asked to take an entrance exam and provide grade point averages. In other words, there was a tacit selection process. In addition, the monthly fee was approximately 1,000 Turkish liras (approximately 55 sterling) which included all food, accommodation, pastoral care and tuition fees. This amount was exorbitant for many parents in the catchment area of Zinnur School.

With regard to motives of the parents for sending their children to the Hidayet Dormitory, I found various explanations. This is because the teachers in the dormitory acted in place of the parents, half of whom lived outside Istanbul, and I could only reach two 'real parents' (*gerçek veli*), as they were called by teachers in Zinnur. The 'real parents' were among the few who lived only a few blocks away from the dormitory and still enrolled their sons at Hidayet. In our unstructured informal interview, two mothers, Nezaket and Fadime, expressed that the dormitory compensated for the 'absence of Islamic teachings' in the state school curriculum. They both told me that they want their children to 'know their religion' (*dinlerini bilsin*). However, Fadime also explained to me how hard she had been working at her job and told me that she decided to send her boy Mustafa to Hidayet in order not to leave him 'unattended' (*başıboş*). In other words, she did not want Mustafa hanging around on the street on the weekdays when she was at work.

In addition, many focus group discussions with the Zinnur's teachers pointed to other parental motivations, such as divorce or a deceased spouse. Neither Nezaket's and Fadime's accounts nor the teachers' partial knowledge about the boys and their parents were sufficient to draw conclusions about the aspirations of the 'real parents'. However, for Hüseyin, the deputy head of Hidayet Dormitory, the parents' motives were too obvious, namely that the pupils would receive both 'education' and 'instruction' in the dormitory. At first glance, the Hidayet Dormitory certainly fits well with 'shadow education system', key features of which are (i) privateness, (ii) supplementation and (iii) focus on academic subjects (Bray 1999; Yung & Bray 2017: 96). Nevertheless, two distinctive features of the dormitory were evident. First, with what Hüseyin called 'education', Hidayet Dormitory aimed to impart *habitus* (in line with the Hidayet community) and promoted itself with this feature of the dormitory. Secondly, what Hüseyin did not mention, but what I observed, is that Hidayet also offered the service of what I call a 'professional' *loco parentis* role. That is why there was a term as 'real parents' as mentioned above, which will be clarified below. In what follows I turn to the relationship between Zinnur and Hidayet Dormitory and the role the dormitory played in marketing the school.

'The dormers' or the 'privileged' boys

That day, when I went to the Hidayet Dormitory for the interview, I also met with some boys in the carpeted corridors of the dormitory. They had just finished ablutions and while drying their faces, some said: 'Peace be upon you my teacher' (*selamun aleyküm hocam*). Others ignored me altogether, including some of my pupils from Zinnur. This was unusual because most primary school pupils greeted the teacher or at least nodded to her/him when they saw her/him regardless of gender. After a split second of perplexity, I realized that I was in a different learning space with a different curriculum as well as a pedagogy based on hierarchy and discipline. In one space, I was 'a total stranger', in the other I was a respected and loved teacher. Obviously, there was no continuity between the school and the dormitory or their temporary homes. At school despite the competitive nature of the contexts in both Hidayet and Zinnur, there was quite a strong fraternal relationship between these boys regardless of age. And this relationship required them to behave in a certain way at school, which was evident in the cases of disputes. For example, when a conflict arose between one of them and an 'ordinary' pupil in Zinnur, all the boys from Years Six to Eight supported their 'brothers'. Certainly, the boys staying in the dormitory had little time to interact with their classmates at school, in contrast to the time they spent in the dormitory, where they prayed, slept, ate and studied together, mostly under the strict supervision of young university students or *abis* – not to mention the possible influence or pressure of their peers or brothers on their behaviour inside and outside the dormitory.

The pupils of the Zinnur deemed the boys 'privileged' (*özel*) and called them 'the dormers' (*yurtlular*). This was not only because 'the dormers' were among the star pupils of their classes and were often praised for their academic achievements. It was mainly because the boys were treated differently as a group, which did not go unnoticed. For example, I learned from young female teachers that these boys often tried to control or disrupt the classes in which they formed a small group. Such instances occurred when only what the boys had learned in the dormitory contradicted the content of the official curriculum of the school (see Chapter 4). I was told that in these instances it was difficult for these teachers to keep the situation under control, as they feared being stigmatized, bullied or harassed by the boys and thus also by the teachers who were members of the Hidayet community. However, a closer look at the activities of the teachers in Zinnur who followed the Hidayet community reveals a rather complex relationship between the school and the dormitory and further explains why the boys were perceived as 'privileged' by the pupils in Zinnur and the reasons for the concerns of the young female teachers, even if they were few.

Hidayet community member at heart, schoolteacher by training

As I mentioned earlier, both Halim and Üzeyir were Zinnur teachers who were followers of the Hidayet community. In other words, both were officially working in Zinnur and at the same time volunteering for the Hidayet Dormitory as members of the Hidayet community. For me, the most important question was whether the interests of the dormitory took precedence. Or did the teachers prioritize the needs of the school and thus all the pupils? As the school year continued, it became clear to me that they were giving priority to market and ideological interests of the dormitory. Firstly, these teachers made Zinnur what I call 'a captive market' for Hidayet community. Üzeyir and Halim at times participated in and partly led various activities of the dormitory that targeted all the pupils in Zinnur. These included selling books published by the Hidayet community-owned publishing companies, offering free mock exams to advertise the dormitory, organizing charity events (e.g., jumble sales) and asking for donations for the community's foundations. Halim also told me that the dormitory offered free Qur'an courses for boys who lived in the Zinnur's catchment area. It was clear to me that this was primarily a marketing strategy to attract boys who might not otherwise had access to the dormitory.

Secondly, they urged the teachers in Zinnur to serve the dormitory. Üzeyir and Halim asked almost all the hardworking teachers, including me, to offer free revision and tutoring to the boys who were staying in the dormitory. For this purpose, they invited male teachers to the dormitory, while they expected female teachers to schedule classes on the school premises. Also, the teachers in Zinnur gave continuous feedback to the teachers who acted in place of the parents, which was not an option for the other parents in the school. Thirdly, they wanted to create continuity between the school and the dorm. Among the many examples of such attempts, I think the boldest and most explanatory were those that showed the intrusion of gender socialization practices. It was in the first week of the school year when Üzeyir presented the blueprint of 'what school is' or 'what a teacher does' in the school to me and other newcomer female teachers:

> The Prophet is the teacher of all human beings, and a teacher in a school is a teacher of all pupils. This school is full of children. When you come through the door, you must leave everything outside this building. For instance, you might hold different ideas … You cannot defend your opinions inside the school.

> Sobriety [*sadelik*] is the most important thing. Sobriety! Whether in your
> opinions or in your dress ...

The word 'sobriety' was a kind of loose umbrella term he used to refer to the
rules of women's acceptable attire as well as gender socialization in the school.
I understood what he intended to do by briefing us only later. His aim was to
identify teachers who could disrupt the school from within by changing the
rules related to cross-gender interactions. And in doing so, as I mentioned
earlier, Üzeyir wanted to balance what he perceived as a discrepancy between
co-educational socialization at school and the gender-segregated socialization
in the male only dormitory Hidayet.

The head teacher and deputy heads did not frown upon Hidayet followers nor
did the other teachers 'raise their voices', as one of the young freshly graduated
teachers put it, against the various activities of Üzeyir and Halim, even when they
intervened in gender socialization at the school. Undoubtedly, the *habitus* of the
teachers in Zinnur contributed significantly to what some teachers at the school
called as 'silence'. As I have already explained, most of the Year Five to Year Eight
teachers at Zinnur, like the boys at Hidayet, socialized in the dorms or in other
educational settings – subsidized or provided by Islamic communities – outside
the schools, or were supported in some way by an Islamic community. However,
their *habitus* offers only a partial explanation. For a full grasp, we need to shift
the focus from the interests of the Hidayet Dormitory to the interests of Zinnur
and follow the marketing strategies of the school, which reveals significant
insights into the rather complex relationship between the dormitory and the
school. It also offers further explanation to the 'value' of boys staying in the
dormitory.

Zinnur's marketing strategies through Hidayet

Taking the risk of repetition here I would like to clarify the marketing strategy
of Zinnur. First, Hidayet Dormitory was not seen by many teachers as a for-
profit dormitory that pursued the goals of the Hidayet community, but as a
representative of the parents of the boarders of dormitory. Üzeyir and Halim
were perceived as mouthpieces of Hidayet teachers, acting in place of the parents
in the school. Therefore, the teachers adapted to the 'wishes' of the 'parents',
even if they were not 'real parents'. In this respect, Hidayet's teachers acted very
much like middle-class parents who 'exploit the education market' with their
cultural capital (Ball 2003). This was also true of Gülen teachers who acted on

behalf of the mothers, as I explained earlier at the very beginning of this chapter. The second equally significant point is the 'value' (Ball & Gewirtz 1997) of the boys who were staying in the Hidayet Dormitory. More precisely boys had value in the education market of Bahçelik district. The boys' academic achievements encouraged parents to continue donating to the school and attracted better-off parents with high expectations of their children. Boys' names were on the top of the list displayed outside the school with the title: 'Our Source of Pride' (*'Gurur Tablomuz'*) – as I mentioned in Chapter 1. Added to that the school's high reputation in the district had also attracted the attention of district officials including the municipality, making the school eligible for donations. In other words, the close relationship with the Hidayet community through the Hidayet Dormitory certainly also played a role in the highly politicized education market, where the Islamist AKP municipality offered privileges exclusively to Islamic communities, constituencies, civil society actors and the schools that show commitment as I have already illustrated above.

Bilgi evi: The new trend in Istanbul

Bilgi evi was among the key centres for afterschool activities for a significant number of pupils, predominantly for girls, in Talip and Zinnur. While there were cultural centres with the same name in other cities, it is fair to say that *bilgi evi* was a predominantly Istanbul-based phenomenon and a shared project of AKP-run municipalities in 2010s. The first *bilgi evi* was established by the AKP-run municipality of Zeytinburnu in Istanbul in 2004 (Aydın 2008: 191).[15] In rapidly growing districts, the demand for services – especially in education – has undoubtedly led to greater municipal involvement. And at the same time, the revision of the legal framework of municipalities had expanded their responsibilities and duties.[16] Within the borders of Istanbul, the numbers of *bilgi evis* reached up to 150 in the mid-2010s (Şolt 2014). In the meantime, growing number of non-AKP-run municipalities also started to adopt some aspects of *bilgi evi*, albeit using a different name. Moreover, 'culture centres' would be an umbrella term for *bilgi evis* which conceals the diversity beneath. In other words, the form, content and organizational structure of *bilgi evi* varied from district to district and even from neighbourhood to neighbourhood within Istanbul's borders. I saw two main reasons for this diversity. The first was that the municipalities were involved in defining the 'needs' of the children, which varied greatly between districts. The second reason was that the definitions of 'services' were not the same in each context. However, a common feature of all the *bilgi evi*s established by the AKP municipalities in Istanbul seemed to be that the preferences of party members took precedence over the content of the school curricula. This was also the case in Bahçelik as will be explained below.

Chameleon like *bilgi evis*: Unmet needs

From the vantage point of Zinnur and Talip, the *bilgi evis* created a kind of symbiotic relationship with the schools in the sense that they were designed around the deficiencies of state primary schools. Four important services that the *bilgi evis* provided in Bahçelik, as in many AKP-run municipalities, explain my argument. First, they functioned as a kind of study centre for children, providing access to libraries, computers and child-friendly study spaces. I learned from both the pupils in Zinnur and Talip and the librarians working for the municipality that access to study spaces was a very important resource in the district. This was simply because many pupils told me that the physical conditions in their homes were not suitable for studying. Secondly, *bilgi evis* offered co-curricular activities. These tutoring sessions functioned as revision classes according to the national curriculum. They consisted of a relatively small group of pupils – no more than fifteen – who were taught Turkish, mathematics, social studies and English by professional teachers. During my visits to the *bilgi evis*, the teachers told me that high demand and pressure from pupils' mothers led to the current form of tutoring. In Bahçelik, the municipality encouraged the mothers' involvement and valued their wishes (see Chapter 6) as long as these 'wishes' did not go against the preferences of the AKP members. Moreover, after the implementation of the 4+4+4 education reform, *bilgi evi* started to offer tutoring in Islamic subjects – such as the Qur'an – during the summer. This expansion was in addition to the Qur'an courses already offered by the DİB through the mosques in the district as well as by Islamic communities such as Hidayet as I explained above. Thirdly, the *bilgi evis* offered a wealth of free recreational opportunities, including clubs, competitions, choirs, bands, arts and crafts, music, sports and so on. In the *bilgi evis* clubs, pupils participated in actual activities, which was not the case in Zinnur and Talip. In both schools there was lack of space, materials, time and guidance from teachers for the clubs to function properly. In terms of content, it is possible to claim that the *bilgi evis* served as a medium to disseminate the tastes, beliefs, ideals and symbols of both the AKP and the now-criminalized Gülen community. Fourthly, *bilgi evis* were a platform to inform pupils about the cultural events that took place in the district in which Islamist intellectuals, writers, thinkers, musicians and more reach children with their books, songs and more. In addition, certain commemorative ceremonies were held in *bilgi evis*, including the Day of Commemoration of the Adoption of the National Anthem and Mehmet Akif Ersoy, and the celebration of Holy Birth Week (which I discuss in detail in Chapter 4). Last but not least, one of the interesting aspects of *bilgi evis* was that, as I have already mentioned, in both Talip and Zinnur it was mainly girls who attended *bilgi evis'* services, clubs, courses and more. I had the impression that *bilgi evi* created public spaces where girls could safely be outside and socialize under the control of the *bilgi evi* teachers. From the boys' and girls' accounts, I learned that boys benefitted from more unsupervised recreational activities, such as playing in the streets, while girls were generally more closely monitored. *Bilgi evi* teachers also suggested that the *bilgi evis* in the district mainly attract girls.

Nevertheless, a complex landscape emerged in Bahçelik with, on the one hand, publicly funded primary schools – Zinnur and Talip – and, on the other hand, again publicly funded cultural centres – the *bilgi evis*. In other words, in a context where both schools had a budget deficit, the Bahçelik municipality stepped in and, as I explained above, offered amenities and services that both schools could not provide. Therefore, many services provided by the *bilgi evis*, which were supposed to be a public good, were to some extent transformed into a municipality-driven and hence AKP-supported service. More importantly, the content of the various recreational activities in the *bilgi evi* indicates that these centres also aim to promote the ideals of the AKP which I will discuss in the following chapter.

Conclusion

As we have seen in this chapter, in Bahçelik, SBM led to establishment of a local education market, which was *literally* a market. The logic of this local market is the answer to one of the key questions of this chapter: Why some schools are 'rich' while others not? Or, more precisely why Zinnur was rich while Talip was not? This chapter consists of three levels of simultaneous analysis of local education market from the vantage point of Talip and Zinnur schools. The first level is devoted to outlining what I call 'tacit marketing structure'. Identifying the roles of almost all actors within this structure forms the second level of analysis. The third level is about finding answers to the significant questions that help us to grasp the inner logic of this market, such as who is valued, who is rewarded or punished, and who exploits this market among the others. I will very briefly explain each level separately.

First, while the relevant literature in the country has mainly analysed the functioning of OABs or examined the schools' budget (i.e., the schools' income and expenditure) (Altuntaş 2005; Candaş et al. 2011; Köse & Şaşmaz 2014; Özdemir 2011; Yolcu 2007), I comparatively followed the context-specific practices in two schools that revealed a 'tacit marketing structure' in which (i) teachers of Year Five, Year Six, Year Seven and Year Eight were responsible for convincing parents to *donate* to the school; (ii) teachers of Year One to Year Four created class-based systems and, in this structure, urged pupils' mothers to take on the role of *sınıf annesi* (classroom mother); (ii) schools engaged in local politics (i.e., for the interests of the AKP-run Bahçelik municipality); (iii) and schools built relationships with Islamic communities. It was significant to set out this tacit structure which illustrated briefly 'who does what' and made the next level of analysis comprehensible.

The second level involved analysis of the main actors that is presented in this chapter: parents, teachers, pupils, the district municipality and the Islamic communities. The starting point was the question of why some teachers were very successful and why others did not succeed in getting parents (predominantly mothers) to donate to the schools. I drew mainly on Bourdieu's (1986, 1996, 2010; Bourdieu & Passeron 1990) conceptual tools of *habitus, capital* and *field* and worked with Diane Reay's (1998, 2004, 2006, 2009) interpretation of *habitus* to find answers, or more precisely explain what I found in the schools and in the local education market. To start with the 'parents', it was clear that those who had distinct *habitus, social capital* and *cultural capital* had advantages. I have highlighted the word 'parents' because we have seen how problematic the term 'parents' is and yet how much we take it for granted. We have seen that (i) mothers, not fathers, were involved in the education of their children; (ii) Islamic community-affiliated teachers interfere in decisions of mothers; (iii) Hidayet Dormitory – a for-profit private dormitory for boys only, owned by the Hidayet community – acted as 'professional' *loco parentis*. In the case of teachers, comparative analysis of the two school contexts revealed that in Talip there was a lack of uniformity among teachers, while in Zinnur teachers with their different individual *habituses* formed an alliance to market the school. Moreover, the teachers who knew how to play to the *habitus* of working-class pious mothers had an advantage. The district Bahçelik municipality was perceived as the 'patron' of the local education market, with the power to determine the rules of the game in the *field* while the role of the Islamic communities was more complex and yet had great influence, as can be seen in the case of the Hidayet community-owned Hidayet Dormitory or the activities of the Gülen-affiliated teachers.

Third level of analysis aimed to explain the 'rule of the game' in the local market from within both schools. I am inspired by analysis of 'education market' of sociologists (Ball 1993, 2003; Ball & Gewirtz 1997; Bowe et al. 1994) which suggest an approach among the others to see the logic of the market – almost like a list of where to look to grasp the inner logic of the market. And I asked questions such as who exploits this market and who is valued or rewarded. The answers, which I have detailed in this chapter, offered further explanations for the sharp difference between Talip and Zinnur. And one of the most crucial findings was that while Zinnur with teachers, mothers (parents) and pupils adapted to this local market Talip was not well adapted.

Having said that, this chapter is the base of this book, the aim of which is finding answers to how Islamization and that of consolidation of neoliberalism transformed education under the AKP in Turkey by focusing on political aspect of neoliberal education policy SBM from the vantage point of Talip and Zinnur Schools, that is, Islamization of primary schooling. The following chapters will add and enlarge this chapter.

4

Culture wars: Fragments from 'lived culture' of Talip and Zinnur

It is possible to re-read almost all literature across all social science disciplines in Turkey from the perspective of culture wars, or hegemonic struggles in the Gramscian sense since the mobilization of political forces opposing the Kemalist modernization project. At the heart of this struggle, discussed in Chapter 2, is the question of whose values will prevail and be passed on to the next generation and how the cadres of the state's power centres will be educated. Since AKP came to power, almost every aspect of state education has been at stake in a cultural tug-of-war that has been intensifying since the mid-2000s. One of the key questions regarding these changes has been whether the ruling AKP regime represents a radical shift or whether it is better understood as another phase in the 'social engineering' of state education displaying some continuities with the pre-AKP past. Is the AKP period the last chapter in the gradual demise of the republican ideal of secular universal state education – an ideal that was first crystalized in the Law on the Unification of Education (*Tevhid-i Tedrisat Kanunu*) of 1924, which introduced a unified universal education system regardless of ethnic, religious and gender differences?

There is no simple answer to this far-reaching question. Approaches to the field of education that are prevalent since the 1980s still dominate discussions and have taken insufficient account of changes in the bigger picture from the 2000s onwards. One such approach is to explain Islamization in education by limiting the analysis to the expansion of state-funded Islamic schools, namely the *imam-hatip* schools, which were originally established to train *imams* (prayer leaders) and *hatips* (preachers) (Aksit 1991; Gökaçtı 2005; Ozgur 2012). This involves scrutinizing *imam-hatip* schools, tracing their development, examining their links to Islamic movements and describing typologies of their students or parents. Another approach examines changes in state ideology and traces the ways in which Islam has been integrated into national identity since the founding of the republic. One of the most discussed official ideologies in this regard is the Turkish-Islamic Synthesis, which incorporated Islam into the national imaginary to indoctrinate students and socialize younger generations after the 1980 military intervention. The dominant versions of this approach, with Sam Kaplan's (2006) ethnographic work being a notable exception, neglect institutional analysis relying, instead, on a close reading of the Turkish-Islamic Synthesis discourse (Kaplan 1999).

Although the term 'cultural struggle' (*kulturkampf*) originated in Bismarck's Germany between 1871 and 1887 and refers to the conflicts between the Protestant civil authority and the Roman Catholic Church, I use the term analogically in the early 2010s Turkish context to denote struggles over resources, personnel and symbols in the domain of state education. These struggles, which initially pitted secular versus religious orientations, have become increasingly complex since the 1980s with the entrance of a variety of Islamic actors into the educational arena as I discussed in Chapter 2. This chapter sheds a light to cultural struggle from the vantage point of Zinnur and Talip by using Raymond Williams' concept of the *structure of feeling* as a point of reference and approach rather than a fixed conceptual tool to trace *lived culture* (Williams 2001: 66) of both school settings. With *structure of feeling*, Williams (1977) suggests that the focus on the 'institutionalized' ways of thinking impedes not only the remnants of the 'residual' but also the 'emergent or pre-emergent' mode of thinking. In doing so, it does not exclude the dominant mode of thought or, as Gramsci (1971) puts it, *hegemony*, but offers a perspective to recognize the 'emergent or pre-emergent' (alternative and/or oppositional) to the dominant ideology. More specifically, *structure of feeling* defines 'a social experience which is still in process, often indeed not yet recognized as social but taken to be private, idiosyncratic and even isolating, but which in analysis [...] has its emergent, connecting, and dominant characteristics. [...] These are often more recognizable at a later stage, when they have been (as often happens) formalized [...]' (Williams 1977: 132). Although *structure of feeling* can easily be linked to changing conventions in literature or art, as Williams argues (1977: 133–4), it also provides a lens through which 'emergent or even pre-emergent' modes of thinking can be discerned in the 'presences' in everyday school life.

In what follows I focus on seemingly 'idiosyncratic' games, or more accurately play forms that pupils invented and enjoyed playing in both schools, and then I look at the some of the very popular songs among pupils, or as pupils called 'hymns'. In addition, I analyse some of the posters the pupils designed albeit selectively. Therefore, this chapter is not about what is said and meant in textbooks, nor is it about already institutionalized practises, ideas and imaginaries. Rather it is mostly about fragments from the *lived culture* (Williams 2001) of both schools. Also, in an attempt to find their sources of inspiration I also touch on two commemorations, namely the Day of Commemoration of the Adoption of the National Anthem and Mehmet Akif Ersoy and Holy Birth Week (*Kutlu Doğum Haftası*) that venerates Muhammad the Prophet which was celebrated in both schools during the 2012–13 school year. Having said that in the first section I focus on the pupils' plays, in the second section I briefly explain the significance of Mehmet Akif Ersoy for the AKP and in the last section I look at the songs that the boys and girls enjoyed singing and the posters they designed during Holy Birth Week.

Iconoclastic play forms: 'Iconoclasm as child's play'

It was after discovering the play forms that the pupils in both schools invented and performed, I realized existence of two parallel symbolic domains. In the textbooks of the 2012–13 school year, Mustafa Kemal (1881–1938) was portrayed as the first educator-in-chief (*başöğretmen*), 'founder of the republic', first president of the Turkish Republic, commander-in-chief of the Nationalist Army in Turkish War of Independence and 'the father of the nation' (*Atatürk*). In the forms of play Year Five, Six, Seven and Eight pupils invented and played, however; he was a '*kafir*' (infidel),' 'a demonic figure' and 'mocked hero' that I illustrate below. I am guided by Joan Huizinga's rather broad yet subtle two main characterizations of play. One is that play is 'free' and the second characteristic of play is that it is '[…] not "ordinary" or "real" life. It is rather a stepping out of "real" life into a temporary sphere of activity with a disposition all its own. Every child knows perfectly well that he is "only pretending", or that it was "only for fun"' (2002: 8).

Inspired by the early ethnographic analysis of Atatürk symbolism by the renowned anthropologists Yael Navaro-Yashin (2002b) and Esra Özyürek (2006) and the discovery of many play forms in which pupils incorporate Atatürk busts, images and more, I also included concept of iconoclasm. In this regard I am intrigued by Joe Moshenska's (2019) in-depth discussion and analysis of 'iconoclasm as child's play'. In particular, at the beginning of his book Moshenska (2019: ix–x) gives example with Roman Catholic preacher Roger Edgeworth who speaks about the practice of Reformers taking sacred objects from churches and giving them to children as toys to break their power in a sermon delivered in Bristol, England, in the sixteenth century. Although Moshenska focuses on Anglo American literary studies, he goes deep in his scholarly search for 'iconoclasm as child's play' and offers significant insights to think about both concepts. In what follows I illustrate and analyse three forms of play which boys and girls invented and enjoyed playing in both schools.

A 'super-funny' play: '*Dabbe*'[1]

In Zinnur, Year Five pupils Muhammed and Furkan started to relate an incident that happened the previous day, right before the end of our class. Muhammed told their classmates (and, to me, in a lower, more serious tone) that they looked at the portrait of Atatürk hanging above the door of the conference hall in the basement, and they found that there was something wrong with Atatürk's eyes. Furkan said, 'Atatürk's eyes turned brown ... And then changed to black. Suddenly, they were filled with blood!' Muhammed added, 'Atatürk's eyes were moving. We saw it! *Vallahi hocam* [I swear my teacher].' Furkan went further, 'Atatürk is possessed by *dabbe*!' The pupils in the class were shocked, amused, excited, laughing, etc., on hearing what Muhammed and Furkan said. They spread the word and it went viral within ten minutes, even if only among the Year Fives during the short break. In the meantime, they were already engaged in a game that I call '*dabbe* play', the rules of which were relatively simple: one had to go to the basement, look the portrait of Atatürk in the eyes, pretend to see the existence of 'evil', and come back with a 'scary' narrative. Pupils found the game funny, hilarious, entertaining and they shaped it continuously in relation to the restraints and limits imposed by teachers.

On the same day, a Wednesday, pupils reshaped the *dabbe* play during the long afternoon break by flocking to the basement in large groups. All the Year Five pupils in the school – more than 200 pupils – attempted to go down to see the picture. Mass entertainment rushed into a vacuum, and it would be hard for it to pass unnoticed by teachers, who did not have the slightest idea about what was happening. The teachers assigned Year Eight pupils the task of stopping the Year Fives from going to the basement by guarding the steps and not allowing any pupils to go down.[2] The admonishments and interdictions did not end the game but increased the tension and made it even more entertaining.

I had immediately recognized the similarities between their play and some of the elements of an emerging Turkish horror genre, in particular films by Hasan Karacadağ who was very popular among the Year Fives.[3] There was a 'creepy' place (basement), an imagined threat ('malignant' *jinn*, *dabbe*, evil) and an ordinary familiar object that had become uncanny, unsettling, strange and demonic (Atatürk's portrait). Pupils were the chief protagonists of this 'play' as 'beholders' and 'storytellers'.

On the second day, Thursday, a group of Year Five pupils (in another class) tried to mock me by telling me that the Atatürk portrait in the classroom was haunted. Again, it was the beginning of a class and they frantically spoke without waiting for each other to finish. 'His eyes were rolling back and forth. It was kind of scary ...', said Beytullah. 'I saw it too', added Kaan. Beytullah thundered, 'Yes, look up at Atatürk's portrait [pointing his hand at the portrait hanging on the board]. His eyes are rolling. Still! Waooo! ... He is possessed.' Kaan interrupted again and said, 'There are *cins* [*jinn*] in his eyes.' 'He is possessed, he is possessed by *dabbe*!' said Mert. Mert and Kaan were pretending to be serious; however, there was an impish and playful smile on Beytullah's face. Following their short dramatization, pupils would either turn their eyes away from the portrait or examine it carefully to see 'whether Atatürk's eyes were moving', as they put it, during the entire class. I also learned from the disclosures of the teachers that the classes were frequently disrupted with different versions of the play.

On the third day, Friday, it was as if the entire lower secondary section of the school (Year Five, Six, Seven, Eight) was already humming about *jinn*. Only when I shared the synopsis of the popular horror films by Hasan Karacadağ with the head teacher, İsmail, did he understand the pupils' sources of inspiration. He addressed the topic that day during the Friday ceremony that marks the end of the week. 'This *dabbe* nonsense is a fabrication of the film industry in Turkey. The film is not real, it is a fiction, and enough is enough! Do you hear me? Enough is enough!' he said at the end of the ceremony, speaking in an angry tone to the entire school. İsmail's words, coupled with the weekend holiday, put an end to the *dabbe* play by Year Five, Six, Seven and Eight pupils who had had a great time for three days.

In all forms of iconoclastic '*dabbe* play' the portraits, pictures of Atatürk became 'hybrid' figure. Joe Moshenska's interpretation of 'doll-idol- "the idoll"' explains this hybridity well which is 'neither obviously valuable or worthless, neither obviously alive or dead, obviously deserving of neither pure reverence nor pure revulsion, neither tentative care nor violent breaking alone' (2019: 43–4). An interesting facet of this game was that it was adolescent play, and younger pupils in Years Two, Three and Four (remember there were no Year One classes in Zinnur due to the transformation of primary schools following the 4+4+4 education reform) did not take part. The *dabbe* never paid a visit to the many gazes of Atatürk in Year Two, Three and Four classrooms, figuratively speaking. In these classrooms, the corners were reserved for collages of Atatürk's pictures, known as Atatürk Corners. These corners have become a significant part of the visual symbolism of schools since 1977 (MEB 1977). In Zinnur, the pupils used poems, quotes, pictures and photographs to depict various aspects of Atatürk's life – personal as well as political (see Figures 1 and 2). I saw a difference between the images that was similar to what anthropologist Esra Özyürek (2006) found in her ethnographic work. There were pictures and photographs of Atatürk that showed him 'as serious, solemn and superhuman' (Özyürek 2006: 123). There were also pictures of him 'engaged in social activities and mundane pleasures' (Özyürek 2006: 123).

I noticed the sharp contrast in the Atatürk Corners of Year Five, Six, Seven and Eight, where most of the photographs were either torn to pieces, or the corner was erected merely to meet the required regulation, which was apparent in the ways in which these corners were presented (see Figures 3 and 4).

Figure 1 Atatürk Corner in a Year Three classroom at Zinnur School.

Figure 2 Atatürk Corner in a Year Two classroom at Zinnur School.

Figure 3 Atatürk Corner in a Year Seven classroom at Zinnur School.

Figure 4 Atatürk Corner in a Year Eight classroom at Zinnur School.

Dabbe play also provided me with an impetus for a fresh look at the portraits hanging on the walls inside Zinnur (and Talip as well). I wondered why, in a figurative sense, Atatürk's portrait was the target of demonic forces. There were several other alternatives, such as the portraits of leaders of 'Turkic Empires', which were chosen to comply with the regulations introduced in the 1980s and elaborated in the 1990s (MEB 1982, 1990). These leaders include Alp Arslan (1029–72), who ruled the Seljuk Empire, or the martyr Hasan of Ulubat, who played an important role in the siege of Constantinople in 1453 as a soldier of Sultan Mehmed II (see Figures 5 and 6). The walls reflected what might be called visual universe of the Turkish-Islamic Synthesis.

When looking at the walls of Zinnur, Ayşe Gül Altınay's argument that masculine heritage is essential to the idea of what she defines as the myth that 'the Turkish nation is a military nation' (2004a) came to my mind. There was not a single portrait of a female leader, author, artist or thinker on the walls, although the actual regulation on decorating the walls of schools recommends the use of portraits of women that encapsulate 'Turkish womanhood', such as those 'who carried bombs during the Turkish War of Independence' (MEB 1990). It was interesting to see the similarity of the walls to content of the old national security

Figure 5 The walls of Zinnur School I.
(From left to right: Mustafa Kemal, Beyazid I, Mehmed II, Hasan of Ulubat, Selim I.)

Figure 6 The walls of Zinnur School II.
(From left to right: Oghuz Khan, Atilla, Alp Arslan, Osman I, Mustafa Kemal.)

studies textbooks of the late 1990s in which there was no image of 'woman' (Kancı & Altınay 2007: 62). On the walls of Zinnur the only exceptions were the images of women appeared alongside Atatürk in collages pinned to Atatürk Corners.

Moreover, rather newly hung portraits of all-male poets, authors and thinkers, including Necip Fazıl Kısakürek, Sezai Karakoç and Mehmet Akif Ersoy who have inspired generations of Islamists in Turkey, figuratively speaking, evaded possession as well. The selection of these authors from the long list of possibilities was no accident. Although there were heated debates about 'cultural unity' at the national level, at the local level an alternative 'repertoire' was already emerged following the lead of the Bahçelik municipality, and the school walls reflected this. Having said that, I observed other forms of play in Zinnur as well. In the following I explain the play forms invented by the boys staying in Hidayet Dormitory.

Spitting on the face of the '*kafir* [infidel]'

I observed several times when Year Six, Year Seven and Year Eight pupils who were staying in Hidayet Dormitory spit on the face of Atatürk's bust in Zinnur. It was a kind of role play which required all these boys to adopt the role of an 'iconoclast', who destroys images, sculptures, statues. It was obvious to me that had it not been overt vandalism, they would have taken one more step and shattered the bust into pieces within moments to make their role playing more shocking, or more accurately persuasive. They never included other pictures or portraits to their play, like Year Five boys and girls who played *dabbe* that I explained above. I think boys' play which I call 'spitting play' served to distinguish themselves from the rest of the Zinnur School. I explained in detail how these boys were valued and treated differently in the school and yet how they remained close to their fraternity and *abis* (elder brother) acting in place of their parents in the previous chapter. In this regard, part of it was to show their belonging to the Hidayet Dormitory, more specifically, loyalty to the solidarity built by *abis*, and their fraternal brothers. As Huizinga put it, play 'promotes social groupings which tend to surround themselves with secrecy and to stress their difference from the common world by disguise or other means' (2002: 13).

Moreover, there was another form of play in which again boys targeted Atatürk. In this version of the play, boys adopted what I call 'provocateur' role and used slogan like statements or sentences in the form of rhetorical questions to disrupt the classes. For instance, in a class that I observed, Year Eight pupil İlhan said, '[Atatürk] *Kuran'ın üstünde dansöz oynattı*' ('[Atatürk] made belly dancers dance on the Qur'an') and then whispered, '*kafir* [infidel]'. Boys did not elaborate but just shouted or whispered to cut the silences in the classrooms or take the attention to themselves. In another class that I taught Year Six pupil Osman shouted, 'he [Atatürk] forced women to unveil', and Semih added, 'no one saw him [Atatürk] praying in any mosque'. Atatürk's personal and political life: his habit of drinking alcohol, his reforms to secularize and modernize society, his attempts to change the role and status of women in society through various reforms were selected by the boys in this play. Again, I think the boys aimed to emphasize their differences. While they were showing defiance to official narrative of Atatürk, they were showing compliance to narratives of *abis* in Hidayet Dormitory.

'Atatürk set his foot on Samsun'

In Talip I was also interested in the games pupils enjoyed playing. I discovered a form of play that Year Four girls liked to play called *Atatürk Samsun'a ayak bastı* ('Atatürk set his foot on Samsun') when I was observing the Physical Education (PE) classes of the Year Two, Three and Four pupils in the school. Both crowding and limited space in Talip, which I explain in the following chapter, led teachers to perform PE classes together in an irregular manner in the open space of the school. Besides, as I illustrated in the previous chapter, the necessary or crucial pieces of equipment (e.g., balls) could not be added to the long 'shopping list' of Talip teachers. Therefore, those pupils who brought skipping ropes and balls from home played games, and those who did not either had snacks (they called it 'having a picnic') or made up games such as 'Atatürk set his foot on Samsun'. In this physical form of play, each female pupil was expected to step on another's feet with one foot; and, when successful, she had to shout: 'Atatürk set his foot on Samsun!' The exclamation they used is among the ritualized expressions derived from the opening sentence of the speech Atatürk delivered, known as *Nutuk* ('The Speech'). Atatürk marks the first step in the Struggle for Independence and the first concrete step against the Ottoman Sultan-Caliph by saying, '*1919 senesi Mayısının 19 uncu günü Samsun'a çıktım*' (I landed in Samsun on the nineteenth day of May 1919) in his own account on the foundation of the republic (1963: 1).[4] These girls were pretending to be Atatürk while trivializing his one of the key steps in the establishment of the republic.

***

Comparing three forms of play I illustrated above allows us to see different features of each. Year Fives mostly boys in Zinnur wanted to haunt the school with scary narratives with *dabbe* while boys who were staying in Hidayet (Year Six to Year Eight) aimed to provoke teachers and pupils in again Zinnur. However, Year Four girls in Talip performed a pretend play with their peers. Definitely, girls and boys were all in search for fun within the limits of under-resourced Talip and Zinnur and how they define 'fun' differed a lot in relation to expected gender roles as well as age differences. However, reading their imaginations was not easy, knowing anthropologist Michael Taussig's brilliant phrase which is 'the adult's imagination of the child's imagination' (2003: 449). At first glance definitely all the forms of play seem 'idiosyncratic'; however when put in the context of the Bahçelik district as well as both school contexts, they also reveal significant insights. All the boys and girls in one or other way, figuratively speaking, attacked only the remains of the republic's most iconic leader, Mustafa Kemal Atatürk. It was at a time when AKP's iconoclastic measures to destroy republican symbols with an extensive campaign of 'de-Atatürkification' (Kandiyoti & Emanet 2017) as a strategy to renounce the Kemalist revolution were becoming only visible. As mentioned in Chapter 2, there had been several failed as well as accomplished attempts to eradicate Atatürk symbolism. Therefore, I think girls and boys also reflect on the 'emergent or pre-emergent' (Williams 1977) way of thinking in the district and in both schools. Having said that, I argue that substitution of an alternative national hero, Mehmet Akif Ersoy, also played an important role in the degradation of Atatürk from a national hero to a 'demonic' flawed historical figure. In what follows I focus on the significance of Mehmet Akif Ersoy for AKP.

***

A substitute 'hero'?: The figurehead for the ideal generation

Figure 7 Office board in the office of the deputy head Ruhi in Zinnur I.

Figure 8 Office board in the office of the deputy head Ruhi in Zinnur II.

Figure 7 shows the card for the celebration of the 'Day of Commemoration of the Adoption of the National Anthem and Mehmet Akif Ersoy' that Ruhi, one of the deputy heads of Zinnur, had pinned, or rather taped, on the board in his busy office. On the card, which was distributed by the Bahçelik municipality, is the picture of Mehmet Akif Ersoy (1873–1936), whose poems and political thought make him one of the most influential Islamist figures in the country (Aktay 2005; Bulaç 2005; Kara 2005; Ünsal 2005).[5] And a quote from one of his most popular poems, *Asım*, is also on the card. It was clear to me that Ruhi was not only paying respect to Ersoy by placing this card next to Atatürk's portrait at the top, which also contains the image of the flag and the national anthem on the left-hand side, and Atatürk's address to the youth and another image of Atatürk on the right-hand side (see Figure 8).[6] He was also 'marketing', as I discussed in detail in the previous chapter, through which Ruhi conveyed his political views to his visitors, be they parents, pupils or high-ranking district officials. It was in a context where a new way of thinking was 'emerging': Atatürk and his deeds were overshadowed by narratives about Ersoy that portrayed the poet as the 'spiritual leader [*manevi lider*]' of the Turkish War of Independence.

In 2007, the 'Day of Commemoration of the Adoption of the National Anthem and Mehmet Akif Ersoy' (12 March) was declared an official day of commemoration. The claim was to honour the author of the national anthem, *İstiklal Marşı* ('March of Independence'), Mehmet Akif Ersoy. Given the detailed preparations and the broad participation expected at the national level, it was a clear competitor to the national commemorations, even though it was not officially declared as such (Official Gazette 2008).[7] The ceremonies that took place on that day in both schools focused mainly on the life of Ersoy, his personality, his thoughts and his moral sentiments. In Zinnur, the focus was on Ersoy's speeches he had given in mosques and on the battlefield, and how he played a key role in conveying the aims of the Turkish War of Independence. It was clear to me that this commemoration did not only serve to honour Ersoy but became a significant part of the AKP government's attempt to revise the master narrative of republican Turkey by transforming Mehmet Akif Ersoy into a 'hero'.

The school bulletin boards of both schools which were designed to commemorate this day remained untouched until the end of the school year, which was not the case for other commemorations. In other words, these boards *de facto* became 'Mehmet Akif Ersoy Corners'. Throughout the school year I found out that Ersoy's life, works and ideals were edited for mass consumption in various forms such as songs, books and documentaries. Bahçelik municipality channelled these cultural products, and schools like Zinnur and Talip were the prime targets – alongside the *bilgi evis*. However, rather than analysing simplistic narratives about Ersoy in books or in reading club circles – known as *Safahat* ('Stages') reading clubs – or arabesque and pop songs that turn Ersoy's poems into song lyrics, in the following subsection I briefly touch on Ersoy's poem *Asım*, which provides a more accurate understanding of the extent to which Ersoy's ideas inspired many Islamists and how Ersoy's verses achieved the pervasiveness of former Kemalist pronouncements.

The fictional character of Ersoy: Asım

In his works, most of which were published in *Sırat-ı Müstakim* ('True Path') and *Sebülireşşad* ('Straight Path') (collected in a compendium called *Safahat*),

Mehmet Akif Ersoy deals with various topics, including but not limited to contemporary political issues of the late Ottoman Empire. *Asım* is one of Ersoy's most popular poems and is admired by various Islamic intellectuals. Ersoy has his characters talk about education in *Asım*, in addition to various other issues such as family and modernization of Islam, which fuelled the ideological debates of the late Ottoman period (Ersoy 1989: 343–431). The significance of *Asım* is that Ersoy also shares his thoughts on education. At that time, the field of education was divided: On the one hand, there were modern educational institutions, and, on the other hand, there were the traditional educational institutions such as *medreses* (Fortna 2002; Somel 2001). In short, in *Asım*, Ersoy fleshes out the ongoing discussions on the question of education with his characters in his poem. Two main characters debate the basic premises of religious *medrese* education in comparison to the ideals of modern institutions, – comparing the capabilities of graduates of these institutions (Ersoy 1989: 343–431). While one character (Köse İmam) is in favour of traditional education, the other (Hocazade) argues for modern education, but both question the implications of the bifurcation of education (Ersoy 1989: 343–431). One of the secondary characters Asım, who gives the poem its name, embodies Ersoy's position on education. Asım is a nationalist and a pious Muslim, a strong, hardworking and intelligent boy who respects his past, traditions and his culture, but also a boy eager to learn the positivist knowledge of the West (Ersoy 1989: 343–431). Ersoy criticizes the educational policies of the Ottoman state, but also proposes his own synthesis by means of separating positivistic knowledge from traditions imbued with Islam. In this way, Ersoy describes the ideal youth he envisioned, calling them *Asım'ın Nesli* (Asım's Generation).

It is fair to claim that Mehmet Akif Ersoy's works are an expression of the mind of an intellectual shaped by the decline of an empire in the wake of colonial impositions and the struggle against modernity. Nevertheless, Ersoy's ideas on education have been a source of inspiration in Turkey especially for the Gülen community and the AKP. As I explained in Chapter 2, these Islamist actors did not share the same worldview, nor did they have the same experience and knowledge of education in the early 2010s. The Gülen community cultivated Ersoy's ideas. The character Asım is reflected in the *Altın Nesil* (Golden Generation). AKP on the other hand transformed these ideas into the cornerstone of its educational policies, which became even clearer after the implementation of 4+4+4 reform which paved the way for the mainstreaming of *imam-hatip* schools as well as injecting Islam to national curriculum that I explained in Chapter 2. Both Islamist actors intended to reshape the country's cultural and social reproduction processes by promising future advantages in education and employment. These privileges were available to those who joined the community or enrolled in *imam-hatip* schools. This was clear in Bahçelik where *imam-hatip* schools were distinct from the other schools with their high budgets, physical and structural advantages, and uncrowded classrooms. Likewise, the pupils selected by Gülen-community teachers had the privileges provided by these teachers in everyday schooling, with continuous feedback, revision and tutorial support that I explained in detail in the previous chapter. Equally significant point is that both actors elide women as members of the sanctioned community that will run the country. Asım is a quintessentially male subject, a beacon for the Islamo-nationalist brotherhood.

Veneration of the Prophet Muhammad: Teaching Islam

Since 2011, the Prophet Muhammad's birthday has been commemorated in state primary schools. The introduction of this commemoration, the details of which are explained below, into the curricula could be seen as part of a rather long process of reforming religious education as a compulsory and elective course in state primary schools in the country in line with the growing global interest in the role of religion in education. One of the most important steps in this regard was the revision of the curriculum for religious education, more specifically for religious culture and moral knowledge (*Din Kültürü ve Ahlak Bilgisi*) courses in primary, lower and upper secondary schools, which became compulsory with the 1982 Constitution that I mentioned in Chapter 2 briefly. This occurred between 2005 and 2006, but its roots lie in studies undertaken by the MEB in 2001 in response to growing international interest in 'religion and schooling' after 9/11 in the context of children's human rights and in response to EU concerns about democratic citizenship and values in schools (Şaşmaz et al. 2011). Nevertheless, it has been argued that the revision did not fundamentally change the aim of these courses, which since the early 1980s had been to promote religious adherence to Sunni Islam (Gözaydın 2009; Kaymakcan 2007).

Recep Kaymakcan's detailed analysis of religious culture and moral knowledge secondary school curriculum, moreover, suggests that one of the recognizable changes was that the Prophet became an important part of the course, which was not the case with the previous approach (2007: 22–3). The second step was the introduction of electives, namely the Qur'an and the life of Muhammad, the Prophet, which are compulsory basic courses in *imam-hatip* schools, under the

4+4+4 reform for primary schools in 2012. In these elective courses, too, the Prophet has central role. In this section, however, I focus on veneration of the Prophet through the arabesque, arabesque-pop and pop songs that pupils sang and posters they had designed. I argue that the veneration of the Prophet in primary schools allowed for a variety of interpretations at local and school levels, to the extent that the commemoration acted as a gateway for Islamic communities to penetrate *lived culture* (Williams 2001) of the schools. And, perhaps more crucially, it provided an opportunity for these actors to influence pupils. I illustrate my point with two examples among many: the children's songs produced by the followers of the Gülen community, and the slogans created by the Kurdish Hizbullah (or Hizbullah in Turkey). Before doing so, I would like to give a brief overview of the history of this veneration and touch on some of the discussions it has provoked.

An 'invented' tradition: From *mevlid* to Holy Birth Week

The celebration of the birth of the Prophet Muhammad was predominantly limited to mosques and the private sphere known as *mevlid* until Presidency of the Religious Affairs (*Diyanet İşleri Başkanlığı*, DİB) established the Holy Birth Week in 1989.[8] No commemoration can avoid reflecting the specific political, social and economic circumstances of its creation or more accurately 'invention' (Hobsbawm 1983) and Holy Birth Week was no exception. In essence, according to Mümtazer Türköne (2012), who was columnist in Gülen community's mouthpiece *Zaman* newspaper, the intention was welcoming Islam into the public sphere by removing spatial boundaries for venerating the Prophet.[9] During the late 1980s, Islamic constituencies closed ranks and secular-religious binarism was becoming recognizable. For more than a decade, DİB had played an important role in shaping the boundaries of the official form and content of the commemoration, which was limited to academic and intellectual discussions about the role of Islam (DİB 1995a: 243). However, through the increased attention given by the Nurcu movements' news media to the DİB events during the week, Holy Birth Week became recognizable in the late 1990s (DİB 1995a: 243, 1996).[10] As early as 1992, members of the parliament, Islamic intellectuals and notable academics had begun to participate in seminars, symposia and forums organized by DİB during the week (DİB 1995a, 1996).

In 1993, the opening speech of the then Prime Minister Tansu Çiller was a defining moment for the week (DİB 1995b, 1996). In 1994, the date of the commemoration was set according to the Gregorian calendar and thereafter the celebrations took place between 20 and 26 April. This change was an attempt to give the event the temporal permanence that secular national commemorations require. Another important change concerns the commemorative practices. While events at the institutional level drew more attention, events at the local level took on different shapes. At the national level, for example, the state broadcast panel discussions on Turkish Radio and Television Corporation (*Türkiye Radyo ve Televizyon Kurumu*, TRT); at the local level, people celebrated the week in various forms such as with free food donations, offering health check-ups for free and more (DİB 1995b: v–ix). In 1995, there were also international symposia and forums (DİB 1997).

In the late 1990s, the 28 February process (when the army struck back and repressed Islamic actors and their activities, as I explained in Chapter 2) suspended the growing public recognition of Holy Birth Week. The military's interference in politics altered the content of the thematic panels, which had become key commemorative practices of DİB. In line with this change, the visibility of local practices ceased in 1997–2002. This change was reflected in the choice of the theme for the 1998 commemoration – Islam and Democracy – and the related discussion panels, which focused on the theme of development (DİB 1999). The content and form of the week began to evolve again after the AKP came to power. The themes of the week between 2002 and 2007 reflected the expansion of identity politics at that time, partly due to the demands of the EU accession process (see Chapter 2). Multiculturalism, the concept of love in the Alevi faith, interfaith dialogue, racism and many other issues were discussed (DİB 2006, 2007, 2008, 2009). In other words, the purpose of the panel discussions during these years was to analyse and promote understanding of important social and political issues, especially in relation to Islam. The number of commemorative events has increased with the growing influence of DİB (2008).[11]

The increasing visibility of Holy Birth Week celebrations across the country in the mid-2000s was addressed in a statement Turkish Armed Forces (*Türk Silahlı Kuvvetleri*, TSK) published online in 2007 just before the presidential election, which I explained in Chapter 2. The main argument of this so-called e-memorandum was that the AKP government aimed at secular ideals of the country. It is possible to claim that one of the most controversial aspects of the week was the date of the Holy Birth Week celebrations. The question was whether Holy Birth Week, which was observed between 20 and 27 April at the time, superimposed onto National Sovereignty and Children's Day which was celebrated on 23 April. This was significant since National Sovereignty and Children's Day not only commemorates one of the foundational landmarks of the republic that is the regime change but also addresses exclusively children. As I have already mentioned, two processes were running in parallel in those years: on the one hand, the form of republican commemorations was revised to limit their scope (i.e., public celebrations were discouraged), and on the other, new commemorations such as Holy Birth Week were incorporated into symbolic domain of schools and public participation was encouraged at both local (even enforced in some local contexts) and national levels. In 2010, the week became among the official state commemorations (Official Gazette 2010).

Moreover, in 2011, a circular letter issued by the then Minister of Education, Nimet Çubukçu, in which Çubukçu recommended the veneration of the Prophet in primary schools (MEB 2011). It is significant that this week was introduced by a circular letter. Apart from foundation day and the key moments of the founding of the Turkish Republic, every festival, observance, commemoration or awareness-raising event has traditionally been included in a long list of Significant Days and Weeks (*Belirli Gün ve Haftalar*). This list did not include the Holy Birth Week, nor did the circular letter mentioned above provide comprehensive information on the content, although a rather sketchy information with regard to form was provided (MEB 2011). In this respect, it is fair to claim that MEB acted beyond the norms, given the discussions that Holy Birth Week had provoked.

In what follows I turn to significant part of the content of Holy Birth Week, arabesque, arabesque-pop and pop songs for children produced by Islamic music producers which were referred to as hymns.

A music class in Zinnur: "'Hymns", not songs!'

It was five months before the commemoration of the Holy Birth Week when I observed Aslı teaching a music class in Zinnur. She was a cheerful young teacher who had studied Turkish literature and had come to Istanbul for the first time after her appointment in Bahçelik. Even though she was supposed to offer Turkish classes, in the absence of a dedicated music teacher at the school, she had been assigned to teach music to the Year Seven and Year Five pupils, like some of her colleagues. About her duties in the music classes, she had to offer, Aslı said:

I know nothing about music, so I decided to teach them folk songs. For instance, in this school many of the pupils are from the Black Sea region, so I teach them folk songs from that area. But I also teach other folk songs, like *Çanakkale Türküsü* [Gallipoli Song]. Mostly, I let them sing the songs they like to listen to and sing. At the end of the day, I am not a music teacher, for god's sake what is this?

She began the class by going over the songs the pupils had learned thus far, trying to teach them to sing in unison. After singing *Çanakkale Türküsü* ('Gallipoli Song'), Aslı asked, 'Who would like to sing today?' Eager pupils raised their hands and came to the front of the classroom, one by one, to sing the songs they loved the most. *Ankara'nın Bağları* ('Vineyards of Ankara') was popular at the time. Aslı and I were nodding our heads and, at times, shaking our shoulders and clapping our hands. Some pupils were dancing happily as well. Then, one of the female pupils Esma raised her hand and said, 'I want to sing a hymn', and went to the front of the class and sang *Yetim Kız* ('the Orphan Girl') (*Peygamberin Gülleri* 2014a). Laughter, dancing and cheerful exclamations suddenly ended as they heard the moaning melody of arabesque music in Esma's voice. The lyrics of this song, which was referred to as a hymn, are as follows:

The sacred hand [of the Prophet Muhammad] that caresses the head of the
  orphan girl,
I am an orphan girl too; please caress me as well!
Muhammad, you regard the orphan girl as your daughter,
I am an orphan girl too regard me as your daughter as well!
Oh, my dear prophet your gracious love is sufficient,
I am so destitute; I shall be grateful for your favour!
Oh *Resulallah* [Messenger of Allah]! My grandfather once told me that you are
  the protector of all orphans.
Kids played hopscotch on the street earlier today and they cast me out.
I felt so sad, and I cried.
My grandfather and my grandmother consoled me.
Oh *Resulallah*! I hug my doll while sleeping.
This consoles me sometimes, however; most of the time I cannot help crying.
If I only had a mother, she would put me to sleep with stories and lullabies.
Oh, *Resulallah* be my mother and father!
Then caress my head and love me!
I guess it is you who caresses my head, and it is you who tucks me into my bed.
This is because I discovered that/I feel as though someone tucks me into my
  bed after I wake up at night.

You are both my father and my mother, dear *Resulallah*! It is you, oh
  Resulallah! It is you, oh *Resulallah*! It is you, oh *Resulallah*!

(Peygamberin Gülleri 2014a)

We moved abruptly from one emotion to another in the classroom. It was not
only the rich texture of Esma's voice, but also the narration of the song that evoked
sadness and despair in the class. For a moment all the orphans from fairy tales
such as Cinderella came to my mind. Aslı said, 'The song is nice.' Esma looked
back at her while heading to her desk and said, 'It is not a song! It is a hymn!' in
a trembling voice that cut through the noise in the classroom. The pupils were
stunned. Aslı was always encouraging the pupils to be articulate, and yet much
of their audacity and fervency came from all the songs they had been consuming
within the school, *bilgi evi*, Qur'an courses provided by Islamic communities. At
the same time, they immediately recognized that Aslı was vacillating between
what she was probably really thinking and what the pupils expected of her. Then,
almost all the pupils repeated three sentences one after the other: 'It is a hymn,
yes, not a song!'; 'It is not a song'; 'It is a hymn teacher, we don't call it a song'. They
studied Aslı's anxious face for a minute or so and they decided that her choice of
the word 'song' had been a slip of the tongue. Aslı responded, 'Oh well, okay is
there anyone else who would like to sing a song or a hymn?' although she did not
think that they were hymns. This nuanced negotiation between Aslı and the pupils
and not to mention Aslı's self-censorship (see Chapter 5) was revelation for me. I
comprehended that these songs were sacrosanct to the pupils. I was just beginning
to realize how popular these songs were among the pupils of both schools.

Popular arabesque and pop songs for children: Fellowship of *ummah* or Gülen community?

In 2006, the popularity of *Yetim Kız* ('the Orphan Girl'), which is also the subtitle
of the album by a children's choir for schoolchildren called *Peygamberin Gülleri*
('Roses of the Prophet') (2014a), soared after it was broadcast on Samanyolu
Haber TV – one of the leading channels of the Gülen community (İlhan 2010).
Yasin İlhan, the group's artistic director, stated that this album sold more
than 400,000 copies (İlhan 2010). The album contains various eulogies to the
Prophet in the form of arabesque, arabesque-pop and pop songs. There are also
poems such as *Nur Yüzlüm* ('My Dear Prophet Who Has Light on His Face')
with the lines 'I am afraid, my rosy dear one [the Prophet], I am afraid of not

being the right *ummah* for you'. It continues, 'please come and enter my dreams …', 'the best of all Mustafas' (*Peygamberin Gülleri* 2014c). The song *Biz Dünya Çocuklarıyız* ('We are the Children of the World') in the album is also striking. An 'African child' with 'shining teeth' (as the lyrics say) is the narrator in this song and he proposes a community among children all over the world that transcends all national ties, with lines like 'we embrace the world; we are the roses of the Prophet' (*Peygamberin Gülleri* 2014b).

This album was also one of the most popular albums in Bahçelik. I discovered it when I attended various ceremonies in the neighbourhood when Holy Birth Week arrived. Many events were held, such as exhibitions, lectures, ceremonies and meetings. The municipality, the District Mufti Office, the District Governorate and the District National Education Directorate all collaborated to organize the week's celebrations. In addition, many Islamic foundations and communities organized special ceremonies and invited teachers and school communities over their pupils. They distributed leaflets, posted invitation cards on classroom noticeboards and delivered them to teachers. Some even personally invited most of us to participate in these various ceremonies. In other words, the commemoration was not limited to the schools or the mosques.

One such ceremony was organized by the District Mufti Office and the District Governorate. The ceremony began with the national anthem, an official introduction and a speech, followed by dances and songs by pupils. Had it not been for two visually impaired pupils reciting Qur'an, I would not have been able to distinguish the form of Holy Birth Week from National Sovereignty and Children's Day. As for the content, the songs chosen for the day were again from *Peygamberin Gülleri*'s album, like *Peygamberi Görmek İçin* ('To See the Prophet') (*Peygamberin Gülleri* 2014d). The lyrics of the song are as follows:

> To see the Prophet, to see the Prophet …
> Anything, anything, anything, I would give up anything.
> Half of my pocket money, the yolk of my egg, my biggest apple.
> I would give up all!
> My favourite toy, my favourite toy.
> My kite, my race car, my cute doll …
> Half of my pocket money, the yolk of my egg, my biggest apple.
> I would give up all!
> My life shall be yours; my life shall be yours!
> The Sultan of my heart!
> My dearest Prophet!
>
> (*Peygamberin Gülleri* 2014d)

The sudden change from praise to self-sacrifice shows the idealized behaviour expected of the singers of the 'hymn' or, more correctly, the nursery rhyme. It was interesting to see similarities between the content of these songs and the study by Benjamin C. Fortna (2016) on reading materials for children, including textbooks and magazines produced in the period from 1880 to 1930 (Turkish and Ottoman periods). Fortna notes two worlds at odds with each other: In the 'world of bonbons', as he calls it, there is an imaginative, 'cartoonish world of sweets, dolls and games' and in the 'world of bayonets', as he puts it, the hard 'world of war, sacrifice and service to the home-land, first to the empire and then to the nation' (2016: 173). In the songs of *Peygamberin Gülleri*, it is not the nation but the overarching *ummah* that becomes an 'imagined community' (Anderson 1991). In the choir's later released album, *Peygamberin Gülleri II*, it is even bolder.

At the ceremony that I attended in Bahçelik, another song from this album was played as well and the pupils danced with it. The content of this song, namely, *Bitsin Artık Bu Savaşlar* ('These Wars Should End') and the rather simple choreography of the pupils' 'dances' were worth mentioning. In short, the song is a girl's account of what has happened on earth since the Prophet left the earth (*Peygamberin Gülleri II* 2010a). It begins with the sounds of bullets and bombs. As the girl cries for help, talks to the Prophet about the wars, the song becomes graphic when she says, 'children were killed in wars' and adds, 'a girl was raped'. At the end she exclaims (almost shouting), 'all the Prophets have called for peace', adding that there are still wars. The pupils with fancy clothes who danced to the song during the event first lay down and pretended to have died, then stood up and swayed, jumping from side to side (but not really dancing).

The second album of the *Peygamberin Gülleri* is dedicated to the Gülen movement. The song *Dön Yoluna Kurbanım* ('Come Back, I Will Sacrifice Myself to Your Path') is a eulogy to Fethullah Gülen (*Peygamberin Gülleri II* 2010b). In this song, a girl asks Fethullah Gülen to return to his country and end his self-inflicted exile without addressing Gülen with his name. In *Sevginin Sultanları* ('Sultans of Love') the ambitions of the Gülen movement around the world are summarized (*Peygamberin Gülleri II* 2010c), and the song *Öğretmenim* ('My Teacher') praises teachers who work for the community (*Peygamberin Gülleri II* 2010d). In *Öğretmenim* ('My Teacher'), the female pupil says: 'Everyone wants to earn more money, but you offered service [*hizmet*] … You chose heaven' (*Peygamberin Gülleri II* 2010d). At the end of the song, a female teacher appears and speaks for herself in the form of a letter she has written to her mother. She talks about her life in the *ışık evi* (house of light) (without mentioning their names) and tells how *abis* (elder brother) helped her find shelter, food, and the necessary clothes. The letter continues. Referring to the schools in Central Asia (with special mention of Kazakhstan and Uzbekistan), the teacher says: 'We emigrated here' – using the word *hicret* (emigration), which refers to the Prophet's emigration from Mecca to Medina (in 622 CE) for political reasons, namely because of the threat of persecution in Mecca (*Peygamberin Gülleri II* 2010d). Through the use of political innuendo, sexist depictions of female characters and the emphasis on the Gülen community's understanding of the *ummah*, these songs turned into a vessel for propaganda. The crucial point is that these songs are categorized and sold as 'hymns'. As we have seen above in Aslı's music class, the pupils perceived these songs as sacrosanct which made these songs indisputable. However, *Peygamberin Gülleri* was not the only album.

Since the 1990s, renowned Islamic composers and singers have played an important role in shaping the emerging market for 'Islamic music' (Özel 2016). Among these composers and singers, there were many who produced songs for children marketed them as hymns or prayers.[12] Among others, Ertuğrul Erkişi also made a name for himself in this market as a well-known composer and singer of Islamic music. Erkişi is known for his compositions of Fethullah Gülen's poetry, and he was the first musician to perform a song with lines from Mehmet Akif Ersoy's *Asım* (the poem that I discussed above). In addition, Erkişi founded several children's choirs and albums that have won awards in the Turkish music industry. *Minik Dualar Grubu* ('Kids Prayer Group'), for example, became famous with the song *Teşekkür Ederim Allah'ım* ('Thank you, O Allah') (*Minik Dualar Grubu* 2005). This album sold 285,000 copies within the first six months of its release (Milliyet 2006) and inspired many other groups such as *İsmail Uslu – Minik Eller, Grup 571* ('İsmail Uslu -Tiny Hands, Group 571') (2007), *Grup Cennet Kuşları* ('Birds of Paradise Group', known in the Arab World as *Toyor Al Janah*) (2008), including *Peygamberin Gülleri*.[13] Obviously, each group has a unique background. *Peygamber Sevdalıları İlahi Grubu* ('Lovers of the Prophet, Hymn Group'), on the other hand, has mainly Kurdish songs for children and were also available on YouTube.[14] In what follows I touch upon the supporters of this group and their claim on *ummah*.

Hidden in plain sight: 'Let's unify under the flag of *tevhid* [the unity of Islam and Muslims]'

The quoted slogan above was taken from the poster in Figure 9 by Büşra, a Kurdish Year Seven pupil. Her poster was one of the twenty posters shortlisted for an exhibition in Talip designed by Ahmet as part of the commemoration of the

Figure 9 A poster by Year Seven pupil Büşra.

Holy Birth Week mentioned in Chapter 3. What interested me about her poster
was that it stood out from the others, both in terms of the slogans she chose and
the symbols she reproduced, such as Zoroastrian Sun, the wheatgrass basket
and the colours she used (green, red, yellow), which are associated with Kurdish
nationalism and white flag of *tevhid* (the unity of Islam and Muslims). Neither
Ahmet nor the members of the upper echelons of the district bureaucracy who

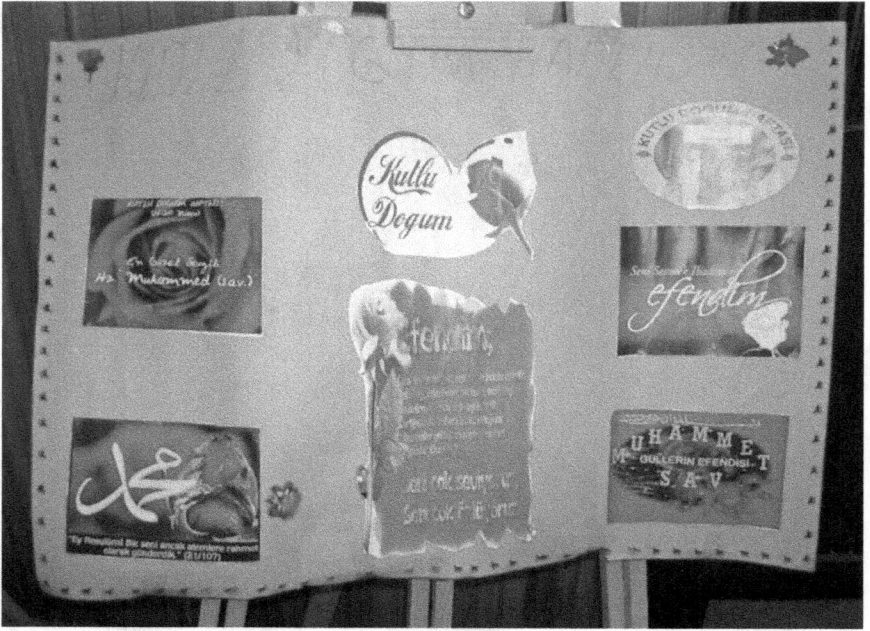

Figure 10 A poster by Year Six pupil Nevra.

Figure 11 A poster by Year Seven pupil Zehra.

opened the exhibition were familiar with these symbols. Figuratively speaking, these symbols on the poster were hidden in the plain sight.

With this exhibition, pupils were given the opportunity to express themselves and share their ideas through posters. However, as I learnt from the pupils, they had downloaded and reproduced the images that were widely circulated on the internet. Their posters were full of symbols such as photos and illustrations of roses, the sun and Arabic calligraphy of the words Allah and the Prophet Muhammad which had become traditional symbols of the week (see Figures 10 and 11). In addition, reproductions of the Kaaba (in Masjid al-Haram in Mecca, Saudi Arabia) were also among the popular symbols to show love for the Prophet. On Büşra's poster, the flag of *tevhid* (the unity of Islam and Muslims) (see Figure 9) and the slogans were visible to everyone in the school, unlike the symbols she reproduced. The slogans on the poster read '*Ezan* [call to prayer] is an invitation to salvation', 'Let's unify with *ezan* [call to prayer]', 'Let's unify under the flag of *tevhid* [the unity of Islam and Muslims]'. I found out that Büşra was inspired by the symbols used during the celebration of Holy Birth Week by the platform *Peygamber Sevdalıları* (Lovers of the Prophet), which is a nationwide organization affiliated with Kurdish Hizbullah (or Hizbullah in Turkey) and its successor Free Cause Party (*Hür Dava Partisi*, Hüda Par). Mehmet Kurt's insightful study of Kurdish Hizbullah offers analysis of the symbolism used by the *Peygamber Sevdalıları* during the Holy Birth Week (2016: 225–40). Kurt argues that veiled girls and the flag of *tevhid* are among the symbolic markers (alongside women wearing *çarşaf*, a black outer garment that looks like an Iranian chador) during the Holy Birth Week celebrations of Kurdish Hizbullah, which seeks public recognition (2016). As I mentioned earlier, the YouTube videos of the *Peygamber Sevdalları İlahi Grubu* (the Prophet Lovers, Hymn Group) that were visible in the 2010s also feature veiled girls. During the school year, the week's celebrations of Kurdish Hizbullah gained national attention as well. The celebrations in the city of Diyarbakır (where the majority of the population is Kurdish) attracted a million attendees in 2013 (2016). Cengiz Güneş argues that the platform for *Peygamber Sevdalıları* use this week as a medium against the Kurdistan Workers' Party (*Partiya Karkerên Kurdistanê*, PKK) (2021: 30, 88). Returning to Talip context, the commemoration of Holy Birth Week morphed into a political platform for *Peygamber Sevdalıları*, which was also visible in the school.

***

The main aim of Holy Birth Week was teaching Sunni Islam through venerating the Prophet. However, in practice it functioned as platform for diverse Islamist political parties, Islamic constituencies and Islamic communities to 'present' or more accurately inculcate their own understanding of Islam to boys and girls in both schools. It was clear in their different descriptions of *ummah* above. In other words, Gülen community's depiction of *ummah* reflected on the songs, or as pupils name them as 'hymns' which involves commitment to Gülen community among the others was sharply different from Hüda Par's interpretation that suggests an establishment of an Islamic state seen in the poster of Büşra above. It is not my intention here to compare the claims of each Islamist actors in terms of their claims on *ummah*, understanding of Islam or the inclusion of Islam in their political ambitions. However, what I have selectively presented above among the others suggest that pupils in Zinnur and Talip were exposed to different narratives about Islam as well as the 'nation' through the 'love of the Prophet' and the *ummah*.

***

Conclusion

Many forms of play by pupils in both schools, which I have illustrated in this chapter, prompted me to reflect on my own experiences as a pupil in primary and lower secondary school. Symbols of Atatürk, whether in the form of his sayings or images, had become platitudes for me simply because I belong to a generation that was educated in the mid-1980s and early 1990s in school when the Turkish-Islamic Synthesis was dominant ideology. Although we were exposed to the repetitive, ritualized narratives about Atatürk that had already emptied of any meaning, I believe that for most of my generation, if not all of them, inventing and playing games like boys and girls did in both Talip and Zinnur would probably end with a slap in the face at best and a beating or expulsion from school at worst. We would probably carry around not only the imprint of five fingers on our faces or the physical pain of the beatings, but also the 'shame' and 'humiliation' associated with it.

The grammar of speaking about and of Atatürk was and is strict: one 'must' either 'love' or 'not love' (hate?) him. Definitely symbols of Atatürk were not only perceived as Atatürk himself, but, as Navaro Yashin aptly put it, one can speak of multiple symbols of the republic 'in the garb of Atatürk' (Navaro-Yashin

2002b: 2). In the 1990s, the symbolism around Atatürk, or in Navaro-Yashin's words 'the aura around Atatürk' (2002b: 202), had been used as a kind of 'shield' to protect the 'secular' state against the rising Islamic politics. In the 2010s, as we have seen in both school contexts, Atatürk became 'doll-idol- "the idoll"' to use the concept of Joe Moshenska (2019), or a demonic figure, a benign *jinni*, a *kafir* – in the hands of boys and girls. Definitely, what we think as a 'child's imagination' is in fact our 'imagination' (fantasy?) as adults or it is 'the adult's imagination of the child's imagination' (2003: 449), to reiterate what anthropologist Michael Taussig has wisely put. Yet at the same time, the iconoclastic moves orchestrated by AKP government to destroy republican symbols, especially the remnants of the republic's most iconic leader, Mustafa Kemal Atatürk, as a strategy to renounce the Kemalist revolution seems to feed the boys' and girls' imaginations. I focused on Day of Commemoration of the Adoption of the National Anthem and Mehmet Akif Ersoy, and touched on how Mehmet Akif Ersoy was crafted. This is because the official claim was to honour the anti-secularist author of the national anthem, Ersoy. As we have seen, portrayal of Ersoy as the 'spiritual leader [*manevi lider*]' of Turkish War of Independence, as 'an ideologue' served in practice to erase the role of Mustafa Kemal Atatürk and create a link with Ottoman past without disjuncture and served to empty the official republican symbols, almost like an iconoclastic attack within the local education market in Bahçelik. However, this was only half the story.

An analogy I have followed within this chapter is the familiar one of 'culture wars'. I used – if not worked with – Raymond William's (1977) *structure of feeling* as a lens through which not only the dominant but also residual as well as emergent and pre-emergent ways of thinking become visible. As I mentioned at the beginning of the chapter, two threads have dominated the relevant literature in education: (i) the analysis of the historical roots of the conflicts that have shaped and informed the Turkish-Islamic Synthesis which has been legitimized by the schools (Kaplan 1999; Kaplan 2006), and (ii) the study of the *imam-hatip* schools (Aksit 1991; Gökaçtı 2005; Ozgur 2012). The former focused on the official ideology of the Turkish-Islamic Synthesis vis-à-vis the contested secular character of the state and its institutions. The latter dealt with various aspects of the *imam-hatip* schools, their role in Islamic movements and their role in imparting distinctive *habitus*. Nevertheless, both approaches offer insights to already 'institutionalized' ways of thinking.

In both schools there were competing ideas, ideals and symbols of different Islamists. As we have seen there were rival generation ideals: On the one hand, there was 'pious generation' which aims to reproduce a loyal base of pious citizens which has become visible following the 4+4+4 education reform that I discussed in Chapter 2. On the other hand, there were *Asım'ın Nesli* (Asım's Generation) and *Altın Nesil* (Golden Generation), both bearing the imprint of Ersoy's 'residual' fictional character Asım, a representation of the traditional idea of masculinity that is heroic, smart, strong. Gülen community and the AKP intended to transform cultural and social reproduction processes, and yet they fragmented degree of unity between and within schools by implying a hierarchical order in which the 'pious generation' came last. And although Day of Commemoration of the Adoption of the National Anthem and Mehmet Akif Ersoy suggested a new understanding of 'nation', the commemoration of Holy Birth Week challenged this seamless narrative. As we have seen, the songs, full of gender stereotypes that swing between the 'world of bonbons' (Fortna 2016) and the 'world of bayonets' (Fortna 2016) and contain political allusions, aim to have pupils in Zinnur and Talip imagine the *ummah* almost replacing the nation but also implying (or inviting?) an alternative collective, namely Gülen community. This was also evident in the posters pupils made, such as the one calling for the establishment of an Islamic state. The 'emerging' way of thinking in both schools was that there was not one new 'imagined community' (Anderson 1991) but rival 'imagined' 'communities', which raises the question, which Islam?

In conclusion, this chapter might sound 'idiosyncratic' on its own, if one does not take into account the previous chapter in which I described in quite some detail how two schools had become hostages to the local politics of the Bahçelik municipality and various Islamic communities. In other words, this chapter deepens the arguments of the previous chapter and illustrates the extent to which the local education market had dissolved the 'unity' that we assumed so far. In the following chapter, I turn on several layers of surveillance and control with different meanings and conclusions.

Controlling gazes and faces of surveillance

If my readers followed me to Talip School, the first sight they would encounter would be a big grey iron gate at the entrance to the school. Now, imagine a small window on the right side of the gate through which you can see the open space of the school. Suppose you have a legitimate reason to ask Efe, the school's gatekeeper, who is in his early fifties, for permission to enter the school. After you get permission, he opens the creaking gate. If the head teacher and deputy head teachers were to look at the closed-circuit television (CCTV) screen now, they would see you enter. Next you arrive at another large grey iron gate with bars. You can hardly see inside, so you have to get closer. Now you must explain to the pupils on guard who you are and who you want to see. These two pupils – a girl and a boy – have been assigned to check the school gate during class time. Again, your movements will be followed. As one walks around Zinnur School, one is struck by the similarities between the structure of the surveillance mechanisms. Both schools have gatekeepers, surveillance cameras and assigned teachers and pupils who monitor certain areas at specific times during the school day. In addition, police officers regularly visit the schools to ensure that everything is under control – so you may come across one of them.

What I have described above that I gleaned from my fieldwork notes captures relatively visible technologies of surveillance in both Talip and Zinnur Schools which brings Michael Foucault's (1995) interpretation of Jeremy Bentham's concept of the *Panopticon* into mind. Here I am referring to one of the well-known explanations of Foucault in which *panopticism*

[i]s polyvalent in its applications; it serves […] to instruct schoolchildren, to confine the insane, to supervise workers, to put beggars and idlers to work. It is a type of location of bodies in space, of distribution of individuals in relation to one another, of hierarchical organization, of disposition of centres and channels of power, of definition of the instruments and modes of intervention of power, which can be implemented in hospitals, workshops, schools, prisons. Whenever

one is dealing with a multiplicity of individuals on whom a task or a particular form of behaviour must be imposed, the panoptic schema may be used.

(1995: 205)

Foucault (1980, 1995) does not take *Panopticon* as fixed blueprint to follow but with his empirical studies of various institutional settings (e.g., hospitals, prisons) in which he elucidates the ways in which power is diffused and exercised to condition the behaviour, mobility, attitudes, dispositions and even thoughts of those who enter these micro-social worlds. In other words, it is a matter of exercising power. In the relevant literature in particular scholars who suggest following context-specific practices of surveillance rather than forcing a template, that is scheme of *Panopticon*, to fit them offer significant insights (Gallagher 2010; Lyon 2006; Taylor 2012; Murakami Wood 2007). In these respects, for instance, Michael Gallagher's (2010) arguments based on his empirical findings in Scottish primary school are insightful. Gallagher argues that 'the school bore more than a passing resemblance to the panoptic model of power' (2010: 266) and adds surveillance is 'profoundly discontinuous, in contrast to the panoptic ideal of total and constant visibility' (2010: 266). Drawing on this literature as well as Foucault's *panopticism*, in what follows, I aim to shed light on an unexplored facet of primary education in Turkey by examining the ways in which both old and emerging surveillance mechanisms come into play in both school contexts.[1] Although it is beyond the scope of this chapter to fill this large gap, I hope to touch on some questions by examining some surveillance mechanisms very briefly that were introduced under the AKP government. I focus on two distinct but interrelated themes: the first is the emergence of surveillance practices such as the use of CCTV and policing in schools. I then highlight one of the older versions of surveillance practices, namely the *nöbet* (guard duty) role of teachers. The 'guarding' was a school-based solution to underfunded, overcrowded and physically undersupplied schools. The second theme of the chapter concerns perceived tactics of political control over teachers who do not define themselves as pro-AKP or supporters of an Islamic community. In the last section I turn to control over bodies starting from debates on teachers' dress codes.

CCTV, policing and 'guarding'

In this main section I present three techniques of surveillance in Zinnur and Talip. I begin with those that were relatively recently introduced during the 2012–13 school year, namely CCTV and police involvement, both of which were originated from the 'secure school' framework with roots in a global action plan to combat violence against children as well as emerging discourses on 'violence' at the national level and the inquiries, debates and policy changes these generated.[2] Definitely, the establishment of discourses on 'violence' by the experts and how they shape 'secure school' framework offers significant insights with regard to how power works in Foucauldian sense to shape our ways of thinking about and on schools. Yet I am more interested in the ways in which these surveillance mechanisms are interpreted within school settings. Nevertheless, in the last subsection, I shift the focus to the central role teachers play with their duties to watch over the pupils known as 'guard duty' (*nöbet*). While above-mentioned surveillance mechanisms carry the imprint of current global concerns national adaptations, the *nöbet* (guard duty) could be claimed as a traditional practice.

Police involvement in schools

I saw the police officer Sami several times when he visited the office of the deputy head Ruhi in Zinnur. Sami did not wear his official uniform during his visits, and he had no contact with teachers or pupils. However, everyone in the school knew that a police officer 'hangs around' and within the school. Therefore, I came to know who Sami was after hearing the Ruhi's jokes about his style of dress in the corridor. I was interested in his visits, but Ruhi did not want to talk about their meetings. In Talip too, the content of the meeting with Ali the police officer was kept secret. What I observed in Zinnur or Talip was certainly not typical of the situation across the country, which varied widely as numerous media reports about police involvement in schools suggest.[3]

Visits of the police officers led me to think about the inherently ambiguous aspects of surveillance, which in the sense that it involves keeping an eye on schools to improve pupils' safety while at the same time implies the threat of being criminalised. Initially, I thought that policing both schools by involving police officers was in line with the basic idea of the *Panopticon*, that is, the pupils know they are being closely watched even if they do not know exactly when the police are watching them. And, I gradually revised my position. The pupils at both schools did not see the police officers because Ali and Sami were not wearing their uniforms. However, the secrecy of their visits suggests that the police officers were indeed 'watching over' all the staff at both schools, but not the pupils at Talip and Zinnur which was the case with the CCTV, as will be discussed below.

CCTV: The all-seeing eye?

The installation of CCTV cameras in schools was one of the measures taken with the claim of protecting the pupils, as I mentioned earlier, as was the involvement of the police. In both Talip and Zinnur, CCTV systems were installed by the Bahçelik municipality during the 2008–9 school years, which was the case for all state schools within the district boundaries.[4] In both Zinnur and Talip, the cameras were very basic compared to the high-tech CCTV cameras used elsewhere, which have various functions such as zoom or face recognition. Moreover, the positions of the cameras were limited in terms of the view they capture, that is, in any given state school in the district, the cameras can only watch when someone enters the premises monitored by the cameras. In both schools, the positions of the cameras were the same: there were cameras that monitored the entrance, the open space and others that had a view of the corridors on each floor. There did not seem to be any difference between the CCTV systems of the two schools, but there were significant differences between the two schools in terms of the actual use of this system and this made the real difference.

Head teachers as 'operators': Eyes or lenses?

Gavin J. D. Smith argues that '[…] CCTV cameras are neither conscious, nor autonomous, and require, in order to be effective, constant monitoring and control by human beings in a work-like situation […]' (2004: 377). In Talip, the deputy head teacher's offices and the office of the head teacher served as CCTV 'control rooms', whereby these heads perform the role of 'operator'. In head teacher Aslan's office in Talip, a huge screen (about sixty inches) for monitoring CCTV footage hung on the wall in front of his desk. Whereas in the offices of the deputy head teachers, there were relatively small screens which were split into two: while the upper one showed the views from the cameras in the corridors, the lower one captured the cameras in the corridors, the entrance and the open area. In the school, everyone knew that the screen was in front of the head teacher and the deputy head teachers.

When I asked about the cameras, Aslan said he wanted to 'force' the teachers to be on time for class. I observed that teachers were often late for class, and this was mainly because of the time-space regime of the double shift. In short, the 'morningers' had their classes between 7.30 am and 12.30 pm, while 'afternooners' had classes between 12.30 pm and 5.00 pm. In this system, the short breaks were five to ten minutes. This imposed a much faster daily schedule on the school. Pupils, teachers and parents felt a lot of pressure, which was noticeable in the school day. There was never enough time to drink a glass of Turkish tea, eat a snack, chat, play, rest, pee and much more. Pupils and teachers were never on time. Even in some classes, pupils were allowed to use class time to eat snacks. Aslan and all the teachers knew that under such strict time-space regime that one might expect in carceral institutions being on time every day in every class was impossible.

Nevertheless, Aslan wanted to secure teachers' compliance by means of hanging a screen in front of his desk, and yet he could not fulfil his aim. That he chose the words 'forcing teachers' was not come out of thin air. He himself knew that he was unsuccessful in this endeavour. In other words, teachers knew when he was watching. And therefore, adapted their behaviours accordingly, for instance, teachers developed the habit of going to another teacher's classroom, which is called 'visiting'. On these occasions, I observed that they made small talk or, as they put it, 'they gossiped'. Knowing that Aslan was watching them or that they could be noticed at any time, they also invented reasons. Significant was the timing, which was not supposed to be at the beginning or the end of the class – but in the middle. It is likely that they wanted to steal time. Definitely, teachers refused to show compliance, and this was clear in their 'jokes' as well. For instance, most of the female teachers spoke of the 'head teacher's "observation habit"'. Whenever I went into a teacher's classroom to observe, one of the first questions was, 'Did you greet him [Aslan] [in a teasing voice]?' The camera became, figuratively speaking, Aslan himself, watching over the teachers. Even some of the jokes contained subtle sexual innuendo. For example, one of the older teachers, Nigar, who liked to tease everyone said, 'He is so fond that he wants to see us before and after every class [she laughs frantically to tease].' They were mocking Aslan. Aslan's use of CCTV clearly does not fit the *Panopticon* scheme.

In Zinnur, however, I found it interesting that classes also started late, although the time regime is not comparable to that in Talip. Head teacher İsmail kept his office door that faced the teachers' common room open. When the bell rang, he could see who was late to class if he was in his office. In other words, he did not need cameras to monitor them; he could see with his own eyes. Teachers adjusted their behaviour accordingly that is to say if İsmail was in his place everyone was punctual; however, when he left his office teachers went to classes late.

Moreover, unlike Talip, there were no screens or monitors in the school in Zinnur, although cameras could be seen inside and outside the school building. During the school year, the CCTV footage was only played during one incident to find out who had tried to open one of the office doors. The head teacher, İsmail, explained to me that the cameras were there to control the entry of 'strangers', as schools equipped with technology had become the target of attempted break-ins. That is why teachers mostly forgot the presence of CCTVs and behaved freely. To conclude CCTV like police involvement targeted teachers in both schools but not the pupils. In what follows I briefly touch upon the surveillance technique that targets pupils.

Teachers on 'guard duty': Being an ear or an eye

Long before the introduction of surveillance mechanisms, some of which I have discussed above, there was an official, well-established practice called *nöbet* (guard duty) by the MEB. My intention is not to offer genealogy of this practice, rather focusing on its use within both school contexts. The basic premise of *nöbet* of teachers in both schools was that the pupils should not be left unsupervised during the short and long breaks and/or when the teacher was absent. Duties of the *nöbetçi öğretmen* (guard teacher) encompass many activities including patrolling the open space and monitoring the classrooms, halls, and toilets during breaks and lunch time. Since the teachers at both schools were almost always late for class (as I explained above), this also meant 'managing' the classrooms until the teachers arrived. During our interview İsmail, the head teacher in Zinnur, explained the 'necessity' of such practice,

> *Nöbet* [guard duty] is a necessity *Hocam* [my teacher]. Firstly, there is no security guard in schools [funded by the state]. Secondly, the schools are crowded, and thirdly, there are threats outside the school. Fourthly, there must be someone in the playground to act in cases of emergency. A child can harm him/herself and can cause harm to his/her surroundings. This practice comes with the need. I know that this duty is a burden for the teachers, but if there is no other solution – like employing security guards – this practice will continue.

İsmail did not literally suggest hiring security guards in his account above. He always knew how to combine irony, absurdity and seriousness, and this time he was criticizing a school context where parents and many teachers believed that any 'problem' could be solved by, as they often put it, 'buying a service', 'hiring 'someone' or 'paying someone to do it'. Or by asking the Islamic communities or constituencies for help – a way of compensating for the services not provided by the state, which I discussed in detail in Chapter 3. And yet İsmail was sure that this work could only be done by teachers.

İsmail gave a brief technical summary for all schools in the district. However, Erman, deputy head of Talip, told me about the structural limitations of the school's infrastructure. During our interview, Erman told me that he performs the role of '*çavuş*' (drill instructor) as part of the *nöbet*. In his opinion, without this performance, the hustle and bustle could easily turn into chaos in the blink of an eye. Erman explained,

> Let me tell you what we did the other day! We made a kind of calculation and found that each pupil has a floor area of less than twenty centimetres, which means one cannot move at all ... Why did we do such a calculation? I must tell you what the typical accidents are here: cuts on eyebrows, knees, and elbows. Do you know why they are so common? [...] Because pupils do not slip, they bump into each other! They bump into each other when they are running [in the open space, corridors, and so forth during breaks], and cuts on the eyebrow occur because of hitting the tooth of another pupil ... There is no adequate space to play with a ball. When a pupil throws a ball, often it hits the face or head of another pupil.

As I have already explained, Talip, with more than 3000 pupils, was what I call a 'titan school'. Erman was right that there was 'no adequate space' in the school, apart from very small classrooms, which, as he mentioned above, posed health and safety risks.[5] In this respect, *nöbet* was a technique of 'crowd management' that literally aimed to protect the pupils from each other. Both Erman and İsmail explained the reason for legitimizing the practice and explained the health and safety risks.

In practice, I thought that the *nöbetçi öğretmen*'s gaze was on possible bullying, fights and accidents, while I carried out *nöbet* and watched over the pupils. While also watching myself, I thought that a *nöbetçi öğretmen* was expected to check classrooms and corridors during the breaks. Her/his ears were searching for an abnormal noise. As Michael Gallagher (2010: 266) quite rightly said, sounds in schools play a very important role in 'surveillance'. I also observed that pupils were aware of teachers' gazes and knew they could hear them. So it is not 'total' surveillance, but a kind of performance that encompasses a wide range of roles, such as being an ear or an eye. Or as with Erman, it is the '*çavuş*' (drill instructor) I mentioned above. It was clear to me that the ears and gazes of the *nöbetçi öğretmen* exerted power on younger pupils to change or limit some of their behaviours only when they saw they were being watched. Relatively older pupils, on the other hand, sought a space where there were no gazes. For example, male pupils often spat in the liquid soap in the toilets as a prank, which I learned when relatively young boys came to me for help. I interpreted this as a kind of negative reaction to gazes of *nöbetçi öğretmen*.

With what I have illustrated so far, I can relate to what Michael Gallagher suggests, 'We might think of surveillance as activities designed primarily to produce the illusion of control in the face of untameable chaos' (2010: 271). I think regardless of the cause, be it necessity or 'crowd management', *nöbet* also aims to create an 'illusion', as was the case above with CCTV and the use of police.

'Big Brother'

In order to illustrate another face of surveillance in this section I give heed to a young female Kurdish teacher in her early twenties, Feryal. During our in-depth interview with Feryal, who described herself as a secular Kurdish nationalist, she offered me an eloquent personal testimony on 'Big Brother',

> Big Brother is watching us! This is from George Orwell, 1984. [In the book] everywhere is full of cameras and the man [the protagonist] cannot do anything about it. They even find his diary. I feel like I am living in the same era, that Big Brother is watching us! No one dictates that I talk about this or that, or even what to do or not to do in the classroom. There is freedom but it is a partisan freedom [*taraflı özgürlük*] to the extent that I know well what to say or not to say ... This is because I know that I can dig my own grave. I know it. When I was younger, when an inspector arrived at the school the head teacher locked the doors of the prayer rooms. I went back to my town, to my own school, and I observed that the first thing a head teacher does when an inspector arrives is to show the prayer room. [...] Each decade has its own rules. No one made it compulsory! Neither the inspector himself nor the state made it compulsory. It is about a kind of psychology. It is everywhere so that everyone knows very well without instructions what to do or not to do. [...] I would fear if I was a Kemalist. However, I would have no fear if I were a teacher who was paying visits to the parents' houses [member of a Gülen community] and work in the service of my community [Hidayet community]. Even if the centre were to receive ten different complaints about me, I would be sure that they [the high-ranking bureaucrats] would dismiss it. [...] I believe this. I do not have any sort

of evidence, nothing; but I know very well if I was to attend a meeting, plan a meeting at the parents' houses, hold religious conversations in their homes [refers to practices of Gülen community affiliated teachers], or even if I were to attend a meeting on the street, say, a street protest [as a pious or religious person] I would have no fear. I would know that my back is strong [*arkam kuvvetli*]. However, if I were a Kemalist, Alevi – or such like – I would fear for my life. [...] It is a partisan freedom!

Her account was definitely what I would call idiosyncratic in the context of Zinnur, as the school was dominated by an alliance of Islamist teachers who described themselves in terms of their relations with Islamic communities and constituencies, which I explained in Chapter 3. And yet it offers significant insights into the power relations within the school and deserves a brief analysis. Certainly there are many layers to her account in which she aptly echoes Foucault's *panopticism* when she explains above how she felt 'watched' by 'Big Brother', by which she meant the AKP government and her colleagues at school, and how her perceptions led her to curtail her own behaviour. She says above: 'no one dictates that I talk about this or that, or even what to do or not to do in the classroom', and admits that she controlled herself. Later during the interview, she also told me candidly that she had been politicized at an early age in a school context where Kurdish Hizbullah (or Hizbullah in Turkey) and the Kurdistan Workers' Party (*Partiya Karkerên Kurdistanê*, PKK) 'had fought to influence pupils through pupils and teachers', as she put it. Presumably, I thought, this was why she had immediately recognized and critically observed the wide range of practices of teachers affiliated with Gülen community and those with Hidayet community in the school.

However, this was not only about the context of the school. Feryal also referred to the political turmoil to encompass more than what she observed, experienced and lived in everyday school life which was clear in the term 'partisan freedom' she chose rather than other terms such as nepotism, favouritism and cronyism. There was the fear of the future, the fear of stigmatization, the fear of prosecution; the threat of violence and intimidation in Feryal's account. Definitely, they were not coming out of thin air; there were two developments that I discussed in Chapter 2. One was the sudden change in the composition of civil society, which marginalized the Kemalist nationalist civil society. The way in which the Association for the Support of Modern Life (*Çağdaş Yaşamı Destekleme Derneği*, ÇYDD) was systematically ostracized was one of the symbolic markers of such marginalization. Additionally, the successful mobilization of teachers' unions, particularly those that established strong bonds with the AKP government, was changing the landscape of civil society. One such example was the rapid increase in members of the Union of Educators' Association (*Eğitim Birliği Sendikası*, Eğitim-Bir-Sen) (Göktürk et al. 2012: 114). The second was the arbitrary privileges offered to members of Islamic organizations and communities (and the Gülen community in particular) and overt favouritism towards *imam-hatip* schools and their graduates which started to decline reputation and credibility of almost all the central exams. And I think the continuous changes that were taking place in the field of education also created a shaky ground. On the one hand, it was not clear how far the AKP government would go in reshaping civil society. On the other hand, it was obvious that only those who pursued strategies with Islamic messages and affiliations would survive.

Dress code

In this final section I turn to another 'face' of surveillance, namely the dress code and the 'self-inflicted' uniforms of teachers. Unlike much of the literature that focuses on the students' uniforms, I focus on teachers' dress code. I begin with an episode showing performances of 'protests' in both schools during the discussions on the civil servants' dress code regulation at the national level. This section I think complements to Feryal's account of 'Big Brother' above by illustrating some elements of the notion of 'partisan freedom' she uses. I then focus on the 'self-inflicted' uniforms and touch on another brief episode where the boundaries between discipline and surveillance become blurred.

Protest episode: 'Partisan freedom'?

At the beginning of the 2012–13 school year, the lifting of the official ban on headscarves in schools had not yet been implemented. However, in Zinnur, almost all of the veiled female teachers wore their headscarves in the classrooms almost from the beginning of the school year. It all started after Zehra, one of the religious culture and moral knowledge teachers in the school in her thirties, decided not to take off her headscarf in class. One day, during lunch, she turned to all the teachers and me and declared, 'Friends, I do not want to read the Qur'an without a veil.' During Qur'an classes, an elective included in the Year Five curriculum after the 4+4+4 education reform, almost all the female pupils brought their headscarves and wore them while reading the Qur'an. Zehra continued, 'And you know ... all the female pupils had brought their veils to class, so it's a bit strange not to veil as a teacher.'

In the following days she kept telling us all that she was worried about the pupils, and that she thought she might appear inconsistent towards them. As a result, she decided to wear her headscarf in school during all class hours. I think that what Zehra did was probably taken as an invitation. The teachers who wore headscarves outside school followed Zehra's lead, with the exception of Nebahat, a Year Three class teacher in her early fifties. Nebahat explained to me when we were at a picnic she had organized. She said, 'Why would I put my head teacher in a difficult position! The rule was clear. It said that you have to enter the school without a headscarf. OK, we take it off at school, but we did not have the right to do that. I can understand the others, but it is my decision.' Nebahat was reluctant.

In the months following these incidents in Zinnur, Eğitim-Bir-Sen – which is known for its political affiliations with the AKP government – initiated a petition seeking to change the dress code of civil servants in Turkey, which was backed by 12,300,000 signatures (EBS 2013). They echoed the prevailing narratives of the high-ranking AKP politicians at the time, arguing that the dress code was an imposition of the junta that came to power with the 1980 coup (EBS n.d.). These arguments were misleading in that the focus was exclusively on the headscarves. In other words, the dress code was hardly criticized in its entirety. At the time, headscarves were explicitly not allowed in the dress code for civil servants in public institutions, including schools and universities. Meanwhile, union members began to protest the dress code by going to schools with headscarves (women) or without ties and with facial hair (men) (NTV 2013). Union of Education, Science, and Culture Workers (*Eğitim Bilim ve Kültür Emekçileri Sendıkası*, Eğitim-Sen) secular union on the political left criticized the campaign of Eğitim-Bir-Sen and accused the trade union of pushing for the status quo of the AKP (Meltem Gazetesi 2013). Specifically, the protest by Eğitim-Bir-Sen was perceived as a sham, a hypocritical and self-serving act that was not seen as a 'genuine' protest. Broadly, the changing tides of political Islam have made the issue a controversial one over the last three decades. In this sense, Eğitim-Bir-Sen essentially sought to lift the ban on the headscarf, and that was all.

The details of the regulation on the dress code of civil servants reveal the extent to which it has been a political issue in Turkey that was exacerbated by the 1980 military *coup d'état*. The dress code's regulations could be summarized in two parts. For men, wearing a tie and suit is obligatory (Official Gazette 1982). The rules with regard to men's attire, however, include rather elaborate and specific details about the trimming of facial and head hair. For instance, the outer edges of the moustache must not hang below men's upper lip line. In the case of hair, sideburns are not allowed (Official Gazette 1982). In an alternative reading of the law, one could surmise that *'komunist bıyığı'* (communist moustache) and *'ülkücü bıyığı'* (right wing nationalist moustache) were not allowed. Thus, men's facial hair and hairstyles can be construed as expressions of political affiliation (Delaney 1994: 168; Kandiyoti 1997: 124). The state does not allow the manifestation of political leanings inside schools, particularly those that were claimed as a 'threat against security', or a 'challenge to the secular state'. Even though the perceived 'threats' had changed, the specifics of the regulation remained. For women, on the other hand, there were (and still are) very specific bans which include sleeveless and/or low-cut revealing shirts/blouses/dresses, stretch or skinny jeans and trousers, miniskirts, slit skirts and sandals. In addition, headscarves were banned prior to the selective, minor revision of the regulation on the dress code of civil servants following the protests, which I explain below.

In Talip, in contrast with Zinnur, female teachers only started to wear their headscarves after the Eğitim-Bir-Sen protest was publicly acknowledged. They hung the poster for the campaign on the bulletin board in the teachers' common room (see Figure 12). All the female teachers who were veiling outside school started to enter the classrooms wearing their veils. They told me that they had a meeting in which they decided to act together. As I explained earlier, there was factionalism in Talip and this collective act by veiled female teachers aggravated these tensions further. Even those who were supporting the freedom of headscarves for civil servants criticized the hypocrisy represented by the Eğitim-Bir-Sen 'protest'.

A genuine protest came in the form of recognizing the dress code as a form of control and refusing all dress codes. In fact, most of the teachers and almost all female teachers had never strictly conformed to the dress code. They had white coats that made them look like health workers in a bid to minimize their gender and their chosen dress style, which I discuss in detail below. During the protest they took off their white coats to attend the protest and some even wore clothes that they would not wear even under their white coat on school days. One day a male teacher came in with a beard, another day female teachers arrived in miniskirts, the following day some of the female teachers wore denim and sports shoes, and male teachers mostly took off their ties. 'Are you protesting?' became a standard joke. There were also those who were 'protesting the protest', that is, protesting the hypocritical stance of Eğitim-Bir-Sen members in the school who

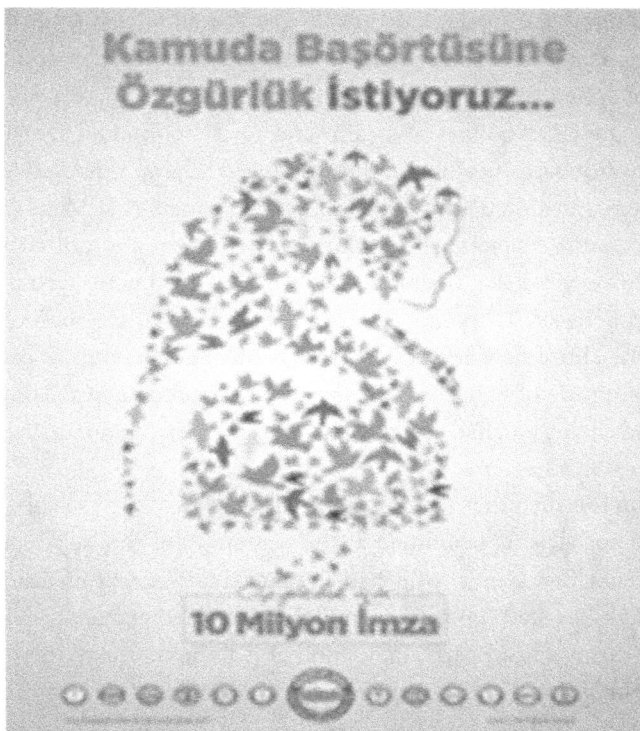

Figure 12 'We want freedom for headscarves in the public space ...' '10 Million Signature'.

selectively focused on the headscarf issue while neglecting the interests of their colleagues. Pupils also participated by coming to school without wearing their uniforms, which happened in Zinnur as well.

Yet the protest by teachers who wore headscarves was prolonged and transformed into 'civil disobedience'. The head teacher Aslan and deputy heads Erman and Ahmet kept silent – like İsmail in Zinnur – though they had to take official action against these teachers. The actions of the teachers and the dismissive manners of the head teachers morphed into a process that highlighted who has the right to temporarily suspend the official regulations. In particular, in Talip the dismissive attitudes of heads towards what was in principle a breach of conduct created an anomaly. During one of the breaks, Başak, a nationalist Kemalist female teacher in her late forties, teased the deputy head, Ahmet. She said, 'Suppose that I came to school in a *çarşaf* [a black outer garment that looks like Iranian chador] today. What can you do? You cannot do anything against this [you cannot take any legal action]!!!' She had an impish smile on her face, but she was mean. Ahmet answered, 'Even the higher ranks hesitate to take any kind of action [referring to the head teacher]. So ... Why should I be the one taking the risk?' Ahmet was calm and rarely took older female teachers' straightforward words personally, though he was young. I thought 'risk taking' was not the right word, because this was beyond a mere risk. Making an official complaint against teachers who prolonged the protest and criticizing Eğitim-Bir-Sen (which acted as a vanguard of the AKP government) would altogether cut the ties between Talip and the district bureaucracy, the municipality, and therefore the entire network of Islamic constituencies as well as communities within and outside of Bahçelik. In order to reinforce these ties, Ahmet had put his time and energy and had accepted the rules for participation in the network – as I explained in Chapter 3.

In Zinnur, on the other hand, İsmail's silence was taken as support by most teachers, if not all – as I outlined at the beginning of this sub-section. What struck me was that Zehra, who had initiated the wearing of headscarves in Zinnur, said in the staff room, 'I was told that even if someone complains [about a teacher wearing a headscarf], they smother it at the centre, so there is no need to worry.' Not only when I heard Zehra's words and noticed her confidence in this matter (a very distinct smile on her face), but also because I knew that her husband was active in politics as a member of the AKP in Istanbul, I realized that she was possibly anticipating upcoming political trends. This was also true for some of the other teachers at the school who were ardent supporters of the AKP. Presumably, this is why she and some of her colleagues felt confident in their actions. Nebahat, however, challenged the collective action of all female teachers in Zinnur (as I explained at the beginning of this sub-section) by daring to be the only woman not to follow Zehra's call. All the nuanced differences in attitudes and silences that this process produced also showed how a relatively 'marginal' issue in education, namely the dress code of teachers and especially female teachers, was charged with highly politicised meanings.

A striking feature of the 'protest' episode, which I refer to as a 'performance', was that it was simultaneously interpreted as an opportunity to challenge the dress code as a form of social control and exposed the pretensions of a union pushing for the lifting of the headscarf ban, which was seen not as a genuine quest for freedom from control, but as cynical political manipulation. It seems that those who 'protested against the protests' were right in their cynicism. Following these protests, the 2013 revision of the dress code affecting female teachers was limited to allowing veiling, nothing more.[6] In addition, in 2014, the veiling of female students was allowed in lower and upper secondary state schools. Nevertheless, the law remains in place, which prohibits the wearing or carrying of political symbols in various forms, including bags, hats or scarves that indicate any kind of political affiliation.[7]

Hiding gender under a white coat: 'Self-inflicted' uniforms

In theory, in both schools, cotton polyester-blend white coats with long sleeves were chosen as a 'self-inflicted uniform' to protect teachers' clothes from the dust, chalk, board markers or an accidental spill of a leaking pen. In practice, however, wearing these coats helped the female teachers to hide their body contours, not to mention the fact that they helped them to neglect the strict details of the dress code that I have explained above. One can encounter a variety of different styles among the female teachers of both schools: miniskirts, low-cut shirts, high-heeled stilettos, jeans and dresses with low backs. Thanks to the white coats, they were able to hide it all. In Talip, the wearers of a white coat could be divided into two groups: those who wore a headscarf to cover their bodies as a form of modesty, and the lower-middle-class female teachers who wanted to protect themselves from the uncouth working-class pupils. 'Who are you dressing for anyway? No one here will understand what you are wearing, so why should I wear proper/fancy clothes?' said one of the female teachers in Talip. The pupils and parents apparently did not have the taste to understand the code that the teacher wants to convey through her clothes.

My initial interest in the white coats came after noticing how elder female teachers interfered in the lives of younger ones in Zinnur by urging them to wear white coats. It was a process that took more than six months. In short, first, elder female teachers kindly advised the young teachers to buy white coats; second, they claimed that it was not possible to distinguish the petite young teachers from the pupils; third, they openly warned them of possible risks, which included becoming victims of bullying – physical and/or verbal – and harassment. I called this 'taming', but the elder teachers defined it as 'support'. Nebahat, one of these teachers, pointed out to all the teachers that there are many adolescent boys living in gender-segregated homes – not to mention those living in the Hidayet community dormitory – who could easily 'misinterpret' a young teacher's dress and easily 'lose respect', as she put it. 'We have to be very careful!' warned Nebahat. It occurred to me that this was a strategic ploy of these elder teachers: the tactic was not to explicitly criticize what the young teachers were wearing, but to make the white coat almost compulsory. At the same time, paradoxically, it did not come out of thin air, but was based on traumatic events they had experienced in their past that they did not share in detail. In the end, after four to six months of 'support work', young female teachers (new to the school) accepted wearing a white coat. I too bought one in the first few months after understanding that it was a self-inflicted uniform of the school without knowing the reasons in detail. It turned out that unwanted panties, skirts that reveal the wearer's legs, tight trousers, lace shirts or skirts and low-cut tops are dangerous elements of women's dress in schools.

It was also interesting to see that the gazes of almost all female teachers were proxy male gazes. The younger female teacher becomes the object of the gaze. She is responsible for being a woman herself and has to hide all the details of her body that draw attention to her gender. Male teachers, on the other hand, have the luxury of over-emphasizing their masculinity, for example, by spreading their legs wide when they sit. Imposing the white coat, which went well in Zinnur's context, as well as discussions on the dress code of teachers were treated as part and parcel of control mechanisms – to the extent that they were related to the 'disciplining' of female teachers' attire.

Conclusion

Looking at the *lived culture* (Williams 2001) of Talip and Zinnur Schools through the lens of Michael Foucault's (1995) *panopticism*, I discovered numerous 'faces' of surveillance. Nonetheless, because of my intention to make meaning of the local education market in which both Talip and Zinnur were situated, as I discussed in Chapter 3, I had to be selective in the extensive amount of data I gathered in relation to surveillance. As we have seen in the first section of this chapter, where I focused on the more mundane level of everyday school life, that is to say the actual nuts and bolts of keeping an eye on pupils and teachers, we see a range of surveillance mechanisms in use. Clearly, new technologies such as CCTV are important, but the ways in which they were used in different school contexts were not specified. CCTV was used to shield the Zinnur from the outside world of the school. In contrast, CCTV was used in Talip to change the teachers' habit of arriving late to their classrooms. Moreover, CCTV revealed another layer of surveillance in Talip, namely the double-shift system with an impossible time-space regime. However, this layer has not been addressed in this chapter. Another surveillance technology was police involvement in schools. It was legitimized by the emerging discourses on violence against children and safe schools, as was the case with the use of CCTV. As we have seen in practice, this implied that teachers were among the possible threats to pupils. Surveillance through more traditional means such as *nöbet* (guard duty) also offered significant insights into the ways in which 'guiding' became 'guarding'.

It was clear to me that none of these surveillance mechanisms fit into the *Panopticon* scheme. When I first started think about the presence of CCTV or police involvement – during the fieldwork – almost every single technology of surveillance seemed to have parallels to *Panopticon*, even as I worked on this book, I began to see many subtle differences in each of the school contexts. In other words, there is no 'total surveillance', everyone knows who is watching them and when. They just create a kind of 'illusion of control' (Gallagher 2010: 271). However, how the power works, became clear in two examples. Female teachers who were 'forced' to be on time for class showed defiance by making jokes about CCTV in Talip. Some of their jokes with subtle sexual innuendos also pointed to the gendered aspect of CCTV. As we have seen in this chapter, boys in Zinnur spitting in the liquid soap and using the toilets as a place where they did not want to be seen to resist the controlling gaze of the teachers who were on *nöbet* (guard duty).

In the following sections, I have first given heed to the young female teacher Feryal. In her account, she explained that she felt that her political leanings and affiliations were closely monitored which offered significant insights to local education market that I discussed in Chapter 3. I then illustrated an episode that captures the controversies and protests over the dress code during the school year. The difference between genuine freedom to choose one's attire and only claiming the right to veil by lifting the ban on the headscarf created a malaise in Talip and Zinnur Schools. And this has led to the paradoxical reaction that is adopting a self-imposed uniform (the white coat) that conceals the body and eludes the controlling gaze. Finally, the white coat expresses, in my view, a symbolic compliance with the norms of modesty and gender segregation by concealing the female form. In this respect, what I have presented so far not only offers an understanding of 'discipline' in the Foucauldian sense, but also reveals significant insights into the gendered aspect of discipline and the ways in which such discipline shapes – if not in its entirety – the gender regime of both schools that I will discuss in the next chapter.

Fashioning gender: Nurturing mothers vs punitive fathers

In this chapter, my intention is to analyse the *gender regime* (Connell 1987, 2000, 2005) of the Talip and Zinnur Schools. The 'four-fold model of the structure of gender relations' proposed by gender theorist Raewyn Connell (2000: 25–6; 2005: 74–5) informed my approach. These consist of *production relations* (division of labour), *power relations, cathexis* (emotional relations) and *symbolism*. A significant feature of a *gender regime* is that no single femininity nor masculinity could be claimed to represent a coherent entity. In other words, there are diverse femininities and masculinities, although the institutional setting could act to privilege specific ones. Connell (1987, 2000, 2005) explains this through the concept of *hegemonic masculinity*, which refers to 'dominant' and 'idealized' masculinity in any given society. Connell (2000) argues that while a specific masculinity is idealized culturally, other forms may be marginalized or subordinated. Connell coins the complementary term of *emphasized femininity*, which refers to culturally idealized femininity constructed in relation to *hegemonic masculinity* (1987: 185). Connell and Messerschmidt explain (2005: 848):

> The concept of hegemonic masculinity was originally formulated in tandem with a concept of hegemonic femininity – soon renamed 'emphasized femininity' to acknowledge the asymmetrical position of masculinities and femininities in a patriarchal gender order. In the development of research on men and masculinities, this relationship has dropped out of focus. This is regrettable for more than one reason. Gender is always relational, and patterns of masculinity are socially defined in contradistinction from some model (whether real or imaginary) of femininity.

Emphasized femininity refers to a type of femininity that complements *hegemonic masculinity* – for instance, motherhood 'in relation to older women' could be claimed as an example (Connell 1987: 187). However, *emphasized femininity* marginalizes 'the experience of spinsters, lesbians, unionists, prostitutes, mad women, rebels and maiden aunts, manual workers, midwives and witches' (Connell 1987: 188). The compliance that *emphasized femininity* entails could be explained with reference to Deniz Kandiyoti's (2013) concept of *patriarchal bargain*. In other words, within the hierarchical structure that Connell constructs to explain gender relations, *hegemonic masculinity* maintains its power over *emphasized femininity* by means of eliciting consent in Gramscian terms. Furthermore, 'patriarchal bargains' 'exert a powerful influence on the shaping of women's gendered subjectivity and determine the nature of gender ideology' (2013: 98). Thus, women's 'active or passive resistance' (2013: 98), under the hegemonic structure, constructs both *emphasized femininities* and those that are 'resistant' in Connell's terms. Most importantly, the wide array of femininities and masculinities are constructed and fluid.

The theory of *gender performativity* developed by Judith Butler (2011) offers an understanding of the ways in which masculinities and femininities are reproduced by being performed on a daily basis.[1] For Butler, *performativity* 'must be understood not as a singular or deliberate "act" but, rather, as the reiterative and citational practice by which discourse produces the effects that it names' (2011: 2). Drawing from Butler, my intention is to trace 'acts' that construct femininities and masculinities in day-to-day interactions. Butler does not limit 'acts' to literal performance (2011: xxi), but she also refers to constructions of 'acts'. Butler's conception of 'doing gender' further clarifies her point. For Butler, 'gender is always a doing'; she explains, 'There is no gender identity behind the expressions of gender; that identity is performatively constituted by the very "expressions" that are said to be its results' (2007: 33).

In this chapter, I illustrate how women's maternal roles are mobilized in the process of education. We have already seen in Chapter 3 how, in the self-funding environment of neoliberal schooling, mothers are used as classroom volunteers, extending their unpaid work at home to providing services for the school. The policies of the Bahçelik municipality targeted at women and children, in line with the gender norms promoted by the AKP, also contribute to constructing a particular version of motherhood. I focus on local policies that target mothers and explore the extent to which school contexts mirror these policies. Connell (1987, 2009) suggests that we look closely at the ways in which institutions condition, construct and reproduce gender roles through a multiplicity of factors including the *gender order* of the society, which offers the blueprint for the perceived gender roles in specific economic socio-political, cultural and historical conditions. However, this does not mean that institutions simply mirror the *gender order* of the society, though the roots of certain dispositions in the institutional setting could be traced to it (Connell 2009: 71). My intention in this chapter is to adopt a bottom-up approach based on my school ethnographies.

The discourse and practice of motherhood as articulated and elaborated by the teachers in both Zinnur and Talip Schools gave me an interesting point of entry. It was intriguing to find that teachers, parents and pupils see the gender roles in schools in much the same way that they define gender roles in the homes. Deriving from the accepted notion among many teachers that school is to a certain extent an extension of the family in terms of gender relations, their approach to femininity and masculinity takes the normative roles of fatherhood and motherhood as a point of reference for interactions between parents, teachers and pupils. Moreover, the family as an institution was not merely used as a metaphor. Maternal and paternal roles in the family became the blueprint for the ways in which female teachers performed 'motherhood', while male teachers acted the part of the paternal 'bogeyman'. Having said that in what follows I first offer a rather brief overview of local policies that target mothers and then I engage with teachers' accounts on motherhood and fatherhood.

Mobilizing women to get involved in schooling: 'The good mothers'

The sharp increase in mothers' involvement in the everyday schooling of their children in both schools that I illustrated in Chapter 3, which includes performing volunteer work such as being a *sınıf annesi* (classroom mother), was a relatively new phenomenon in the 2012–13 school year. Seeing this engagement of mothers, one might easily claim that the situation reflects the *gender order* (Connell 1987) of wider society, where mothers who are not in the paid labour force have flexible time to pay frequent visits to the schools. Nevertheless, as I will explain below, such a claim would fall short. In Bahçelik, mothers in the past were expected to refrain from stepping out of their homes and rarely received permission from their husbands to enter public spaces, including schools, due to concerns about possible encounters with unrelated men. In this section, I aim to offer a rather overview of the local policy measures of the Bahçelik municipality directed at mothers of pupils. Women, who worked for the AKP-run municipality, were successful in mobilizing pious working class mothers to get involved in education of their children. However, by informing them how best to nurture, educate and care for their children, and by supporting the mothers by providing education services to their children (such as those in *bilgi evi* that I explained in Chapter 3), the women working for the AKP not only legitimized the lack of father involvement in schooling but also played a role in defining the boundaries of mother involvement with the notion of 'good mothering'.

Local policies

Hanife, in her early fifties, was one of the hard-working AKP *mahalle başkanı* (neighbourhood head) in Bahçelik. When I first met her, it was her turn to run the cafeteria in the district's giant education centre that offered courses on a wide range of subjects exclusively to women living in the area. In this cafeteria, any woman could sell *börek*, cake, salads, etc. that they prepared at home without paying fees to the municipality, albeit occasionally. Hanife told me that the waiting list was very long. It was, in theory, intended to create an opportunity for working-class women in the district to earn extra income; however, in practice women like Hanife also used these opportunities. What I mean is that all the members of Hanife's family were already working for the municipality and had regular incomes. Many of the practices that I knew of were theoretically available to 'everyone' in the district, however; mostly women, who were ardent followers of the AKP, benefitted from such practices- not to mention those women who were working for the Bahçelik municipality.

While drinking the tea that Hanife had offered, I listened to her talking about what she had done within the borders of the streets that she was responsible for, how she had touched the lives of people – women in particular – in need. I mentioned the expansion of a wide range of facilities (such as educational facilities, sports centres and more), developed projects and ongoing seminars, courses targeting women in the district. I expressed my surprise at the high visibility of women everywhere I went in the district, and she confidently replied, 'Without us [women] such mobilization would not be possible. We work a lot! A lot! Without us it wouldn't be what it is now.' Hanife further explained her political past and told me that she was working for the Welfare Party (*Refah Partisi*, RP) in the 1990s and she said, 'When Erdoğan [Recep Tayyip Erdoğan] established the AKP, we followed him because I trust him … We all worked together when he was mayor of Istanbul.'[2]

In line with Hanife's account, the AKP women's branch in the district reflected context-based party politics and practices, some of which were cloned from the grassroots women's mobilization of the 1990s. In other words, it was only a matter of reframing a well-established tradition in the district. Also, following the municipal reforms in 2005 referred to in Chapter 3, municipalities started to encourage residents' voluntary involvement in informing local policies. Following these developments, a variety of platforms were established across district municipalities in Istanbul. The women's platform in Bahçelik was one of them. It served to address wide range of issues affecting women by women, albeit under the leadership of the mayor. These women initiated innovative local policies that women wanted and/or desired by providing platforms for women to talk about their needs, problems, concerns and aspirations. The aim of these platforms was not only to motivate women to participate in local politics by encouraging them to express their needs, but also to gather information in order to develop policies that address these needs. However, one should not be misled by this provision of a participatory approach, in practice women working for AKP provided gender-segregated spaces and offered women-only activities in order to motivate women living in the district to step outside their homes. Hacer explained this shift:

> When I was directing the women's council [in the past], it was so difficult to make mothers do something for the council, so I was doing all the tasks. I was allocating tasks to mothers to fulfil for a coming seminar, but in the end, I was doing all the work. In general, you decide on a topic [to discuss in the meetings and/or seminars] and then want them to do research on the topic. We have free library access ... Yet, we would say 'bravo' if we can make women step outside their home. I am talking about five years ago. I was calling them to attend the Women's Council. I was telling them that there is going to be a seminar on health for instance ... They would never attend. Within the last five years, this [pattern] changed so much so that now in every seminar you see women and children.

Yet, this went beyond what Hacer suggested. Clubs, courses, classes, meetings, seminars and activities were tailored to address the perceived needs of the women in the district. In addition, the municipality often targeted mother-child dyads to equate the 'needs' of the children with the 'interest' of the mothers, as was the case for *bilgi evi* that I discussed in Chapter 3. What I found interesting was that Hacer took the gender segregation of the spaces, as well as activities, for granted. None of the women working for the municipality that I interviewed mentioned this fact while describing the change in the habits of mothers. The local policies paradoxically mobilized women by encouraging them to play an active role in local politics while at the same time reinforced the nurturing mother stereotype, as will be briefly discussed below.

A captive audience

In various platforms, seminars, meetings, events and celebrations related to the education of children, I saw that a particular version of motherhood and/ or womanhood was created. This was done by means of inviting mothers to hear from 'scientific experts' such as scholars from psychology departments, graduates of sociology, 'popular voices' such as journalists (only from newspapers that are known as the official voice of the AKP) and 'moral experts' such as civil servants working for DİB. Mostly these meetings were very similar to the popular television shows on Turkish television channels that targeted women. While on one side there was a large group of women, I call the 'captive audience' representing the 'uneducated', 'ignorant', 'poor' working-class religious women waiting to become 'enlightened', on the other side there was a bunch of 'respectable', 'educated', 'knowledgeable' middle-class women expecting deference.

The 'captive audience' was able to pay full attention to this presentation of a 'perfect' combination of scientific, popular and moral perspectives on the mother/woman archetype – a mother who is selfless, nurturing, caring. This was also because the 'captive audience' experienced ambivalence, fear, confusion, a sense of responsibility, a sense of inadequacy and at times a sense of guilt about their mothering practices – and the 'experts' were touching their weak spots by means of constructing an 'ideal' mother who shall take all the responsibility for childcare. There was neither an attempt to challenge gender inequality in the family or society, nor was there an intention to aim at economic, social or political empowerment. Moreover, the 'absence of men' in the education of the children was unquestioned. They all frequently referred to a hadith of the Prophet Muhammad which states, 'heaven is under the feet of your mothers'; at times Mehmet Akif Ersoy's ideas on the family and mothers were quoted, in which mothers were the key actors.

After meeting, observing, chatting, having unrecorded interviews, and participating in classes and activities with numerous mothers during the entire school year in both schools, I reached the conclusion that mothers were first and foremost eager to be 'good mothers', who are nurturing, caring and involved in the education of their children in a way that their own mothers had not been involved during their own childhoods.

A brief touch on welfare policies

It is possible to trace the resonance between the partial illustrations I offer above and the welfare regime of the AKP. The AKP government emphasized 'motherhood' by means of supplying what Carole Pateman defines as 'private welfare' (1992: 32). First, we have the constructed motherhood of conservative political discourses, which reference Sunni interpretations of Islam. The debate on abortion during the 2012–13 school year could be offered as an example. The wish that women should bear a minimum of three children, as expressed by the then-prime minister Recep Tayyip Erdoğan, has become the epitome of the statements of the AKP parliamentarians on women's rights and particularly motherhood. This ideology of motherhood is far from the more assertive statements regarding women's maternal and caring vocation, which have become more prominent and to a great extent 'mainstream' under the AKP. Politicians have perpetuated and endorsed understandings of womanhood that for decades a wide range of feminist strands in Turkey have been attempting to challenge.

Secondly, the structural reforms and welfare regime changes that were introduced in the mid-2000s as a part of the EU reform process have not challenged the role of women. On the contrary, the AKP government further consolidated the role of women as wives and mothers (Dedeoglu 2012) and emphasized the caregiving role of women (Buğra 2012). Studies suggest that the limited number of childcare services, as well as their cost, prevent mothers from entering formal sector jobs, particularly those from low-income households in urban areas (Beşpınar 2015: 106–7; WB 2015). These policies structurally confine women to their homes and impose a particular notion of motherhood. Incentives offered for additional children and basic pay for stay-at-home mothers give strong policy signals in the direction of pro-natalism.

The mobilization of mothers in Talip and Zinnur schools – and in Bahçelik – could paradoxically be seen as an attempt to further protect what the AKP government promotes as traditional family values.[3] Therefore, it is possible to fall back on the link between the *gender order* of society and the *gender regime* (Connell 1987) of homes and schools which could lead one to detect similarities between the division of labour in wider society and the home settings, while also explaining the *gender regime* of the schools. Additionally, women are expected to display *emphasized femininity* in the district (Connell & Messerschmidt 2005: 848) as part of a *patriarchal bargain* (Kandiyoti 2013) between the mothers and the party, whereby they display compliance to receive the wide range of services provided in the district. This compliance, however, is not necessarily based on calculation but on their own guilt, doubts and vulnerabilities concerning their adequacy as mothers. This understanding of motherhood is so pervasive that it becomes synonymous with femininity in Talip and Zinnur contexts.

The construction of motherhood in school settings: 'Mothering' or teaching?

Being a female teacher was perceived as synonymous with being a mother in the Talip and Zinnur Schools. The key similarity between a mother and a female teacher was their 'unpaid' care work. On the one hand, the gender disparity over childcare was perceived as a norm in homes, to the extent that it was the key-defining feature of being a mother. On the other hand, the female teachers regardless of their marital status or even if 'they had not given birth to a child' – as they frequently stated – were seeing themselves as the 'mothers' of their pupils or at times as mother substitutes. Given these normative understandings in both school contexts, all female teachers explained the distinguishing features of being a female teacher with reference to motherhood, which also reinforced the Bahçelik municipality-orchestrated attempts to socialize women into appropriate maternal roles, as I touched upon above. Most especially, they define the 'doing' (Butler 2007) of a specific femininity. Emine, who had been teaching for more than twenty years, explained to me how she views her role:

> **Emine:** I do not see my job as teaching, my friend. You know in the family there is a father and a mother. They take care of everything involving their children, are you with me, my friend? And it is the mother who looks after the child, though there might be situations where the father also engages with childcare. In my class I see myself as their mother. […] I work as if I am living in my house … I am a mother in the classroom. Okay there is the curriculum as well and I must teach them, but I focus on the behaviours. They are so young to test. Female teachers see the details like mothers see the details at home my friend. Even when I go home, I think about the pupils one by one. Even before I sleep, I say to myself for instance, 'Esin did

not look well today, I have to check her tomorrow'. Do you understand what
I am saying my friend?

Zühre: You feel like they are your kids, don't you?

Emine: Exactly! But I don't [just] 'feel like' [it] – it is beyond 'feeling' – it is a
reality. You do literally everything!

Emine, who taught Year Three in Talip School, did not see a difference
between herself and the mothers of the pupils. In other words, being a successful
teacher requires her to present her understanding of motherhood (e.g., as
nurturer, care giver, emotional, involved). During our interview she kept
referring to her relationship with her own children to explain her perception
of the pupils in her classroom. It was clear to me that her internalized norms
of motherhood created a positive image of herself in her mind. Emine's ideas
were a succinct summary of those I heard from numerous other female teachers
who were teaching Year One, Two, Three and Four – the age group between
five and ten in both schools. Most asserted that they are the 'mothers' of their
pupils. Therefore, the sexual division of labour in the home was mapped onto
the sexual division of labour in the school setting in terms of caring, nurturing
and disciplining the children.

Fatih, a male teacher in his mid-thirties and a pious Muslim who taught Year
Three in Zinnur, concurred with these ideas:

Women are emotional, they have the potential to feel deeply. You know a bad
male teacher would be called indifferent, but a bad female teacher is unacceptable.
This is what I observed so far, and it is hard to generalize. A bad female teacher
is an awful female teacher. She hates, and she could even say things like, 'I hate
this work [teaching]'. [...] If I were a female teacher who loves her job ... What
would it be like? My relationship with the mothers would be better ... Ok, I
have a good relationship with them [mothers] ... Yet, if I were a female teacher,
mothers would feel more comfortable with me.

Like most of the teachers in both schools, he started to question some of the
norms that he took for granted after hearing my questions. Also, Fatih always
enjoyed thinking aloud, as can be seen in the excerpt above where he talks about
the pros and cons of being a female or male teacher. Yet what I found interesting
was his statement that 'a bad female teacher is an awful female teacher'. With
this expression Fatih was referring to female teachers who do not perform
'motherhood' properly by showing their positive emotions, such as compassion,
towards pupils. In other words, according to Fatih, motherhood and femininity
are the norms for women who teach. However, he never questioned his own

lack of emotional labour, since the display of emotions would marginalize him as a male teacher. In other words, showing emotion particularly towards pupils was not perceived as a masculine performance, which will be addressed in the sections to come.

Unlike Fatih, who felt a sort of barrier between the mothers and himself due to his gender, most female teachers and particularly those teaching the five-to-ten age group developed a very close relationship with the mothers. I shared my observations with a group of female teachers, who were married with children; most of them had more than fifteen years of teaching experience. I told them that, metaphorically, the teachers enter the spatial realm of the homes and have access to the privacy of the family. Moreover, I shared my interest in understanding the extent to which such close relationships blur the lines between being a teacher and being almost a 'member' of the family. This led them to a discussion on the role of female teachers, which, again, foregrounded motherhood. Banu, Adile and Nebahat in Zinnur School took part in the discussion:

Banu: Teacher becomes a mother and a father.
Adile: Even the child might call you 'mother'. Well, I am teaching Year Three and there are pupils in my classroom who still call me mother. When she/he [pupil] comes next to you she/he addresses you with 'mother' and later she/he calls me teacher. They perceive us as mothers. For them we are mothers and for us they are like our kids. Otherwise, you cannot do this job.
Banu: Sure, even the parent perceives you like that. They see you like an older or young sister, and they share their problems, and they talk about their troubles and private problems, they even call you and share it on the phone …
Nebahat: Yes.
Banu: She tells you about her private problems in her marriage. You build such a relationship that they trust you. Because there is a significant link which is the pupil …
Nebahat: Yes, true. It happens frequently.

There was a wide range of shared maternal tasks including playing with the children, instructing and supervising them, caring for them when they are in need. Here I am not only referring to the maternal involvement in the form of the *sınıf annesi* (classroom mother), which was the norm in both school contexts as I discussed briefly in Chapter 3. Here I am referring to what I term 'teachers' involvement at home'. Banu, Adile and Nebahat all stressed that the construction of the female teacher vis-à-vis mothering, figuratively speaking, abolished the spatial difference between the classroom and the sitting room in her own home.

On the one hand, female teachers act as a counsellor to the young mothers and give suggestions on their marriages. On the other hand, again female teachers support these young mothers in disciplining, educating – and more – the children at home. For instance, Banu told me that she and one of the mothers developed a strategy to prevent a Year Two male pupil staying up late at night. To develop a sensible sleeping pattern, they told the male pupil that Banu – his teacher – had been watching him with hidden cameras. Yet, after seeing that the male pupil resisted taking a shower, presumably because he thought that his teacher would see him naked, they decided to put an end to this disciplining strategy. This is only one graphic example demonstrating the extent to which female teachers are involved in the lives of the pupils in general; although the strategy seems pedagogically problematic, I am less interested in this aspect of disciplining than in detecting the blurring of the lines between school and family life.

For the female teachers who were teaching Years Five to Year Eight, 'maternal instinct' was the key word to refer to motherhood. Although they did not claim to be substitute mothers, they emphasized the 'instinctiveness' of motherhood as a key feature of being a woman. Ahu, who taught Year Six, Seven and Eight in Zinnur, explained this instinct by comparing male and female teachers:

> I think female teachers are more emotional. They show their maternal instinct, but male teachers don't have any emotional bond with pupils. He gives the instructions in the classroom and that's it – then he goes home. Because we have maternal instinct, it is, I think, different for us. I think it has pros and cons ... The good side is that you approach the pupils with love [compassion], and you feel as if the pupil is your own kid. The bad side is that when you are emotional the pupils take advantage of it, and you lose your logical thinking ... I am not sure if we are objective enough. Maybe it is my own personal issue, I hesitate to generalize. But when I observe other female teachers, I see the same behaviours as well, which means that it is an innate feature of women. It is an instinct.

'Innate' maternal instinct, according to Ahu, influences the ways in which female teachers take on more duties compared to male teachers. Another significant point is that Ahu distinguishes female from male teachers in terms of their attitude to their profession. For instance, while female teachers are concerned with the emotional needs of the pupils, male teachers only 'give instructions', which will be further discussed in the following section.

To sum up, female teachers' 'performance' of motherhood in school settings mimics mothers' 'performance' in the family. This reproduces and reinforces the normative 'performance' of femininity. Yet, not all female teachers meet the criteria of 'ideal' motherhood, as we shall see below.

The deviant 'working mothers', 'single mothers' and 'single women'

It was intriguing to encounter portrayals of 'femininities' that fail to comply with the normative expectations of femininity in both schools. In particular, the perceptions of the male teachers revealed significant insights into marginalized femininities. Osman was an ardent follower of the Nationalist Movement Party (*Milliyetçi Hareket Partisi*, MHP) and his perspective on the 'Turkish' nation was that it was a military nation in which every 'boy' was a born soldier.[4] Moreover, throughout the course of my fieldwork he insisted on the idea that there has never been inequality between men and women, by referring to the Turkic heritage. His ideas were mere reflections of narratives of the nationalist ideologies.[5] According to Osman, some Kurdish families have inequality problems in their homes. Osman explained his views during our interview:

> We do not separate people as woman and man in our minds. In the [parent-teacher] meetings there is no difference between the mother and father. But I see a difference between man and woman, if you ask me. I see a huge difference ... The woman is more hesitant [*tutuk*]. I see that mothers have no authority. You know in our families the father has the authority. Okay there are dominant mothers as well. I must confess this reality. There are also families in which there is a [power] balance [between the couple], but this constitutes twenty per cent of all cases. Eighty per cent of the families lack this balance. Both mothers and fathers are powerful and active in the families where mothers are working; especially if the mother works, she has power. If she doesn't work – which is the case for most of the mothers in this region and school – she doesn't have power or a voice, so she does not have authority. She is the one to yell at. Mother is the one who absorbs the problems. She is the one who protects her child from the father and society. She sacrifices herself. Yet what does she get? [...] As I told you before we are in a [social] structure in which if you have authority people respect you, but if you are more democratic and if you value people – like mothers do – help them and teach them, they don't respect you. So, mothers are in this [social] structure ... I think in general there is no difference between the female or male pupils until they get married. When they enter social life [get married], with marriage the woman becomes the mother, and the man becomes the father. Then the power of women becomes limited and yet their responsibilities and burdens become unlimited.

Although, in principle, Osman believes in democratic values, he sees the 'undemocratic' values of the family structure as inevitable. He also reflected on his own past and family while elaborating on his point. During the school year, he constantly referred to the 'oppressive nature of the family structure', as he put it. However, he was allergic to the word 'inequality' when it was used in connection to 'Turkish' family structure. He, nevertheless, thinks that family structure and the unequal division of labour in the home have detrimental effects on women. Women only gain power when they enter into the labour market, he claimed.

Although Osman's ideas were contradictory at times, Üzeyir, who was the 'gatekeeper' of the Hidayet Dormitory in Zinnur and a member of the Hidayet community, was quite consistent. His ideas were in line with those of the community and yet they were not peculiar to the community in question. On the contrary, they were prevalent among most of the pious Muslim male teachers who owe their past education to wide range of Islamic communities (see Chapter 3). He justified his opposition to women's employment:

I think mothers influence each other a lot [in a negative way]. They are also influenced by television series [in a negative way]. They become more open to harassment by men or maybe they want to experience what they see on the television [he refers to Turkish television series and dramas]. For instance, I know a mother who is working. She came closer to the man that she was working with [in the workplace] and then the man used her [*kullanmış*].[6] Nowadays she does everything to make her husband cheat on her so that she will feel relieved of her guilt. There are also mothers who are coming [to school] just to see us [male teachers]. One can easily grasp their intention at first sight. I can give more than twenty examples of such [mothers]. I always leave my door open when I meet them. There are so many women, who got married just to leave their homes, and there are a lot of women who started to wear chador [*çarşaf*] not to cheat on their husbands. I think those [mothers] who are not working over-estimate/ exaggerate the [freedom of] working mothers. But when they experience that life [working life], they feel like they are re-discovering America [the continent]. They cannot differentiate the fictional life depicted in the television series and real life. Even my daughter looks for a handsome man like James Bond with his sports car. She assumes that she is going to get married to someone like him and have a baby. Television shows and films affect them all. [...] This also affects men. I have a rich friend who holds high status and manages a big business. He said, 'if the man becomes urbanized, and the woman behaves like a peasant it becomes a problem [*erkek şehirleşir kadın köylüleşirse sorun oluyor*].' He says, 'I don't want women wearing long leg knickers [*tuman*] in my bed', and he says, 'my wife had forgotten me and turned her back [lost interest in sex]'. I think the responsibilities of the women at home are as important as their social responsibilities ...

Üzeyir talked very explicitly, considering the setting of Zinnur and knowing that he was a member of the Hidayet community. Being exposed to his keen reference to sex and sexuality, I felt a bit uncomfortable at times and at times it was puzzling. It was not the subject matter as such, but his motivation to intimidate me through the choice of detailed examples he provided in his account. Some of the male teachers often used explicit language or such narratives, as seen in Üzeyir's account. One reason was that these male teachers were raised in gender-segregated settings and had difficulty in socializing with women (I learned this from the disclosures of younger male teachers). Another reason I observed was to show off their power, like Üzeyir did, by deciding on the details of the subject matter. This was because female teachers in Zinnur either got embarrassed or shunned speaking in these instances. Hence, the more I maintained my cool while listening to him, the more explicit his account became. I think the other reason for his explicit language was his perception of me, an unmarried woman studying abroad, an instance of 'resistant' (Connell 1987) non-conforming femininity. Those who do not comply with normative expectations become 'vulnerable' to the explicit innuendos of some of the male teachers.

Having said that, Üzeyir thinks that women who enter the labour market are looking for 'sexual adventure'. For him, the domain of paid work is where the women are 'used' [kullanılmak] (or 'raped'?). That is why he put pressure on both pupils and young teachers for same-sex socialization. Fatih, the male teacher from Zinnur mentioned above, shared some of his thoughts, which were in line with Üzeyir's perceptions. Fatih told me that until he started university, he had believed the idea that 'women who are not veiled are prostitutes'. 'Such a shame!' he added, having revised his position. Üzeyir's arguments and Fatih's past beliefs reminded me of the Islamic novels of the 1980s that pupils consumed in Zinnur.[7] In most of these works, 'secular' women's 'depraved identity' is depicted with hateful, crude stereotypes, while 'religious' women essentially embody the morality that 'secular' women lack. However, what I have explained should not mislead one in the sense that the male teachers I observed had not distinguished teachers according to their attire when it came to showing power.

Another stigmatized femininity is that of single mothers. The discussion among Adile, Banu and Nebahat is a graphic summary of how single mothers were perceived among teachers:

Adile: These [the pupils living with single moms] are on the streets because the mother is working. She [one of the single mothers] was divorced so she is responsible for everything in the home. She took the child [custody rights] and the child needs nurturing. What can she do? She must work from morning to late night. Mothers generally do not have anything [skills and diplomas] so they work in the textile workshops. This job wears them out.

Nebahat: They come home very late.

Adile: They come home late. They spent all the time in the workshops, so the child is all by himself. The child is alone so those children older than him influence him in a negative way [on the street]. The older children made him tell the girls in the classroom that 'this and that is done to the girls' – I cannot go into details – And then I was angry with him, and he said, 'teacher, the older brothers told me these things.' He repeated what he was told to all the girls in the classroom. And there was another incident; one of my girls [pupils] in the classroom did not come to school for more than twenty days ... Suddenly mother called me she said '*Hocam* [My teacher] she doesn't want to come to school.'

Banu: Why doesn't she want to come to school?

Adile: There is no information; no explanation – I don't know what happened but – Because I think separation is a big issue! It is a wearing experience. She must be working day and night. The child is neglected. In the morning we talked about this with one of the teachers [male teacher] and he said, 'the most important need is bread. She must work. The most important need is feeding the child not the school or the classes [education]'.

Banu: It is about awareness/consciousness ...

Adile: Okay but is there really something a woman can do *Hocam* [My teacher]?!

Banu: I think what the male teacher told you is wrong.

Adile: But come on. If you think about his logic, he is right.

Banu: Yes, well you cannot stay hungry but ...

Adile: She does not have a university diploma.

Banu: Okay but look –

Adile: There is nothing in her hands. What can she do? She goes to the unrelated men's workshops and works from morning till late at night.

Banu: I think it is about developing oneself ...

Adile: Oh, come on how can she develop herself if she had left school [dropped out] ...

Banu: I think socio economic factors are important here. [...] In my classroom there is a single mother as well and she does everything for the education of her child. She doesn't eat or drink in the workplace and brings that money home to buy books for her child. I think this is also about someone's heart [disposition] ... Well does she have a diploma? No. I am sure she barely graduated from primary school, and she migrated to Istanbul and got married at an early age. She is the daughter of a poor family, but she sees education as a liberation/an exit from here ... Their psychological situation is bad. Do you know that I have more than fifteen mothers who are seeing psychiatrists? You would say we are in a low-income neighbourhood [*varoş*]; but every mother knows how to go to the psychiatrist.

Nebahat: My mothers [my pupils' mothers] are like that as well.

The constructed 'neglected children' image was used against the single mothers to further stigmatize them or used against women, who were considering separation, as a threat.

Adile, who was a pious Muslim teacher in her early fifties, candidly talked about the difficulty she faced in her Year Three classroom due to the increasing number of children of single mothers. She explained to me that the divorce of more than ten parents in her class had a negative impact on the education of pupils who would otherwise be successful. Moreover, teachers suggest young mothers should stay in the marriage even if they were experiencing the most oppressive forms of marriage or polygamy. The teachers in Talip were even more relentless when it came to single mothers. The children of single mothers constituted the majority of the 'problem kids' or 'trouble kids' as they were referred to.

I was also struck by the fact that it was not only the teachers, but the AKP women's branch in the district and Offices for Family Religious Guidance (*Aile İrşat ve Rehberlik Bürosu*) of DİB were also struggling to persuade women not to get divorced.[8] Another significant outcome of the increasing number of single mothers is the prevalence of informal religious kindergartens which are called *sıbyan okulları* (infant schools) in the district, since there is great demand for childcare.[9] Female teachers, themselves, were definitely not untouched by this phenomenon; among the others, Ceylan's candid account was informative. Ceylan was a young teacher in her early thirties in Zinnur; she told me that she got divorced shortly after her marriage; however, she had not shared this information with her colleagues or pupils' parents for more than two years. 'This way is better …' she said. What was striking was that she kept her wedding photos on the table in her flat to give the impression that she was still married. 'I turn them down when everyone leaves,' she added.[10]

The *gender regime* of the school – allocating stereotypical roles to male and female teachers – reinforces and reproduces the perceived *gender regime* of families. In a way, school mimics the *gender regime* of the home where the female teacher 'performs' 'normative' femininity, which is maternal. Those that do not comply with the requirements of *emphasized femininity* (Connell 1987) are marginalized. The complement to these constructions is *hegemonic masculinity* and the ways it is lived out in schools.

Beware of fathers and male teachers: Male teachers as bogeymen, aka fathers

Nil in Zinnur, who believed that teachers and pupils engaged in what she called 'psychological warfare', spoke openly about how desperate she was to maintain control in her classes. She explained,

> If you are a female teacher, you always clash with male pupils. Disobedience, not listening to [what you say]. This is because you are a woman. [...] It might be because the ones they listen to are their fathers or uncles and brothers in their families and/or in their culture. The children fear them. Mothers are always passive, or they show compassion. [...] They [mothers] are willing to forgive and be tolerant. They [the children] feign reluctance. But when it comes to fathers – ... When you tell them 'I will tell your dad'. You know mothers always use this [expression] as a weapon. [They say] 'I will tell your dad'. When they cannot cope with the child. The child gets scared [*tırsar*]. It is the same in the school. They don't take heed of a female teacher.

The main difference between a male and female teacher, according to her, was authority. For Nil, gender role expectations and beliefs are clearly shaped by family socialization, particularly the relationship between both parents. Male pupils see their mothers as helpless, and powerless in the face of fearsome father, uncle and brother figures, which reproduce the social construction of the 'passive' mother whose sole 'weapon' is to threaten by saying, 'I will tell your dad'. In Nil's very graphic explanation, which is quite a common one among teachers, the actual parenting role of the father is very thin and limited to what I call a 'bogeyman': summoned in need. More precisely, a disciplinarian who employs coercion, threats of violence and/or insults.

Moreover, although Nil criticized fathers and mothers of pupils, she was imitating them in her classes 'to establish authority', in her words. She explained how she insulted Year Five pupils:

> They [the pupils] are all stupid ... One day I told them [the pupils] to write down the subjects that they could not remember on small pieces of paper and then I said roll those papers and swallow them with a glass of water [laughs]. You could hardly forget, I said [laughs]. The next day I asked those who did what I had said to raise their hands. [...] And I saw that almost the half of the pupils did what I said. Then I told them [pupils] 'you are all stupid' [laughs].

Seeing that I was listening with a frozen face, Nil suddenly stopped laughing. I was in an utter shock not only about her maltreatment of the pupils but also about her obvious enjoyment of such an act to compensate for her poor class performance where she kept yelling at pupils. After this incident, she never shared her impressions again. Yelling and 'showing wit' in front of 'stupid' pupils were in fact replicating the very features of fatherhood that she described during our interview.

'Children fear the male teachers' (*çocuklar erkek öğretmenden korkuyorlar*) and 'pupils shun/avoid/fear the male teachers' (*öğrenciler erkek öğretmenden çekiniyorlar*) were two sentences repeated continuously in both Talip and Zinnur. My in-depth interviews suggest that fathers' gender identities and male teachers' gender overlapped to such an extent that they could hardly describe male teachers' attitudes without referring to the fathers of the pupils. In other words, the categories of 'fatherhood' and 'male teacher' became coterminous and made sense in relation to each other in the narratives of the teachers, which was in line with their behaviour in everyday schooling.

Most especially, violence or the threat of violence is a key expression of the fathers' role or one of the key features of fatherhood as imagined by the teachers. The teachers constructed 'fatherhood' around essentialist and totalizing assumptions, imagining it as disciplinarian, emotionally distant, aggressive and violent. Interestingly, the teachers who were criticizing this 'poor, inadequate fatherhood', in practice, imitated, mimicked and replicated the assumed roles, behaviours and attitudes of fathers. Thus, implicitly, violence and the threat of violence emerge as the key determinants of masculinity. In what follows, I illustrate my arguments about the ways in which masculinities, which are a significant component of the *gender regime* (Connell 1987, 2000, 2005) of the schools, are reproduced.

Aziz, a male teacher, and Ceylan, a female teacher, in Zinnur came out with more or less the same ideas as Nil – yet they expanded further on the coercive power of fathers as well as male teachers. The discussion went as follows:

> **Aziz:** […] the kids are wary of their fathers, not of their mothers in the family … It is the father who uses punishment or falls back on punishment and even though it is not right for fathers to resort to beating. So, I think the father figure at school is the male teacher.
> **Ceylan:** They [fathers] can be meaner and more serious.
> **Aziz:** For sure …
> **Ceylan:** For instance, when I get angry in some situations and if the pupil becomes sad, I do not feel okay. Either I go and nudge him/her or – Well, I try to make amends … After I get angry, I can hardly contain my anger. The pupil knows it, so easily manipulates it.

Aziz: Exactly, women are very sensitive in that ... They [female teachers] are more fragile in all senses. Our female teachers are full of love [compared to male teachers]. In fact, this is a good characteristic. If we were able to show more love to our pupils, their academic success would increase up to 100 per cent. But unfortunately, we are not able to do it because of the infrastructural shortcomings. It is hard to realize this. Teachers do their best. [...] Teaching is not limited to teaching during the class, you are involved with all the needs of the child.

Again, the comparison of female teachers and male teachers frequently ends with sexist stereotypes, such as the sensitive and fragile female teachers versus the relatively more mean and serious male teachers. Moreover, female teachers lack the very 'essential' feature of masculinity that is being 'bogeymen' and at times being the relentless disciplinarian, while the male teacher can easily mimic the attributes of normative fatherhood. As one of the teachers put it, 'it is in their blood'.

In the previous chapter, I discussed the extent to which the infrastructural limits of the schools transform schooling into a kind of 'crowd management' situation, and I also analysed the duties required of teachers with respect to keeping the pupils in check. It seems to me that these structural shortcomings prompt teachers to develop different approaches, such as searching for tools to intimidate pupils to control them; constructed fatherhood is one of those tools. According to Aziz, the overcrowded classrooms prompt male teachers to be 'meaner and sterner', and yet he also thinks that this is an essential feature of manhood.

Nevertheless, these ideas were also prevalent among the teachers in Talip. Kevser's ideas suggest that the *gender regime* of schools and families is similar due to the expectations that pupils developed in their homes. Ironically, their own perception barely differs from those of their pupils. Kevser explained,

How can I say this? [...] Those pupils who are warned in a mean tone ... I mean those pupils who are exposed to physical violence at home fear male teachers. The male teacher takes the role of the father. It is because he/she [the pupil] is afraid of violence whether in the form of physical violence or in other forms. He has the authority. But again, if the teacher has certain attributes such as dominance in the classroom and knowledge, pupils grasp it easily.

As could be gleaned from Kevser's narrative, the pupils who are 'scared' of male teachers are the ones who are exposed to violence in their own homes and, again, teachers mirror the role of the fathers to show their authority.

Elmas, when she was giving examples from Talip and her earlier experiences in other schools, said that when they faced difficulties, they asked male teachers to handle the issues, 'I do not know if there is some sort of fear against males in society in general, but I guess there is such a thing [this perception].' We could conclude that teachers as role models operate on the assumption of sex-typed and stereotypical paternal roles which also reveal the extent to which *hegemonic masculinity* is performed in school settings by, among other things, 'scaring' pupils with the threat of violence.

Fantasy or real fear?

The fantasy of fear was a reflection of the real fear pupils experience in families, according to some female teachers. In both schools, the description of fatherhood by female teachers involved all forms of violence including abuse, physical violence and even incest. Nazlı's personal experience and her dilemma after seeing a pupil who was exposed to physical violence at home confirm this bleak landscape:

> The child [pupil in Nazlı's class] came to school with a bruised face. He was beaten up. I asked the mother what happened. She said he had fallen. He had not fallen. His dad beat him up. During the breaks, he didn't leave the classroom. After a while … I was angry toward the mother. She said, 'we couldn't do anything he [her husband] is neurotic and when he gets angry, he would do anything'. So, this is the kind of family that I am talking about. […] Most of the time you get shocked, and you don't know what to do. I said, 'why are you allowing your husband to beat this kid?'

During our interview Nazlı continued to describe to me the details of the seven-year-old male pupil's injuries and she became frustrated. Many teachers, especially male ones, do not talk about such incidents because they think they cannot intervene in home. In Zinnur, the violence that pupils were subjected to came up again during the interviews. Aslı candidly explained how she found out that one of her Year Five male pupils was beaten by his father,

> After I examined his neck, I saw that it was purple. I asked, who did this to you? He said, 'my father did it'. His peers said, 'check his arm'. I said take off your t-shirt. He resisted. I forced him to take it off. All his body was purple. He was beaten up and his entire body was bruised. When you raise this issue with the school administration, you say, 'this kid is beaten up'. And this is not

a normal beating; the kid's entire body was bruised. And this kid works at the weekends and besides he is one of our problem pupils. They would say, '*Hocam* [My teacher] we have a lot of pupils here who are beaten up [at home]'. I said we can raise this issue there are various places to go. There are the police, the child protection agency and they must do something. Again, they would say, '*Hocam* [My teacher], it would get us into a lot of trouble'. I said, well okay to them. And I said if something happens to this kid, for instance, if he is killed while he is beaten up wouldn't it be our responsibility? Wouldn't they ask, 'doesn't this kid have teachers, deputy head teachers, head teachers?' 'Don't these people exist?'

Aslı lost her temper and told me that she was not supported by the deputy head teachers in her proposal to take action against the father who beat his son. Some of the teachers do not want fathers to be involved in the education of the pupils because the pupils might be exposed to violence at home. Aziz told it clearly: 'When a father visits the school, we tell him what is bothering us … And unfortunately, fathers see violence as a solution. We tell them not to resort to violence.' It was interesting that Aziz did not want to see the fathers because pupils might experience violence at home, while Gülşen, another teacher in Zinnur, asked the fathers to visit the school to control the pupils, to – as she put it – 'scare them'. In other words, although Gülşen was critical of violence against children in all its forms from the outset, she used 'fear' – of paternal violence – as a threat to create authority in her crowded classrooms. Gülşen was not alone in this respect, and this was normalized in the context of both schools – to the extent that it was assimilated as gender norms. In other words, within the *gender regime* (Connell 1987, 2000, 2005) of both schools, performing normative masculinity meant the ability to exercise violence.

Conclusion

In this book I attempted to illustrate how Islamization and neoliberal education policy SBM have shaped primary education by discussing various aspects of local education market in Bahçelik district from within where I stand, the Talip and Zinnur Schools. Although I have not deliberately designed each chapter to lead to conclusions about axes of differences in particular gender, each chapter so far has offered significant insights and threads to follow. In Chapter 3, I looked at the political local market in Bahçelik district through the lens of two schools. For example, I briefly discussed the role of mothers and their significant role in the education market through the practice of the *sınıf annesi* (classroom mother) – among the others.

In Chapter 4, I looked at *lived culture* (Williams 2001) and the fragments of this culture showed that Islamic piety was privileged. I have found that, for example, women did not exist in the visual universe of the schools, such as among the all-male portraits hanging on the walls, nor in the imaginary of the ideal youth reflected on rival generation ideals. In Chapter 5, I explored technologies of surveillance and mechanisms of control that offer significant insights into the disciplining of female bodies. Certainly, readers will know that there are more examples to be given. Nevertheless, as we have seen, this chapter follows on from the previous chapters, albeit with the key argument of Raewyn Connell (1987, 2000, 2005) which is that all institutions (including schools) have *gender regime*.

With an intention to lay out *gender regime* of both schools in this chapter I first looked at gender dynamic operating within Bahçelik district. I briefly touched on local – and national – social policies that define 'motherhood' in a specific way. And then I returned to the school contexts. Giving heed to teachers' accounts was helpful in drawing my attention to masculinities and femininities *performed* (Butler 2011) by teachers in their interactions with pupils. However, this approach also inevitably led to some 'blind spots' in the sense that peer group interactions between pupils, which play an important role, could provide important additional insights and yet remained outside the scope of this chapter. Having said that with these two sections I have reached to significant conclusions.

First, I showed that mothers played a central role in local politics in the education market in the district. The material available in this regard was extensive and yet I have focused on the hegemonic one that is 'good mothers'. As we have seen, both the district municipality and the AKP women's branch staged women-only events and seminars intended to equip mothers to engage better with the community and with their children's education. These women-only events legitimized the public presence of women who could not ordinarily step out of their homes without permission from their husbands or their male kin. In other words, the gender segregated nature of the venues and their endorsement by official bodies gave them a latitude they would otherwise lack. However, the messages transmitted at these events about 'good mothering' reinforce their exclusively domestic roles and their primary vocations as mothers, requiring their acquiescence to hegemonic norms of femininity or *emphasized femininity* (Connell 1987; Connell & Messerschmidt 2005). Therefore, the 'idealized femininity' within the district education market, or more precisely *emphasized femininity*, was pious, hardworking, active, engaged motherhood *performance*.

Secondly, as we have seen, the schools mirrored aforementioned *emphasized femininity*. The details and contours of *emphasized femininity* became clear with the dichotomy between 'bogeyman', violent, indifferent, ignorant fathers and 'ideal motherhood' that teachers constructed to explain *femininities* and *masculinities* while at the same time blurring the lines between teaching and parenting. I also have repeatedly observed that parental roles and the femininities and masculinities attached to them were routinely *performed* (Butler 2011) by teachers in the school context. These performances not only reproduce idealized femininities and masculinities, but also define the *gender regime* of the school. The normative expectations attached to this *gender regime* are in line with the local – and national – social policies that define 'motherhood' in a specific way. Mothers or female teachers who do not conform to these norms are considered deviant. While appearing seemingly critical of the parental non-involvement of fathers and their resort to actual or threatened violence, this violence is normalized by being assimilated into masculine gender norms both in the home and the classroom and becomes an expression of *hegemonic masculinity* (Connell 1987; Connell & Messerschmidt 2005).

Conclusion

My immersion in the *lived culture* (Williams 2001) of two state primary schools, Zinnur and Talip, in the Bahçelik district of Istanbul during the early 2010s gave me a unique vantage point to analyse the complexity of the interactions between Islamization and neoliberal education policy SBM under AKP government in Turkey. It is possible to summarize my findings with three themes that this book centres around and yet the boundaries between these themes are not seamless.

A sketchy broader context

Since it came to power within ten years of time the AKP government enacted social and economic policies grounded in the prescriptions of the global governance institutions, such as UN agencies, UNICEF and regional trading block EU. Within the context of the resulting tensions, a wide range of reforms and policies were enacted in education. These included but not limited to SBM and wider decentralization (mid-2000s). As well, voucher schemes – well-known examples of public-private partnerships framework and privatization – were introduced (early 2010s). One also notes a move towards ranking diverse education systems via international exams such as PISA (Program for International Student Assessment) (2000s and 2010s) and the introduction of child-centred pedagogy (mid-2000s). Within this policy environment, the AKP government not only followed prevalent policy trends in compulsory education. It also prioritized the role of education in the consolidation of neoliberalism, which had detrimental impact on provision of state primary education (Yolcu 2014).

The AKP's agenda in the field of education was also marked by two distinct phases during these years. Initially the government protected the vested interests of the Gülen community that had gradually established itself as a major player in the education domain through its network of private schools, *dershanes* (tutorial college). This was followed by a phase of open hostility after the emergence of a power struggle between the Gülen community and the AKP since 2012, leading to attempts to eradicate the Gülen community from the education sector and, finally, an all-out purge of its cadres and sympathizers after the failed coup of 15 July 2016. During the heyday of the alliance between the Gülen community and the AKP after the mid-2000s, the community with an established expertise and a considerable market share in the education sector was not only influencing national education policies but had also become the source of well-educated workforce for the AKP.

It is within this context I explain how SBM led to establishment of a local education market and more importantly played a role in Islamizing primary schooling.

Talip and Zinnur in local education market

This book adds to ongoing discussion on the trendy global education policies and supports the arguments that although the blueprint of neoliberal reforms may appear to introduce global similarities, the manner of their implementation introduces very diverse patterns locally (Anderson-Levitt 2003; Steiner-Khamsi & Stolpe 2006). As we have seen, even if community involvement is glorified (Caldwell 2009; Caldwell & Spinks 1988), in practice as I illustrated in this book SBM could become a Trojan horse – in other words, the mobilizing agent of ruling party AKP that aimed to transform the education in line with its political priorities. In the relevant literature in Turkey the main argument has centred upon three arguments: (i) SBM functioned in financing schools (Altuntaş 2005; Candaş et al. 2011; Köse & Şaşmaz 2014; Özdemir 2011; Yolcu 2007; Yolcu & Kurul 2009); (ii) SBM transformed educational provision by turning state education into quasi-private (Candaş et al. 2011) model; (iii) and all scholars in the literature agree that SBM increased already-existing inequalities among primary schools. In this book, I aimed to enlarge this literature by illustrating how SBM established local education market and how this market played a role in Islamization of everyday school life. In other words, I look at political role of SBM.

One of the key questions that guided my ethnographic research was 'why some schools were "rich" and while others were not', even though the catchment areas of both schools were in working-class neighbourhoods in Bahçelik. Looking for similarities and differences between the two primary schools in this regard, I explained the details of what I call the 'tacit marketing structure' and showed how SBM has established a local market in Bahçelik from the perspective of Zinnur and Talip Schools. Inspired by significant studies by sociologists of education on the 'education market' and the 'marketization of education' (Ball 1993, 2003; Ball & Gewirtz 1997; Bowe et al. 1994), I asked the key questions of who is punished and rewarded in this market, who exploits this market, who has advantages and who is valued in this market. Answers to these questions helped me to capture the logic of this local market which also revealed political function of SBM.

The first key question in understanding the logic of the micro-education market was who is punished or rewarded. The findings in both schools led me to broaden this question by asking 'by whom' as well. I found that the Bahçelik district municipality played the role of 'patron', that is, the municipality had important role in setting the 'rules of the game' – in Bourdiue's sense – in the local market. The Bahçelik municipality, like other AKP municipalities, has adopted and mastered the local policies of its predecessors – the Islamic movement – National Outlook (*Milli Görüş*). In other words, the municipality has combined the tacit knowledge of the National Outlook with the entrepreneurial spirit of the AKP period to maximize its influence. Unlike other municipalities, the AKP-led municipalities had access to a pool of local, national and global networks because of their privileged relationship with the party and the AKP government. With these powers, the Bahçelik municipality not only became the leading decision maker in the local education market, cultivating both formal and informal networks to palliate for shortfalls in state primary education, but also sought to change 'the rules of the game' by creating alternative educational spaces – such as *bilgi evi*, which I discussed in detail in Chapter 3 – that provide services that are mostly 'unavailable' in state education, or more precisely, free services that are in principle public goods and should be provided by state primary schools.

Nevertheless, at the local level, the municipality also demonstrated commitment to the social engineering (or re-defining aims of education) endeavours of the AKP government, leaving no room for the ideal of the universal. From the vantage point of Talip's and Zinnur's contexts, it was clear that only schools that conformed to the municipality's political priorities would have access to services and networks of influence. In other words, without engaging in local politics by means of being the mobilizing agent of Islamic movement, schools could not benefit from a wide range of donations in many forms, let alone the basic services that the municipality had to offer. Returning to the question of who is rewarded or punished in this local market, the answer is that schools that submit to the priorities of the ruling AKP were rewarded by being included in the network, while those that do not were punished by not being 'invited'. This was evident in the case of Talip School. As we have seen in Chapter 3, Talip received support through celebration of Holy Birth Week which meant showing commitment to the political priorities of the municipality in Bahçelik.

Who exploits this market was the second question. This question led me to the notion of *loco parentis*, which revealed two very important insights: (i) Islamic communities acted in *loco parentis*; (ii) teachers with distinctive individual *habituses* (Bourdieu 1986, 1996, 2010) blurred the line between home and school by intervening to the decisions and choices of mothers (parents). To begin with the Islamic communities: In Zinnur School, the Islamist for-profit Hidayet Dormitory, which was located in the catchment area of the school, took in the place of the parents of the pupils enrolled in Zinnur. The *abis* (elder brothers) in the dormitory, which were followers of Hidayet community (that has links to an old Islamic *tariqa* order in the country), gained the upper hand with their *social* and *cultural capital* (Bourdieu & Passeron 1990) and exploited the market. This was also evident in the way the boys who were 'housed' in the Hidayet Dormitory gained advantages in Zinnur School, which I will explain below. In other words, Hidayet Dormitory played the 'professional' *loco parentis* role and had the advantages which are mostly ascribed to middle class parents. And this role of *abis* allowed Hidayet Dormitory to turn the Zinnur School into a 'captive market'.

Another striking finding was that teachers with their distinctive individual *habituses* (Bourdieu 1986, 1996, 2010) blurred the relations between home and school and interfered in the decisions of working-class mothers (parents) who lacked educational knowledge. This was evident in the actions of Gülen-affiliated teachers in the Zinnur. By selecting 'smart' pupils, developing a tutoring programme that took place in the pupils' homes, the Gülen-affiliated teachers took the place of the mothers (parents) in making decisions about the pupils' education. Although they claimed to support the pupils by offering *hizmet* (service), this meant realizing the ideal of reproducing *Altın Nesil* (Golden Generation). Yet they were also exploiting the local education market and further reinforcing inequalities in the school. In other words, the actions of the Gülen community-affiliated teachers were similar to what is seen as 'parental strategies to reproduce the class' (Ball 2003), while their goal was to reproduce *Altın Nesil*.

The third question was who had advantages. Most fathers were hardly involved in the education of their children; in contrast, mothers were mobilized for the education of their children in this local market. As I discussed in both Chapters 3 and 6, the Bahçelik municipality had developed various formal and informal policies to meet the needs of its residents, which were aimed exclusively at mothers. In the school context, mothers were given the role of *sınıf annesi* (classroom mother). By fulfilling this role and giving their time, energy and money, they played a role in this local market and therefore had advantages. Moreover, mothers who attended to idealized motherhood 'good mothering' also had advantages that I discuss in the last section. The last question is who is valued in this market. The boys (Year Six, Year Seven, Year Eight pupils) who were staying in Hidayet were valued in this market. They were considered 'privileged' (*özel*) by pupils and addressed as the dormers (*yurtlular*) by the rest of the school in Zinnur. Selecting 'smart' pupils and 'transforming' them into some kind of community 'asset' was a leading trend amongst in all the Islamic communities I observed in the schools, but the boys staying in Hidayet were more than just an 'asset'. For Zinnur School, the academic performance of the boys was important in 'selling' the school to working-class mothers and increasing the profit from 'donations', protecting the high reputation of the school and receiving donations in-kind from the Bahçelik municipality.

Having said that, looking at local education market in Bahçelik from the vantage point of both Talip and Zinnur Schools makes political role of SBM, that is Islamization of schooling crystal clear. As we have seen in this book, Zinnur adapted to the local education market, but Talip did not, and this made Zinnur 'rich' and Talip not.

'Islam': Which Islam?

This book is also a contribution to the ongoing debate on secularism versus Islam in Turkey. As I mentioned earlier, there have been two standard approaches to understanding the role of Islam in relation to education: (i) limiting it to *imam-hatip* schools (Aksit 1991; Gökaçtı 2005; Ozgur 2012); (ii) or focusing on institutionalized ideology Turkish Islamic Synthesis (Kaplan 1999) or its reception in schools (Kaplan 2006). One of the aims of this book also has been to expand this literature by looking at amalgam of scenes I have gleaned from the *lived culture* (Williams 2001) in both Talip and Zinnur Schools. In other words, this book illustrates how Islamization permeates everyday life in schools. Although '*de facto* gender segregation' could also be discussed under this heading, I will postpone it to the last section where I discuss the gendered aspect of this local market.

I have approached the *lived culture* (Williams 2001) of both schools with Raymond Williams' (1977: 132) concept *structure of feeling*, which provides a lens through which 'emergent or even pre-emergent' and 'residual' (1977: 133–4) ways of thinking become visible. If I were to focus only on the dominant elements of *lived culture* in the schools, all the nuanced narratives that were told in the schools, the subtle ideas that crept into many of the play forms that the pupils invented and played, the political allusions planted in the lyrics of the songs the pupils loved to sing, the walls of the corridors where there was not a single woman's face among the portraits, and much more would become invisible in the shadow of the dominant ideals, symbols and narratives (see Chapter 4). The 'presences' of school life required more than an approach that only recognizes the 'institutionalized' or the dominant (Williams 1977: 133–4). With the *structure of feeling* Williams offers a way of thinking that allows one to see the whole picture, figuratively speaking, by proposing a relational analysis that takes into account the process within the *lived culture*. Certainly, it was not my intention to turn the daily lives of Talip and Zinnur into a text, but Williams' concept, among others, influenced me to think about and give meaning to what might at first glance be considered as 'idiosyncratic' (1977: 132).

In this book, I was interested in 'idiosyncratic' fragments, such as '*dabbe* play' in which the pupils pretended to see a benign *jinni* in the Atatürk's eyes, or the songs that pupils liked to sing such as *Yetim Kız* ('the Orphan Girl') (*Peygamberin Gülleri* 2014a) that I illustrated in Chapter 4. In other words, I became interested in aspects of education that received less attention, such as the school walls, the popular songs (referred to as hymns) the pupils enjoyed singing, the play forms they invented. These findings led me to reflect on the inherent contradictions in the local education market in Bahçelik. First, the national curriculum still conveyed a dominant narrative of republican ideals and Kemalist reforms. Second, there were newly institutionalized commemorations such as the Day of Commemoration of the Adoption of the National Anthem and Mehmet Akif Ersoy and Holy Birth Week, which in practice became events that challenged the conventional narrative of the national curriculum by suggesting a new 'imagined community' (Anderson 1991). Third, there was a counter-narrative emerging or more precisely narratives in the form of books, songs and documentaries – and more – not only vilifying Kemalist reforms but also challenging this new 'imagined community'.

As we have seen in Chapter 4, a new 'substitute' leader, a new ideologue, namely Mehmet Akif Ersoy, and a new past linked to the Ottoman past were significant components of 'new Turkey'. There was also *Çanakkale ruhu* ('the spirit of Gallipoli'), referring to the fallen soldiers of the Ottoman state during the Gallipoli campaign (1915–16), which symbolized the defence of the Islamic realm headed by the sultan-caliph against the infidel foreign invaders, and which I have not included in my analysis in this book. Nevertheless, it was presented as a new founding moment to upstage founding moment of the republic. The narrative in the local education market in Bahçelik was that there is an Islamic unity independent of subnational identities, a strong reference to the Ottoman past, an implicit and explicit reference to the *ummah* and transformation of Islam into the *sin qua non* element of the nation. However, this seamless narrative of the 'new Turkey' was also being challenged by other Islamic communities or movements in the schools and in the local education market. Indeed, this was hardly surprising, as none of the Islamic communities I analysed with regard to marketing of Talip and Zinnur had the same claim on 'nation' or the overarching *ummah*. As we have seen, each community has different ideal generations, such as Gülen community or the Hidayet community. The pupils' imaginaries (e.g., Atatürk as a mocked hero), the source of their 'ideas' (e.g., various songs or 'hymns' that promote Gülen community) and ideals (e.g., Asım's Generation reflecting the AKP's ambitions in education) and their slogans, whether shouted in class to break the silence or written on the posters they designed, raise the question, to which Islam? Or to whom should pupils be loyal? Or which *ummah*? Which Islamic community or movement?

In conclusion this book argues that education is Islamized, and the question of which Islam will dominate is not clear. Hence if to return to the analogy I used of that is cultural struggle in Chapter 4, it was clear that these struggles were not only pitted secular versus religious orientations from where I grounded in the 'everyday' of Talip and Zinnur.

Gender: Tainted by 'Islamization' and marketization

In this last section which is among the three key themes of this book, I briefly summarize my findings diffused in several chapters. I will follow two threads: one is *de facto* gender segregation and the other one is *gender regime* of schools that offered significant insights with regard to 'idealized' femininity as well as *hegemonic masculinity* (Connell 1987; Connell & Messerschmidt 2005).

To start with *de facto* gender segregation, although state schools are and were still co-educational and there are and were no legal restrictions to mixed sex socializing, within both schools and within the local education market there was *de facto* separation. As I illustrated throughout various chapters, the fraternity of 'dormers' (*yurtlu*) living in Hidayet Dormitory imported their Islamic gender norms into the school setting and influenced socialization in Zinnur School, and teachers affiliated with the Gülen community explicitly reinforced the separation of the sexes. This was also visible throughout the local education market. The predominance of girls registered in the municipality-run *bilgi evi* that I discussed in Chapter 3 and the increasing number of 'women only' public spaces established by the municipality further reinforced gender segregation. As I explained in Chapter 6, the Bahçelik municipality also offered women-only activities and events which had changed the attitudes of women who couldn't leave their homes without permission from their husbands (or male kin) in the past. As we have seen in Chapter 3 these measures of the municipality also changed the involvement of mothers in education of their children, although this was also part of 'good mother' ideal that I will explain below. These instances of *de facto* segregation are at odds with norms that are diffused by a wide range of international actors, which mandate certain standards of gender equality.

Moreover, implicit forms of segregation and control are also visible in mechanisms that mainly aim to control female teachers. This is most evident with respect to teachers' dress codes that I discussed in Chapter 5. The protests over the ban to wear headscarves in public offices resulted in numerous teachers deciding to veil in Zinnur even before the relevant legislation was passed. More interestingly, even teachers who did not wear the headscarf decided to wear a white coat over their clothes to conceal both their choices in clothes (such as wearing low cut tops) and their bodily contours. The white coat almost acts as a 'shield' in a context where gender segregation cannot be legally practised, as the Islamic communities would wish, but is imaginatively enacted through dress and deportment. Not surprisingly, many teachers found the entrance of women into the mixed-sex labour force hazardous and objectionable, although opinions were divided on this subject depending on the political orientations of teachers. Gender segregation also generates paradoxical outcomes, especially for the mothers of pupils. Chapter 3 highlighted the ways in which mothers were pressed into service in schools as teachers' helpers, where such activities become extensions of their nurturing roles in the domestic sphere. Now I turn to *gender regime* (Connell 1987, 2000, 2005) of schools.

Feminist critiques of the Kemalist *gender regime* argued that behind the ideal of gender equality lay a traditional understanding of gender roles (Kandiyoti 1992, 1989). However, these debates were sidelined by an alternative Islamization project, which does not consider gender equality as an acceptable norm but refers to gender complementarity based on essential differences between the sexes (expressed in the language of *fitrat* indicating natural dispositions). What my data suggests is that above and beyond the rhetoric of Kemalism and Islam what *really* gets transmitted to the pupils does so through daily interactions as in the case of *de facto* gender segregation and practices in the context of the school where role models act out specific understandings of masculinity and femininity.

In Chapter 6, I looked at both school contexts as gendered institutions; my intention was to examine how diverse femininities and masculinities are constructed in everyday school setting. I started this chapter by touching on the local policies of the municipality. As we have seen Bahçelik municipality mobilized mothers to involve in their children's education actively and at the same time promoted the notion of 'good mothering' which legitimized the non-involvement of fathers in education of their children. This was also evident in the gender-segregated spaces which were transformed into avenues to construct 'idealized femininity' that is *emphasized femininity* (Connell 1987; Connell & Messerschmidt 2005), which is active, pious, hardworking, nurturer and engaged in the education of their children. And both Talip and Zinnur Schools mirrored this 'idealized femininity'. In the schools I observed that female teachers *performed* (Butler 2011) the role of *emphasized femininity* – in other words, almost mimicking normative femininity of mothers. And complement to this femininity was again normative masculinity, which is paternal. In other words, male teachers performed the role of fathers, although these teachers constructed 'fatherhood' as aggressive, emotionally distant and violent. Teachers' accounts revealed *hegemonic masculinity* (Connell 1987; Connell & Messerschmidt 2005) as aggressive violent 'bogeyman' almost the opposite of *emphasized femininity*. Paternal authority vs maternal nurturance further supported the mothers' role in parenting almost equating while 'working mothers', 'single mothers' and 'single women' were marginalized due to failing to comply with the normative expectations of femininity. Therefore, *gender regime* (Connell 1987, 2000, 2005) of the schools almost imitates the *gender regime* in the home and by doing this reproduces and reinforces gender stereotypes.

A tangible observation emerging from this study is that one of the key premises of republican education, that of gender equality, already underwent a radical transformation with a very subtle relationship between Islamization and the consolidation of neoliberal market reforms. The basic assumptions of the foundational education act of the republic – Law on the Unification of Education (*Tevhid-i Tedrisat Kanunu*) passed in 1924 – which introduced the underpinnings of gender equality in education – are being rapidly re-interpreted. This study analysed some of the key arenas through which this 're-interpretation' might be apprehended and enacted.

***

Nevertheless, this book captured a particular moment in the alignment between the AKP and diverse Islamic actors and their effects on education. After the break-up between the AKP and the Gülen community, the diverse educational providers capitalizing on the education market are no longer seen as an opportunity but as a threat. This has ushered in a period of re-centralization whereby only government-sponsored, -vetted and -approved governmental and non-governmental actors are allowed to operate such as the Turkish Youth and Education Foundation (*Türkiye Gençlik ve Eğitime Hizmet Vakfı*, TÜRGEV). Moreover, the schism reached a dramatic climax with the failed coup of 15 July perpetrated by the Turkish Armed Forces (*Türk Silahlı Kuvvetleri*, TSK) members affiliated to Gülen movement. The purge of cadres following this attempt could be claimed as one of the largest shake-ups of education sector in post-republican Turkey. It will be the task of future studies to trace and document its deep impacts.

***

Appendix

List of interviews

1. Zinnur School teachers

Name	Gender	Age	Marital status
Kutsi	Male	Mid 30s	Single
Yakup	Male	Late 20s	Single
Ahu	Female	Late 20s	Single
Banu	Female	Mid 40s	Married
Nebahat	Female	Early 50s	Married
Adile	Female	Early 50s	Married
Üzeyir	Male	Late 30s	Married
Yekta	Male	Early 50s	Married
Bahtiyar	Male	Late 20s	Single
Osman	Male	Mid 30s	Married
Fatih	Male	Mid 30s	Single
Feryal	Female	Early 20s	Single
Ayça	Female	Late 30s	Married
Aslı	Female	Early 20s	Single
Nil	Female	Late 30s	Married
Aziz	Male	Mid 20s	Single
Handan	Female	Early 50s	Married
Kübra	Female	Mid 30s	Married
Aybike	Female	Mid 20s	Single
Halim	Male	Late 20s	Single
Ceylan	Female	Early 30s	Single
İsmail	Male	Mid 40s	Married
Gülşen	Female	Early 40s	Married
Macit	Male	Mid 50s	Married
Ruhi	Male	Early 40s	Married
Hüsnügül	Female	Early 20s	Single

2. Talip School teachers

Name	Gender	Age	Marital status
Nazlı	Female	Late 30s	Married
Emine	Female	Early 40s	Married
Gül	Female	Late 40s	Married
Sema	Female	Late 40s	Married
Erman	Male	Early 40s	Married
Ahmet	Male	Early 30s	Single
Müge	Female	Late 30s	Single
Nükhet	Female	Late 30s	Married
Nigar	Female	Early 50s	Married
Sevda	Female	Mid 30s	Married
Başak	Female	Late 40s	Single
Kevser	Female	Early 40s	Married
Berrak	Female	Mid 20s	Married
Beşir	Male	Late 30s	Married
Vakkas	Male	Mid 50s	Married
Kadim	Male	Early 50s	Married
İdris	Male	Mid 40s	Married
İkbal	Female	Late 30s	Married
Aslan	Male	Early 40s	Married
Narin	Female	Early 20s	Single
Elmas	Female	Early 30s	Married
Merih	Female	Late 20s	Single
Kadriye	Female	Late 30s	Married

3. OAB members of Talip School – focused group interview

Name	Gender	Age	Marital status	Occupation
Habibe	Female	Early 20s	Married	Housewife
Rümeysa	Female	Early 20s	Married	Housewife
Esin	Female	Mid 30s	Married	Housewife

4. OAB members in Zinnur School – focused group interview

Name	Gender	Age	Marital Status	Occupation
Fazilet	Female	Early 40s	Married	OAB member
Müjgan	Female	Early 40s	Married	OAB member
Sevil	Female	Mid 30s	Married	OAB member

5. Year Eight pupils in Zinnur School – focused group interviews

	Name	Gender	Age
Group I	Melis	Female	14
	Şimal	Female	14
	Rojda	Female	14
	İlayda	Female	14
Group II	Sena	Female	14
	Dicle	Female	14
	Kadriye	Female	14
	Valide	Female	14

6. Year Eight pupils in Zinnur School – focused group interviews

	Name	Gender	Age
Group I	Meryem	Female	14
	Ronya	Female	14
	Sevim	Female	14
	Fadime	Female	14
Group II	Furkan	Male	14
	Muhammed	Male	14
	Tarık	Male	14
	Samet	Male	14

7. Teachers in Zinnur School – focused group interview

Name	Gender	Age	Marital status
Banu	Female	Mid 40s	Married
Adile	Female	Early 50s	Married
Nebahat	Female	Early 50s	Married

8. Teachers in Zinnur School – focused group interview

Name	Gender	Age	Marital status
Aziz	Male	Mid 20s	Single
Ceylan	Female	Early 30s	Single
Kübra	Female	Mid 30s	Married
Gülşen	Female	Late 30s	Married

9. Experts in the field of education

Abbas Güçlü: Education columnist in newspaper *Milliyet*. Güçlü also produced and presented the television show *Genç Bakış* ('the View of the Youth') (2002–16).

Batuhan Aydagül: Executive Board Member and Director of the Education Reform Initiative (*Eğitim Reform Girişimi*, ERG) (2013–2019).

Çiğdem Kağıtçıbaşı (1940–2007): Professor in the Department of Psychology and Director of Centre for Gender and Women's Studies, Koç University. Kağıtçıbaşı was co-founder of The Mother Child Education Foundation (*Anne Çocuk Eğitim Vakfı*, AÇEV).

M. Aytuğ Şaşmaz: Education Policy Analyst in Education Reform Initiative (2008–2013).

Rıfat Okçabol: Emeritus Professor in Boğaziçi University, Education Faculty. His research interests are adult education, educational policy, teacher training, higher education system in education, system theory.

10. Interviewees from outside the school contexts

Name	Gender	Age	Marital Status	Affiliation
Hacer	Female	Early 30s	Married	Municipality
Seda	Female	Late 20s	Single	Municipality
Hanife	Female	Early 50s	Married	Municipality
Mine	Female	Early	Married	Municipality
Rukiye	Female	Late 40s	Married	District Office of Mufti
Arif	Male	Mid 40s	Married	Eğitim-Bir-Sen
Altan	Male	Early 40s	Married	Eğitim-Sen
Babür	Male	Early 50s	Married	Türk-Eğitim-Sen
Yeşim	Female	Mid 30s	Married	The Platform of Unassigned Teachers
Hüseyin	Male	Early 30s	Married	Hidayet Dormitory Deputy Head

Notes

Chapter 1

1   For an excellent account on poverty and its media representations and some of the myths regarding the poverty in Turkey, see Erdoğan (2007).
2   This is pervasive in the context of the world – *Favelas* in Rio de Janeiro (Perlman 2010), council estates in London, ghettos in the United States (Wacquant 2008), slums in India or in China, *el-arafa* in Cairo to name a few.
3   For a detailed account of this process in the Ümraniye district of Istanbul, see White (2002).
4   Adapted from the *The Star Thrower* by Loren Eiseley (1978: 172). There are a wide range of adaptations of this story on the web, in both English and Turkish. I cited the version that is popular in Talip.
5   Here *mevlid* broadly refers to the rituals on life cycle events, including but not limited to death and birth, at which the Prophet Muhammad is venerated. For a very detailed explanation, see Chapter 4. I participated in a *mevlid* after one of the teachers in Zinnur lost her father. A *kına gecesi* (henna night) is a pre-wedding celebration event and significant part of wedding ritual. Again, I attended to *kına gecesi* at the invitation of one of the female teachers in Zinnur, who was getting married. Both events were gender segregated.

Chapter 2

1   See Avar (2004).
2   Arzu Öztürkmen (1998) illustrates the ways in which these houses played a role in the construction of a 'national' Turkish folk dance, and Öztürkmen (1996) analyses the role of these houses in giving a standard form to the commemorations of foundational days in Turkey.
3   See Kirby (2010) for a comprehensive account; for a relatively new perspective, see Karaömerlioğlu (1998, 2006). See also Altunya (2010), Arikan (2012), Gokalp (2015) and Özsoy (2004).
4   See Makal (2008) for an excellent account from Mahmut Makal, who was a teacher.

5 For instance, Necdet Sakaoğlu (2003: 192) and Ayşe Gül Altınay (2004a: 71–2) argue that compulsory military service played a significant role in increasing the literacy rates of men.

6 There have been numerous revisions to the curriculum; see Kancı (2007: 10–11).

7 *İmam-hatip* schools are religious vocational schools established to train *imam* (prayer leaders) and *hatip* (preachers). In the beginning, the main purpose of the *imam-hatip* school was to train religious functionaries; throughout Turkish history, the function of the schools has changed dramatically.

8 See İnce (2012: 133) for an analysis of the constitution in terms of citizenship rights.

9 See Baykurt (2000: 126) as well.

10 Çimen Günay-Erkol with a focus on 'ideology and identity in Turkish literature' offers great insights to understand the extent to which the memories of this trauma moulded a significant part of Turkish literature, while at the same time touching on Islamist writers who 'put stronger emphasis on the cultural colonisation of Turkey' such as Hekimoğlu İsmail and his novel *Minyeli Abdullah* ('Abdullah From Minye') that pushes 'Islam as a remedy' to the ills of communism and Westernization (2013: 119). See İsmail (2019).

11 See Toprak (1984). For a comprehensive contemporary analysis, which also provides the link between the National Outlook and the AKP, see Lord (2018) and Tuğal (2009).

12 For the historical background of the eight-year compulsory education, see Akyüz (2006). For instance, Akyüz (2006) suggests that eight-year primary schooling was first mentioned by the third *Milli Eğitim Şûrası* (National Education Council) in 1946 and started to be negotiated in 1961.

13 Graduates from *imam-hatip* schools were only qualified to attend theology faculties, even though many graduates wanted to pursue careers in other professions.

14 The goals set by the World Declaration Education for All in Jomtien, Thailand, in 1990 (UNESCO 1990) and the World Education Forum in Dakar, Senegal, in 2000 developed strategies that introduced country-level action planning to eliminate inequalities in education (UNESCO 2000). See UNESCO (2007, 2015).

15 For instance, the municipal law – introduced in 2005 – authorized municipalities to: (i) open nursery schools; (ii) build, renovate and/or refurbish school buildings, as well as outsource these services; (iii) provide all kinds of materials and equipment; (iv) provide social and cultural services to the elderly, women, the disabled, youth and children; and (v) offer technical and vocational training courses (*beceri kursları*) (Official Gazette 2005a). Although the right to open nursery schools was repealed, the municipalities offer this service by referencing the 'needs' of the communities.

16 See Gök and Şahin (2003), Gürtan and Tüzün (2005), Gümüşoğlu (2008), Kancı and Altınay (2007) and Tanrıöver (2003).

17 This was an outcome of strict academic grade calculations, which meant that graduates from vocational schools, including *imam-hatip* schools, could rarely meet the requirements for entrance to four-year university programmes.

18 Although secularists mostly emphasized Türkan Saylan's endeavours by means of almost transforming her into, what Daniella Kuzamanovic calls, a 'secular saint' (2013: 177), she had become a controversial figure as well. For instance, some accused her of assimilating and favouring Kurdish children (2013: 183–5).

19 Aytuğ Şaşmaz (2012) succinctly summarizes the ways in which the reshuffles of the AKP changed the composition of the Council of Education six months before the launch of the 4+4+4: a notable decrease in the percentage of academics was visible (reduced to 8.9 per cent from about 12 per cent). There was a decrease in the members from civil society (from 7.2 per cent to about 5 per cent), and the most striking change was that the percentage of those members, who are going to be selected by the Ministry in line with the agenda of the Council, increased from 4 per cent up to about 11 per cent (Şaşmaz 2012).

20 The Gülen community, one of the most influential Islamic movements in the country, has aimed to shape society according to the guiding principles of Fethullah Gülen, the leader of the community (Yavuz 2003). Gülen, who worked as DİB-appointed *imam* for more than twenty years until 1981, was inspired by Said Nursi's thoughts, as manifested in *Risale-i Nur* ('Epistels of Light') and started to be influential since 1980s with his well-known speeches and preaches (Lord 2018: 219). Many aims have been attributed to Gülen since then, such as 'searching for a middle way between Islam and modernization' (Kuru 2003); 'an educator'; the leader with a meticulously crafted image or *imam* (Balcı 2005); and, more recently, a subverter and infiltrator of the state and a 'terrorist'. These mixed attributions among the others from academia and outside the academia are also true for the Gülen community. Its aim had been evaluated either 'benign' or 'positive' (Lord 2018: 219). Ceren Lord offers an excellent summary of the literature on the Gülen community. See Balcı (2005), Bekim (2003), Çobanoğlu (2018), Turam (2007), Özdalga (2003) and Yavuz (2003).

21 For *dershanes*, see Gök (2005), Özoğlu (2011), Tansel (2013), Tansel and Bircan (2005) and Yelken and Büyükcan (2015).

22 A massive corruption scandal was triggered by the leak of audio recordings of a phone call between the Prime Minister at the time, Recep Tayyip Erdoğan, and his son, Bilal Erdoğan, referring to money held in their residence (Orucoglu 2015). In the course of this process, the police found 17.5 million US dollars in cash in the houses of those detained. For instance, 4.5 million US dollars in cash was found in the possession of the director of Halkbank, a state-owned bank (Orucoglu 2015).

Chapter 3

1   The legal basis for the introduction of the regulation on OAB is in the law passed in 2004 which is amendment to the 16th Article of the Basic Law on National Education (Official Gazette 2004).

2   In short, the buildings of the primary schools are owned by the state (special provincial administrations), the state pays for electricity, water and heating of the schools and pays the salaries of the permanent and contracted teachers. After these expenditures, which are made centrally by the state, the schools do not receive a subsidy that can be spent on various budget items (Candaş et al. 2011). For a meticulous detailed analysis, see Köse and Şaşmaz (2014) and Yolcu (2007).

3   The regulation on the role of OAB has been revised three times since the SBM was introduced in 2005. Twice in 2012 (Official Gazette 2012a, 2012c) and another time in 2019 (Official Gazette 2019). It is not possible here to undertake an in-depth critical analysis of these revisions but suffice it to mention four important ones from 2012. One concerns the composition of the boards of OABs. In the revised version of the 2005 regulation, head teachers and teachers were removed from the boards of OABs and only parents and donors can become members of such boards (Official Gazette 2012a). The second major revision concerned the details of renting school buildings and/or renting or leasing school property such as sports fields, school halls or gymnasiums, outdoor facilities, etc. The practises as such were abolished in the 2012 revision (Official Gazette 2012a). The third issue concerned internal cleaning and security arrangements in schools. With the 2012 revision of the regulation, it is the duty of OAB to ensure that social security contributions, taxes and similar payments are made for staff employed in schools, such as security guards or cleaners (Official Gazette 2012a). The fourth revision worth mentioning concerns the guiding principles of OAB. In the 2005 version, 'Atatürk's Principles and Reforms' were the guiding principles, whereas in 2012 it was 'national and moral values'. The basis for this change seems to be the revision of the MEB's organization and obligations, see Official Gazette (2011).

4   Broadly speaking, the MEB intended this system to control and monitor the income and expenditure of all state schools. See Balcı and Öztürk (2014) and Köse and Şaşmaz (2014: 59).

5   Among others, for example, *dershanes* (tutorial college) and private schools owned by Islamic communities advertised their services by offering free mock exams to the schools. In Zinnur, four different mock exams were held during the 2012–13 school year. What Zinnur gained in return was not spelt out, however some in-kind donations were visible, such as stationery supplies.

6   Here, I must note that all the currencies I mention in the book are as of 2022 – the beginning of the year. This information is significant given the constant fluctuation of currency exchange rates in the country.

7   Broadly speaking, classroom teachers (e.g., Classroom teacher of Year 5 B or
    Classroom teacher of Year 7 A) of Year Five, Six, Seven and Eight refer to teachers
    who accompany and support pupils in these years. In other words, Years Five to
    Eight receive guidance services from 'classroom' teachers and school counsellors.
    In practice, the latter provides career guidance specifically for Year Eight pupils,
    while the former is assigned to classes to provide guidance (Year Five to Eight).
    Regardless of subject area, almost every teacher teaching through Year Five to Eight
    is responsible for counselling all pupils in a classroom. Teachers on temporary
    contracts were exempt from this responsibility in Zinnur and Talip.

8   In detail, there was one teacher who was affiliated to the Haydar Baş community,
    which is among Kadiri *tariqa* order. Of the Naqshbandi *tariqa* orders, there was one
    teacher who regularly visited the İsmailağa community centre in Fatih, one teacher
    who defined himself by his connection to Menzil community and there were four
    Nurcus who were followers of the Gülen community. Three teachers were followers
    of Hidayet community (pseudonym). These Islamic communities are among
    the most influential Islamic orders that have played an active role in the social,
    economic, and political life of the country. See Çakır (2002) and Lord (2018).
    Prominent journalist Ruşen Çakır (2002) provides a concise summary in his work
    on *tariqa* orders as well as what he calls 'faith movements [*inanç hareketleri*]'.
    Ceren Lord (2018) on the other hand, offers an in-depth understanding of *tariqa*
    orders as well as Nurcu movements within the 'religious politics of Turkey' in her
    excellent work.

9   As Hakan Yavuz put it well that '[a]lmost all Islamic political movements derive
    their popular legitimacy by framing their activities as *hizmet* […] (serving people
    for the sake of God)' (2009: 41). In a sense, Islamic political movements, and
    Islamic communities (*cemaat*) claim to combine the benefits of the movement and/
    or community with the benefits of the nation and the state. Gülen community was
    no exception, and yet *hizmet* (service) is the key to understanding the community.
    The literature on the Gülen community suggests conceiving *hizmet* as a multi-
    layered concept, (i) with broader explanations that offer an understanding of
    the community's motivations, stated goals, commitments as well as activities on
    the economic, social and political levels within and outside Turkey (see Balcı
    2005; Turam 2007; Yavuz 2003, 2009); (ii) differentiated terms at the level of the
    individual (see Çobanoğlu 2018; Yavuz 2013: 77–8; Özdalga 2003) and/or the
    context (see Balcı 2005; Turam 2007). Hakan Yavuz explains, '[t]hrough *hizmet*
    the values of the community [Gülen community] have been transformed, access to
    "power" and "domination" is sanctified on moral and religious grounds' (2013: 78).
    Certainly, the historicity of the concept is also crucial, as the community started
    to define itself as a *Hizmet* movement (2013: 76). Here, the *hizmet* is considered
    to be vast array of activities of teachers in educational settings (e.g., community-
    subsidized dormitories known as *ışık evis*, secular for-profit private schools

and state schools), with the ambition to realize the ideal of *Altın Nesil* (Golden Generation) (see Çobanoğlu 2018; Özdalga 2003; Turam 2007).

10 The literature on Gülen community, especially that dealing with the role of women in the community, also points to this aspect of gender socialisation. See, for example, Çobanoğlu (2018), Özdalga (2003) and Turam (2007).

11 The findings of Elizabeth Özdalga's (2003) study of female teachers' accounts of their work in for-profit private Gülen schools are consistent with what I found in interviews with female teachers. In particular, in Özdalga's study, paying attention to how teachers translate Fethullah Gülen's philosophy into their daily lives, a female teacher also expresses that she perceives teaching as 'the Prophet's profession' (2003: 102–3).

12 I learned from the disclosures of the female teachers that they never sent the pupils to the toilet alone. Nigar explained that 'younger pupils [girls and boys] could be abused by older boys in the toilet during class time'. Another female teacher told me that one of her pupils had been 'on the verge of being abused' (as she put it) in the past. I observed that teachers kept these stories very secret for various reasons, for example, to protect the anonymity of the pupil. Some teachers teaching Year Three and Year Four found a solution by sending pupils to the toilet in groups. Most of these teachers referred to the physical constraints of the school while searching for a reason.

13 See Buğra and Savaşkan (2014).

14 This episode of my fieldwork clearly coincided with the time when the AKP government was promoting the Kurdish Opening, an initiative first launched in 2009 to improve the human rights of Turkish citizens of Kurdish origin and to resolve the conflict between the Kurdistan Workers' Party (*Partiya Karkerên Kurdistanê*, PKK) and TSK. A dramatic change in discourse on this question has become quite evident since the renewed conflict with the PKK that led to the death of the process.

15 Murat Aydın (2008), who at the time of writing is the current mayor of Zeytinburnu, wrote a thesis on local governance and this information is gleaned from his published MA thesis.

16 In particular, Article 15 of the Municipal Law authorizes municipalities to 'carry out all kinds of activities and undertakings to meet the local municipal needs of the residents of the district'. See Official Gazette (2005a).

Chapter 4

1 According to *Neml Suresi* (An-Naml Sura) in the Qur'an, *dabbe* is a sign of the impending apocalypse. Also known as *Dabbet'ül Arz* (the Beast of the Earth), *dabbe* is expected to appear just before the end of the world. There are many different

interpretations and understandings of what shape *dabbe* will take. Fethullah Gülen (2007), for example, began a debate about whether *dabbe* could be a disease like the plague, cancer or AIDS; yet he also argued that *dabbe* cannot be reduced to just one disease, AIDS. Yaşar Nuri Öztürk (2009), on the other hand, argued that *dabbe* will appear in the form of a human to warn his or her fellow humans, and he suggested Stephen Hawking as an example. The horror film *D@bbe* (2006) by Hasan Karacadağ prompted these debates and questions around *dabbe*.

2   I found that Year Fives often needed more teacher support due to the abrupt introduction of the 4+4+4 education reform. More specifically, they were not mentally prepared to leave their classroom teachers and had difficulty adjusting to lower secondary school teachers (had the education reform not been introduced, they would be Year Fives again but in primary schools with their classroom teachers). Teachers teaching Year Five, Six, Seven and Eight also had difficulties adjusting to Year Fives. I observed that most of these teachers could not adapt their classes to match the pupils' age and had hard time to hold the pupils' attention during the classes.

3   Director Hasan Karacadağ (2012) claimed that he is adapting real-life *jinn* stories from 'Turkish-Islamic culture' and that he used *jinn* footage in his films. Inspired by Japanese horror, Karacadağ directed several films. See, for instance, *D@bbe* (2006), *Semum* (2008), *D@bbe 2* (2009) and *Dabbe: Bir Cin Vakası* (2012).

4   Atatürk gives his own account of Turkey's independence struggle in this six-day speech (October 1927). See Atatürk (1963).

5   For those readers who are not familiar with Mehmet Akif Ersoy, a brief sketch of his life is necessary. Mehmet Akif Ersoy, who was trained as a veterinarian, belonged to the first generation of intellectuals who advocated pan-Islamism in the face of European colonialism and initiated the idea of reformation to alter the influence of Western institutions (Bulaç 2005: 56–8; Kara 2005). Before the establishment of the republic, during the rule of the Committee of Union and Progress (1908–18), Ersoy supported the Islamist faction of the Young Ottomans. In the following years, he actively participated in the Turkish War of Independence (1919–23) in various positions (Aktay 2005). Ersoy, like many other key figures of his time, became a member of parliament in 1920. He penned the national anthem, *İstiklal Marşı* ('March of Independence'), in 1921. Moreover, the abolition of the Islamic caliphate, the banning of the Sufi orders and the closure of the *medreses* changed the lives of many Islamists in the early years of the republic and Ersoy was no exception. In 1922, Ersoy resigned from his post in parliament and moved to Egypt in 1926, which was a self-imposed exile (Aktay 2005). His writings from the post-caliphate period reflect the alienation of Muslim identity following the Kemalist reforms (Aktay 2005). Ersoy wrote for the popular, radical Muslim-modernist periodical *Sırat-ı Müstakim* ('True Path'), which later became

Sebülireşşad ('Straight Path') (Arabacı 2005; Ünsal 2005). According to Yasin Aktay (2005), Ersoy created the roots of the 'diasporic literature' discourse, which describes the Muslim identity that was excluded from society through the reforms of the single party period. Ersoy's followers elaborated further on his ideas – particularly Necip Fazıl Kısakürek, Erdoğan's favourite author, who expounded upon Ersoy's 'self-imposed exile' narrative through lines such as '*kendi vatanında parya*' (a pariah in one's own nation). Such writings became symbolic, critical expressions of the republican ideals in the 2000s.

6   In both schools, deputy heads showed their political views by putting up a photo cut-out of a newspaper or a quote as part of their display. Erman, who was one of the deputy heads in Talip, for example, hung a photo of a martyr's funeral on the board in his office. Erman kept this photo on the board throughout the school year to show his nationalist stance.

7   The regulation on the Day of Commemoration of the Adoption of the National Anthem and Mehmet Akif Ersoy prescribed the establishment of an all-inclusive administrative committee for this commemoration (Official Gazette 2008). Some of its members are representatives of non-governmental organizations as well as high-ranking officials from the Presidency, DİB, the state television channel TRT and so on (Official Gazette 2008). There are also requirements at the local level – including local state officials, municipalities and civil society (Official Gazette 2008).

8   Venerating the Prophet Muhammad on his birthday has been a common tradition across the world since the twelfth century (Kaptein 1993). There have been many debates over whether celebrating the birth of the Prophet, or venerating him on his birthday, is legitimate – i.e., whether it has a basis in the Qur'an and/or hadith since the fifteenth century (Katz 2007: 169–208; Woodward 2011). This controversial status of the commemoration had repercussions in the twentieth century, which was in line with the discussions on the modernization of Islam and the reactions of Islamic intellectuals towards the colonial existence of the West in various Islamic contexts. For instance, Wahhabis in Saudi Arabia strictly condemned – and still condemn – the commemoration, arguing that such a tradition is a religious innovation (known as *bidat*), while in the context of Asia, for example, this commemoration has gained more significance. Nevertheless, it is a public holiday in a wide range of contexts across the world. The Ottoman Empire must have played a significant role in institutionalizing this ritual; for instance, Benjamin C. Fortna's (2002) depiction of commemorative practices of *mevlid* in *Mekteb-i Sultani* shows the ways in which Sultan Abdülhamid II transformed *mevlid* into a state sponsored commemoration. During the Kemalist era, one of the striking developments regarding *mevlid* was the decision to commemorate the newly established National Sovereignty Day (*Milli Hakimiyet Bayramı*), which marks regime change, together with *mevlid* (Taş 2002). However, during the Kemalist reformation process in 1935 this national holiday was outlawed (Taş 2002) and

until the establishment of the Holy Birth Week it has been a ritual that only aimed to (i) venerate the Prophet on one of the five sacred evenings (known as *kandil*) (broadcasting these events on state television channel TRT started from 1950s onwards); (ii) venerate the Prophet during the rituals of life-cycle events including death, birth and marriage. See Tapper and Tapper (1987).

9 Türköne's (2012) article has been often cited to argue that the Gülen community had played a central role in the 'invention' of Holy Birth Week. This became even more evident after the failed coup attempt of 15 July with the arguments such as that Holy Birth Week is 'a FETÖ [Fethullahist Terrorist Organization] project' (Türkiye 2017). And the name of the week was officially changed in 2018 when *Mevlid-i Nebi Haftası* (The Birth of the Prophet Muhammad Week) was introduced, and the dates of the celebrations were set according to the Islamic calendar (Official Gazette 2017).

10 Here I refer to newspapers such as *Zaman*, which is considered the official mouthpiece of the Gülen movement, and *Yeni Asya*, to name a few. The magazine *Sızıntı*, the official mouthpiece of the Gülen community and its leader Fethullah Gülen, also published an article on the importance of venerating the Prophet in public sphere. See Gülen (1991). This article later served to support the claim that Holy Birth Week is an invention of Gülen community in post-15 July Turkey.

11 The thematic titles from the late 2000s to 2014 indicate that the panels and symposia functioned as 'think tanks'. See DİB (2005, 2006, 2007, 2008, 2009, 2010). At this point it is important to mention that DİB gradually became one of the most influential institutions in the country and had a budget to match (Lord 2018: 94–5) – an extremely important change. The role of DİB shifted from an institution that provides and supervises religious services to one that combines religious services with social policy (Lord 2018: 113–19). This was also evident in the commemorations, which became venues to further promote community relations at the local level. The week became a public event with celebrations in stadiums across the country, television broadcasts, dances for pre-school children, children of all ages singing and writing letters to the Prophet, and competitions and exhibitions to celebrate the week.

12 While the number of cultural products that target children has increased greatly since the mid-2000s, the rather limited scholarly interest in the subject makes a large area virtually opaque. Cultural products such as children's books could be considered an exception. See, for example, Azak (2013), Saktanber (1991) and Neydim (2001). With regard to television broadcasting that chases young consumers, the work of Kader Tuğla (2012) on the children's channel Yumurcak TV owned by Gülen community is also notable one.

13 The *Birds of Paradise*, for example, are a group of six Palestinian girls who have become famous throughout the Arabic-speaking world. But the 'Birds of Paradise' is also a provider of content for children, as their album of Arabic songs is sold in Turkey

under the name *Grup Cennet Kuşları* ('Birds of Paradise'). The Birds of Paradise Group, known in the Arab world as Toyor Al Janah, sparked a major debate after the release of their song *When We Die as Martyrs*. Especially the lyrics, 'When we die as shaheeds [Islamic martyrs] we'll go to paradise. No, don't say we're young. This life has made us old. Without Palestine, what significance is there to our lives? Even if they give us the whole world, we'll never forget her [Palestine]' (Nahmias 2010).

14 Here I refer to the videos uploaded to YouTube by anonymous accounts – not the official accounts. The number of music videos by the *Peygamber Sevdalları İlahi Grubu* (the Prophet Lovers, Hymn Group), which mainly performs Kurdish songs (or rather 'hymns') for children, was high in the 2010s. While writing this book, I noticed that there are very few videos on YouTube. This is significant to mention because during my classroom observations, I noticed that among the online platforms, teachers preferred YouTube the most.

Chapter 5

1 The literature on surveillance in the context of Turkey mainly focuses on the relationship between the neoliberal turn and the emergence of surveillance mechanisms. See, for example, Güven (2012) and Özbay et al. (2011).

2 Briefly it was in part a response to changing governance dispositions at the global level, that is the launch of the world report on violence against children by the UN with the impetus to eliminate violence against children. The second layer of influences had to do with changing discourses on 'safe school' at the national level and the debates and policy changes these generated. The involvement of the police in schools began after the MEB and the Ministry of Interior signed a protocol in 2007 to collaborate on the prevention of violence in and around schools, the 'Collaboration Protocol Concerning Prevention and Protection Enhancing Measures for Ensuring Secure Schools'. It was established under the 'Safe School – Safe Education' project based on the recommendations of an ad hoc parliamentary commission, the Commission for Investigating the Causes of Violence against Children and Women and of Honour Killings of the Grand National Assembly of Turkey. See TBMM (2006).

3 In practice, in the early years of the 2010s, three main tasks could be identified among the others assigned to police officers. One was to check the catchment area of schools; this included checking public spaces that children/youth might prefer (e.g., internet cafés or parks). The second task was to monitor and work with those who have close contact with children, such as shuttle bus drivers and security staff hired by OABs. The third task was to visit the schools at regular intervals and obtain information from a designated contact person (e.g., the deputy head teacher

or the head teacher) and write a report. If deemed necessary, or in exceptional circumstances, head teachers may involve the police. For example, police officers could work in the schools in an office provided by the head teachers and/or police officers could have full access to the CCTV systems in the schools. See, for example, Hürriyet (2009) and Radikal (2011). In some contexts, the relatively new approach of the national police (i.e., community policing which refers to community-oriented policing) was also integrated into school policing projects developed at local level which included involvement of police officers in the school through extracurricular activities such as games. Definitely, media yield a one-sided account that legitimizes police involvement.

4   Within last decade, the use of CCTV has become increasingly widespread throughout Turkey as a security measure – particularly after the installation of the expansive CCTV system, Mobile Electronic System Integration (*Mobil Elektronik Sistem Entegrasyonu*, MOBESE). MOBESE has various features, one of which is monitoring city centres and urban areas with the intention of investigating and detecting crime in Turkey (Güven 2012).

5   Indeed, building new classrooms has been one of the priorities of successive governments since the late 1990s. This is in line with the main global governance agendas of the last decades, namely Education for All (EFA), the Dakar Framework and the Millennium Development Goals (MDGs). In this spirit, about 20,000 classrooms have been built between 1997 and 2007 (ERG 2008: 68). Another important policy objective was to limit the size of classrooms for pupils in primary schools to a maximum of thirty pupils. Nevertheless, overcrowding, the double-shift system and schools reaching their infrastructural limits remained in certain regions, such as the south-eastern part of the country and in densely populated cities like Istanbul (ERG 2014). In this context, Talip was one of the overcrowded schools that did not have 'adequate space'. Moreover, there were only a few classrooms in the school with thirty pupils; most classrooms were overcrowded, with the number of pupils varying between thirty-five and thirty-seven. This was also the case in Zinnur, but the school building offered enough space compared to Talip.

6   See Official Gazette (2013).

7   See Official Gazette (2014).

Chapter 6

1   In the gender and education literature, the concept of *performance* is not a new term, and yet it has different references, meanings and connotations. For instance, Valerie Walkerdine (1994) coins the term to refer to the performances of the boys and girls in school settings. Studying the performance of girls and boys in

mathematics, Walkerdine (1994) comes to conclusion that teachers' expectations play a significant role in the construction of particular understandings of femininity and masculinity.

2 Jenny B. White's (2002) study in Ümraniye provides rich insights concerning the very first stages of the mobilization of women within informal networks during the 1990s. Yet, after the AKP came to power, it seems that the past informal networks have evolved into formal, transparent and legitimate networks of the AKP party. As I illustrated above, motherhood and children's education have become one of the key motivations for women's mobility and, unlike the 1990s of Ümraniye, in Bahçelik the wide range of projects, seminars, activities, courses, meetings and so on target all the women in the district – not exclusively party members.

3 See Buğra (2012).

4 Osman's depiction of the nation summarized 'the myth of the military-nation' (Altınay 2004a) almost word for word.

5 See Kandiyoti (1989, 1992).

6 The word '*kullanmak*' (use) also means abuse and in slang it also means rape. Üzeyir sees 'rape' as the fault of the woman – a mother in Zinnur. In other words, for Üzeyir, the labour market is available for men and when a woman enters it, she is/would be 'used'.

7 I found out that Year Five pupils read, among other Islamist authors, Emine Şenlikoğlu's (2012) *Bize Nasıl Kıydınız?* ('How Did You Sacrifice Us?') and Şule Yüksel Şenler's (2000) *Huzur Sokağı* ('The Peace Street'), which belong to the popular genre of books categorized as 'salvation novels' (Çayır 2007: 56). According to Kenan Çayır (2007), in these novels, Muslim identity is created as a stable character who is largely separated from society and only engages with characters who are portrayed as 'degenerates'. In a sense, the encounter of the pious Muslim character with his/her 'Other' defines the contours of Muslim identity, as Çayır's analysis (2007) suggests. These books were not on the national curriculum; however, they were very popular among Year Five pupils.

8 For a critical account on the Offices for Family Religious Guidance, see Adak (2015).

9 In Bahçelik there were numerous *sıbyan okulu* mostly referred to affordable unofficial kindergartens that provides Islamic education. The naming of these kindergartens seems to have been inspired by *sıbyan mektebi*, which were referred to broadly primary schools that were usually located near mosques in the Ottoman Empire.

10 Ceren Lordoğlu's (2018) study of 'life as a single woman' in Istanbul shows comparable tactics women use to keep up appearances of not being divorced. Lordoğlu cites, among the others, the example of a woman who, even after her husband had left the house, put his shoes outside the flat door every evening so that the neighbours could see them (2018: 80).

References

Primary sources

Atatürk, M. K. ([1927] 1963), *Nutuk [The Speech]*, Ankara: Türk Dil Kurumu.

DİB, 'Diyanet İşleri Başkanlığı [Presidency of Religious Affairs]' (1995a), *Kutlu Doğum: 3, Hz. Muhammed ve Gençlik (Kutlu Doğum Haftası: 1992) [Holy Birth: 3, Prophet Muhammed and the Youth]*, Sempozyumlar ve Paneller Serisi: 5, Türkiye Diyanet Vakfı Yayınları: 171, Ankara: Türkiye Diyanet Vakfı Yayınları.

DİB, 'Diyanet İşleri Başkanlığı [Presidency of Religious Affairs]' (1995b), *Kutlu Doğum: 4, İslamda İnsan Modeli ve Hz Peygamber Örneği (Kutlu Doğum Haftası: 1993) [Holy Birth: 4, Prophet Muhammed as a Role Model]*, Sempozyumlar ve Paneller Serisi: 6, Türkiye Diyanet Vakfı Yayınları: 172, Ankara: Türkiye Diyanet Vakfı Yayınları.

DİB, 'Diyanet İşleri Başkanlığı [Presidency of Religious Affairs]' (1996), *Kutlu Doğum: 5, Doğu'da ve Batı'da İnsan Hakları (Kutlu Doğum Haftası: 1993–1994) [Holy Birth: 5, Human Rights in the East and the West]*, Sempozyumlar ve Paneller Serisi: 14, Türkiye Diyanet Vakfı Yayınları: 201, Ankara: Türkiye Diyanet Vakfı Yayınları.

DİB, 'Diyanet İşleri Başkanlığı [Presidency of Religious Affairs]' (1997), *Kutlu Doğum: 7, Değişim Sürecinde İslam (Kutlu Doğum Haftası: 1996) [Holy Birth: 7, Islam in the Wake of Transformations]*, Sempozyumlar ve Paneller Serisi: 19, Türkiye Diyanet Vakfı Yayınları: 233, Ankara: Türkiye Diyanet Vakfı Yayınları.

DİB, 'Diyanet İşleri Başkanlığı [Presidency of Religious Affairs]' (1999), *İslam ve Demokrasi: Kutlu Doğum Sempozyumu-1998 [Islam and Democracy]*, Sempozyumlar ve Paneller Serisi: 27, Türkiye Diyanet Vakfı Yayınları: 291, Ankara: Türkiye Diyanet Vakfı Yayınları.

DİB, 'Diyanet İşleri Başkanlığı [Presidency of Religious Affairs]' (2005), *Üçüncü 100'e Girerken İslam, Kutlu Doğum Sempozyumu-2000 [Millenium and Islam]*, Yayın No: 330 Sempozyumlar Paneller Serisi: 34, Ankara: Türkiye Diyanet Vakfı Yayınları.

DİB, 'Diyanet İşleri Başkanlığı [Presidency of Religious Affairs]' (2006), *Kutlu Doğum 2005 Dinin Dünya Barışına Katkısı [The Role of Religion in World Peace]*, Yayın No: 365 Sempozyumlar Paneller Serisi: 36, Ankara: Türkiye Diyanet Vakfı Yayınları.

DİB, 'Diyanet İşleri Başkanlığı [Presidency of Religious Affairs]' (2007), *Kutlu Doğum 2004 Din-Kültür ve Çağdaşlık [Religion-Culture and Modernity]*, Yayın No: 378 Sempozyumlar Paneller Serisi: 38, Ankara: Türkiye Diyanet Vakfı Yayınları.

DİB, 'Diyanet İşleri Başkanlığı [Presidency of Religious Affairs]' (2008), *Kutlu Doğum 2007 İnsan Sevgisi [Humanity]*, Yayın No: 395 Sempozyumlar Paneller Serisi: 43, Ankara: Türkiye Diyanet Vakfı Yayınları.

DİB, 'Diyanet İşleri Başkanlığı [Presidency of Religious Affairs]' (2009), *Kutlu Doğum 2008 İslam Medeniyetinde Bir Arada Yaşama Tecrübesi [Islamic Civilizations and the Experiences of Peaceful Co-existence]*, No: 433 Sempozyumlar Paneller Serisi: 44, Ankara: Türkiye Diyanet Vakfı Yayınları.

DİB, 'Diyanet İşleri Başkanlığı [Presidency of Religious Affairs]' (2010), *Kutlu Doğum 2009 Küreselleşen Dünyada Aile [Family in a Globalizing World]*, No: 486 Sempozyumlar Paneller Serisi: 46, Ankara: Türkiye Diyanet Vakfı Yayınları.

EBA, 'Eğitim Bilişim Ağı' [Education Information Network]' (2016), '15 Temmuz Demokrasi Zaferi ve Şehitlerimiz: Anma Programı' Available online: https://img.eba. gov.tr/897/98a/3df/b4a/8f9/3a4/a0f/818/944/99f/1f4/615/154/a34/001/89798a3dfb4a 8f93a4a0f81894499f1f4615154a34001.PDF (accessed 28 January 2022).

Ersoy, M. A. (1989), *Safahat*, Ankara: Başbakanlık Basımevi.

Grup Cennet Kuşları [Birds of Paradise Group] (2008), 'Ya Taiba Ya Taiba', on *Ya Taiba Ya Taiba (Islamın Şartı): The Album* [sound recording], Turkey: Sentez Müzik.

İsmail Uslu – Minik Eller, Grup 571 (2007), '571'de Bir Güneş Doğdu [A Sun Rose Up in 571]', on *Ismail Uslu- Minik Eller Grup 571: The Album* [sound recording], Turkey: Truva Müzik.

MEB, 'Milli Eğitim Bakanlığı [Ministry of National Education]' (1977), 'Atatürk Köşeleri Hakkında', Genelge Sayı 3953/6, 21.03.1977, Talim Terbiye Kurulu Başkanlığı.

MEB, 'Milli Eğitim Bakanlığı [Ministry of National Education]' (1982), 'Atatürk Köşeleri Hakkında', Genelge Sayı 1982/128, 1.09.1982, Talim Terbiye Kurulu Başkanlığı.

MEB, 'Milli Eğitim Bakanlığı [Ministry of National Education]' (1990), 'Kahramanlık Tabloları ve Türk Büyüklerine Ait Resimler', Genelge Sayı 1990/44, 12.11.1990, Talim Terbiye Kurulu Başkanlığı.

MEB, 'Milli Eğitim Bakanlığı [Ministry of National Education]' (2005), '*OECD PISA-2003 Araştırmasının Türkiye İle İlgili Sonuçları: PISA 2003 Projesi Ulusal Nihai Rapor [PISA 2003 Report –OECD]*'.

MEB, 'Milli Eğitim Bakanlığı [Ministry of National Education]' (2011), 'Kutlu Doğum Haftası', Genelge, Sayı 2011/22, 07.04.2011, Talim Terbiye Kurulu Başkanlığı.

MEB, 'Milli Eğitim Bakanlığı [Ministry of National Education]' (2016a), '15 Temmuz Demokrasi Zaferi ve Şehitleri Anma Etkinliği', Genelge Sayı 2016/18, 07.09.2016, Talim Terbiye Kurulu Başkanlığı.

MEB, 'Milli Eğitim Bakanlığı [Ministry of National Education]' (2016b), [Brochure] '15 Temmuz Demokrasi Zaferi ve Şehitleri Anısına'.

MEB, 'Milli Eğitim Bakanlığı [Ministry of National Education]' (2016c), [Video] '15 Temmuz Demokrasi Zaferi ve Şehitleri Anma Programı'. Available online: https://www.youtube.com/watch?v=0UnIrb-EML0 (accessed 29 January 2022).

MEB, 'Milli Eğitim Bakanlığı [Ministry of National Education]' (2017), '15 Temmuz Demokrasi ve Millî Birlik Günü'. Available online: https://ookgm.meb.gov.tr/ www/15-temmuz-demokrasi-ve-mill-birlik-gunu/icerik/1067 (accessed 28 January 2022).

Minik Dualar Grubu [Kids Prayer Group] (2005), 'Teşekkür Ederim Allah'ım [Thank you, O Allah]' on: Minik Dualar Grubu [Kids Prayer Group]: Album [sound recording], Turkey: Metin Gim Prodüksiyon.

Official Gazette, (1982) no. 17849, 25 October 1982, 'Kamu Kurum ve Kuruluşlarında Çalışan Personelin Kılık ve Kıyafetine Dair Yönetmelik'.

Official Gazette (2004), no. 25642, 13 November 2004, 'Millî Eğitim Temel Kanununda Değişiklik Yapılması Hakkında Kanun'.

Official Gazette (2005a) no. 25874, 13 July 2005, 'Belediye Kanunu'.

Official Gazette (2005b), no. 25831, 31 May 2005, 'Millî Eğitim Bakanlığı Okul-Aile Birliği Yönetmeliği'.

Official Gazette (2008), no. 26809, 07 March 2008, 'İstiklal Marşinin Kabul Edildiği Günü ve Mehmet Akif Ersoy'u Anma Günü Hakkında Yönetmelik'.

Official Gazette (2010), no. 27492, 13 February 2010, 'Kutlu Doğum Haftası İle Camiler Ve Din Görevlileri Haftasını Kutlama Yönetmeliği'.

Official Gazette (2011), no. 28054, 14 September 2011, 'Milli Eğitim Bakanlığının Teşkilat ve Görevleri Hakkında Kanun'.

Official Gazette (2012a), no. 28199, 9 February 2012, 'Millî Eğitim Bakanlığı Okul-Aile Birliği Yönetmeliği'.

Official Gazette (2012b), no. 28261, 11 April 2012, 'Millî Eğitim Bakanliği İlköğretim ve Eğitim Kanunu İle Bazı Kanunlarda Değişiklik Yapılmasına Dair Kanun'.

Official Gazette (2012c), no. 28473, 20 November 2012, 'Millî Eğitim Bakanliği Okul-Aile Birliği Yönetmeliğinde Değişiklik Yapilmasina Dair Yönetmelik'.

Official Gazette (2013), no. 28789, 8 October 2013, 'Kamu Kurum ve Kuruluşlarında Çalışan Personelin Kılık ve Kıyafetine Dair Yönetmelik'.

Official Gazette (2014), no. 29132, 27 September 2014, 'Milli Eğitim Bakanlığına Bağlı Okul Öğrencilerinin Kılık ve Kıyafetlerine Dair Yönetmelikte Değişiklik Yapılması Hakkında Yönetmelik'.

Official Gazette (2016), no. 29818, 1 September 2016, 'Olağanüstü Hal Kapsamında Kamu Personeline İlişkin Alınan Tedbirlere Dair Kanun Hükmünde Kararname'.

Official Gazette (2017), no. 30255, 29 November 2017, 'Kutlu Doğum Haftası İle Camiler Ve Din Görevlileri Haftasını Kutlama Yönetmeliğinde Değişiklik Yapılmasına Dair Yönetmelik'.

Official Gazette (2019), no. 30714, 14 March 2019, 'Millî Eğitim Bakanliği Okul-Aile Birliği Yönetmeliğinde Değişiklik Yapilmasina Dair Yönetmelik'.

Peygamberin Gülleri [Roses of the Prophet] ([2006] [2008] 2014a), 'Yetim Kız [the Orphan Girl]', on *Peygamberin Gülleri: The Album* [sound recording], Turkey: Nil Production.

Peygamberin Gülleri [Roses of the Prophet] ([2006] [2008] 2014b), 'Biz Dünya Çocuklarıyız [We are the Children of the World]', on *Peygamberin Gülleri: The Album* [sound recording], Turkey: Nil Production.

Peygamberin Gülleri [Roses of the Prophet] ([2006] [2008] 2014c), 'Nur Yüzlüm [My Dear Prophet Who Has Light on His Face]', on *Peygamberin Gülleri: The Album* [sound recording], Turkey: Nil Production.

Peygamberin Gülleri [Roses of the Prophet] ([2006] [2008] 2014d), 'Peygamberi Görmek İçin [To See the Prophet]', on *Peygamberin Gülleri: The Album* [sound recording], Turkey: Nil Production.

Peygamberin Gülleri II [Roses of the Prophet II] (2010a), 'Bitsin Artık Bu Savaşlar [These Wars Should End]', on *Peygamberin Gülleri II: The Album* [sound recording], Turkey: Yedi Nota.

Peygamberin Gülleri II [Roses of the Prophet II] (2010b), 'Dön Yoluna Kurbanım [Come Back I Will Sacrifice Myself to Your Path]', on *Peygamberin Gülleri II: The Album* [sound recording], Turkey: Yedi Nota.

Peygamberin Gülleri II [Roses of the Prophet II] (2010c), 'Sevginin Sultanları [Sultans of Love]', on *Peygamberin Gülleri II: The Album* [sound recording], Turkey: Yedi Nota.

Peygamberin Gülleri II [Roses of the Prophet II] (2010d), 'Öğretmenim [My Teacher]', on *Peygamberin Gülleri II: The Album* [sound recording], Turkey: Yedi Nota.

TBMM, 'Türkiye Büyük Millet Meclisi [Turkish Grand National Assembly]' (2006), '*Turkish Grand National Assembly Special Investigation Commission Report/Research for Specific Measure against Honour Killings and Violence against Women and Children*'.

TCCB, 'Türkiye Cumhuriyeti Cumhurbaşkanlığı [Presidency of the Republic of Turkey]'(2021), 'Olağanüstü Hal İşlemleri İnceleme Komisyonu Faaliyet Raporu 2021'. Available online: https://ohalkomisyonu.tccb.gov.tr/docs/OHAL_FaaliyetRaporu_2021.pdf (accessed 29 January 2022).

TD, 'Tebliğler Dergisi [The Journal of Notifications of Ministry of National Education]' (2005), 2576: 637.

TÜİK, 'Türkiye İstatistik Kurumu [Turkish Statistical Institute]' (2009), 'Statistical Indicators (1923–2008)', No: 3361, Ankara: Turkish Statistical Institute.

TÜİK, 'Türkiye İstatistik Kurumu [Turkish Statistical Institute]' (2012), 'Statistical Indicators (1923–2011)', No: 3890, Ankara: Turkish Statistical Institute.

Secondary sources

Abadan-Unat, N. (1982), 'Social Change and Turkish Women', in N. Abadan-Unat in collaboration with D. Kandiyoti and M. B. Kıray (eds), *Women in Turkish Society*, 5–36, Leiden: Brill.

Abu-Duhou, I. (1999), *School-based Management. Fundamentals of Educational Planning 62*, Paris: UNESCO, International Institute for Educational Planning.

Acar, F. and A. Ayata (2002), 'Discipline, Success and Stability: The Reproduction of Gender and Class in Turkish Secondary Education', in D. Kandiyoti and A. Saktanber (eds), *Fragments of Culture: The Everyday of Modern Turkey*, 90–111, London: I.B. Tauris.

Adak, S. (2015), '"Yeni" Türkiye'nin "yeni" Diyaneti ["New" Diyanet of "New" Turkey]', *Birikim*, 319 (Kasım): 78–85.

Ahmad, F. (1991), 'Politics and Islam in Modern Turkey', *Middle Eastern Studies*, 27 (1): 3–21.

Ahmad, F. (2002), *The Making of Modern Turkey*, London and New York: Routledge.

Aksit, B. (1991), 'Islamic Education in Turkey: Medrese Reform in Late Ottoman Times and İmam-Hatip Schools in the Republic', in R. Tapper (ed.), *Islam in Modern Turkey: Religion, Politics, and Literature in a Secular State*, 145–70, London: I.B. Tauris.

Akşit, E. E. (2005), *Kızların Sessizliği: Kız Enstitülerinin Tarihi [The Silence of the Girls: The History of Girls' Institutes]*, İstanbul: İletişim Yayınları.

Aktay, Y. (2005), 'Halife Sonrası Şartlarda İslâmcılığın Öz-diyar Algısı [Islamic Perception of Homeland in Post-Caliphate Era]', in T. Bora and M. Gültekingil (eds), *Modern Dünyada Siyasi Düşünce Cilt 6 İslâmcılık*, 68–95, İstanbul: İletişim Yayınları.

Akyüz, Y. (2006), *Türk Eğitim Tarihi [Turkish Education History]*, Ankara: Pegem Yayıncılık.

Altınay, G. A. (2004a), *The Myth of the Military-Nation: Militarism, Gender, and Education in Turkey*, New York: Palgrave Macmillan.

Altınay, G. A. (2004b), 'Eğitimin Militarizasyonu: Zorunlu Milli Güvenlik Dersi [Militarization in Education]', in A. İnsel and A. Bayramoğlu (eds), *Bir Zümre, Bir Parti: Türkiye'de Ordu*, 179–200, İstanbul: Birikim Yayınları.

Altuntaş, S. Y. (2005), 'İlköğretim Okullarının Finansman İhtiyaçlarını Karşılama Düzeyleri [The Level of Meeting the Financial Needs of the Primary Schools]', MA diss. Yüzüncü Yıl University, Van.

Altunya, N. (2010), *Köy Enstitüsü Sistemi: Toplu Bakış [Village Institute: Broader View]*, İstanbul: Cumhuriyet Kitapları.

Anderson, B. (1991), *Imagined Communities: Reflections on the Origin and Spread of Nationalism*, New York: Verso.

Anderson-Levitt, K. M. (2003), 'A World Culture of Schooling?', in K. M. Anderson-Levitt (ed.), *Local Meanings, Global Schooling: Anthropology and World Culture Theory*, 1–26, New York: Palgrave.

Arabacı, C. (2005), 'Eşref Edib Ergan ve Sebîlürreşad Üzerine [On Eşref Edib Ergan and Sebîlürreşad]', in T. Bora and M. Gültekingil (eds), *Modern Dünyada Siyasi Düşünce Cilt 6 İslâmcılık*, 96–128, İstanbul: İletişim Yayınları.

Arat, Y. (1997), 'The Project of Modernity and Women in Turkey', in S. Bozdoğan and R. Kasaba (eds), *Rethinking Modernity and National Identity in Turkey*, 95–109, Washington, DC: University of Washington Press.

Arikan, C. (2012), *Neden, Köy Enstitüleri? [Why Village Institutes?]*, Istanbul: Markiz Yayınları.

Atasoy, Y. (2009), 'Islamic Engagement with Europe Universalism: State Transformation in Turkey', in Y. Atasoy (ed.), *Hegemonic Transitions, the State and Crisis in Neoliberal Capitalism*, 166–85, London/New York: Routledge.

Avar, S. (2004), *Dağ Çiçeklerim (Anılar) [My Mountain Flowers]*, Ankara: Berikan Yayinevi.

Aydagül, B. (2007), 'Turkey: Country Case Study', *Education for All Global Monitoring Report 2008*. Available online http://unesdoc.unesco.org/ images/0015/001555/155505e.pdf (accessed 3 February 2022).

Aydın, M. (2008), *Sosyal Politika ve Yerel Yönetimler [Social Policy and Local Governments]*, İstanbul: Yedirenk.

Azak, U. (2013), 'The New Happy Child in Islamic Picture Books in Turkey', in C. Gruber and S. Haugbolle (eds), *Visual Culture in the Modern Middle East: Rhetoric of the Image*, 127–43, Indiana: Indiana University Press.

Balcı, B. (2005), *Orta Asya'da İslâm Misyonerleri: Fethullah Gülen Okulları. [Islamic Missionaries in Central Asia: Fethullah Gülen Schools*, İstanbul: İletişim Yayınları.

Balcı, A. and İ. Öztürk (2014), 'Türkiye'de Eğitimin Finansmani Ve Eğitim Harcamaları Bilgi Yönetim Sistemine (TEFBİS) İlişkin Okul Yöneticilerinin Görüşleri ve Yaşadıkları Sorunlar [Views of Head Teachers on Information Management System of Education Financing and Education Expenses]', *Milli Eğitim*, 204 (1): 63–87.

Ball, S. J. (1993), 'Education Markets, Choice and Social Class: The Market as a Class Strategy in the UK and the USA', *British Journal of Sociology of Education*, 14 (1): 3–19.

Ball, S. J. (2003), *Class Strategies and The Education Marketplace: The Middle Classes and Social Advantage*, London: Routledge-Falmer.

Ball, S. J. and S. Gewirtz (1997), 'Girls in the Education Market: Choice, Competition and Complexity', *Gender and Education*, 9 (2): 207–22.

Baykurt, F. (2000), *Özyaşam 5: Bir TÖS Vardı [Autobiography 5: Once There Was Turkish Teachers' Union]*, İstanbul: Papirus Yayınları.

BBC News (2012), 'Turkish MPs Fight as Controversial Schools Bill Passed', *BBC News*, 31 March. Available online: http://www.bbc.co.uk/news/world-europe-17571131 (accessed 4 February 2021).

Bekim, A. (2003), 'The Gülen Movement's Islamic Ethics of Education', in M. H. Yavuz and J. L. Esposito (eds), *Islam and the Secular State: The Gülen Movement*, 48–68, Syracuse, New York: Syracuse University Press.

Beleli, Ö. (2012), *All Children in School by 2015: Turkey Country Study*. UNESCO and UNICEF.

Beşpınar, F. U. (2015), 'Between Ideals and Enactments: The Experience of "New Fatherhood" among Middle-Class Men in Turkey', in G. Ozyegin (ed.), *Gender and Sexuality in Muslim Cultures*, 95–110, Surrey: Ashgate Publishing.

Berkes, N. ([1964] 1998), *The Development of Secularism in Turkey*, London: Hurst & Company.

Boli, J., O. F. Ramirez and J. W. Meyer (1985), 'Explaining the Origins and Expansion of Mass Education Reviewed', *Comparative Education Review*, 29 (2): 145–70.

BOUN, 'Bosphorus University' (2012), 'İlköğretim ve Eğitim Kanun Taslağı'

Bourdieu, P. (1986), 'The Forms of Capital', in John G. Richardson (ed.), *Handbook of Theory and Research for the Sociology of Education*, 241–58, New York: Greenwood Press.

Bourdieu, P. (1996), *The State Nobility*, Stanford: Stanford University Press.

Bourdieu, P. (2010), *Distinction: A Social Critique of the Judgement of Taste*, Oxon: Routledge.

Bourdieu, P. and J.-C. Passeron (1990), *Reproduction in Education, Society and Culture*, London: Sage Publications.

Bourdieu, P. and L. Wacquant (1992), *An Invitation to Reflexive Sociology*, Chicago: University of Chicago Press.

Bowe, R., S. Ball and S. Gewirtz (1994), '"Parental Choice", Consumption and Social Theory: The Operation of Micro-Markets in Education', *British Journal of Educational Studies*, 42 (1): 38–52.

Bozan, İ. (2007), *Devlet ile Toplum Arasında Bir Okul, İmam Hatip Liseleri; Bir Kurum, Diyanet İşleri [Between the Society and the State: İmam Hatip School and Directorate of Religious Affairs]*, İstanbul: Tesev Yayınları.

Bray, M. (1999). *The Shadow Education System: Private Tutoring and Its Implications or Planners*, Paris: UNESCO, International Institute for Educational Planning (IIEP).

Brockett, G. D. (2011), *How Happy to Call Oneself a Turk: Provincial Newspapers and the Negotiation of a Muslim National Identity*, Austin: University of Texas Press.

Buğra, A. (2012), 'The Changing Welfare Regime of Turkey: Neoliberalism, Cultural Conservatism and Social Solidarity Redefined', in S. Dedeoglu and A. Elveren (eds), *Gender and Society in Turkey: The Impact of Neoliberal Policies, Political Islam and EU Accession*, 15–30, London/New York: I.B. Tauris.

Buğra, A. and O. Savaşkan (2014), *New Capitalism in Turkey: The Relationship between Politics, Religion and Business*, Cheltenham: Edward Elgar Publishing.

Bulaç, A. (2005), 'İslâmcılığın Üç Siyaset Tarzı veya İslâmcıların Üç Nesli [Three Political Forms of Islam and Three Generations of Islamists]', in T. Bora and M. Gültekingil (eds), *Modern Dünyada Siyasi Düşünce Cilt 6 İslâmcılık*, 48–67, İstanbul: İletişim Yayınları.

Butler, J. (2007), *Gender Trouble: Feminism and the Subversion of Identity*, New York and London: Routledge.

Butler, J. (2011), *Bodies That Matter: On the Discursive Limits of Sex*, London/New York: Routledge.

Çakır, R. (2002), *Ayet ve Slogan [Islamic Verse and Slogan]*, İstanbul: Metis Yayınları.

Caldwell, B. J. (2009), 'Centralization and Decentralization in Education: A New Dimension to Policy', in J. Zajda and D. T. Gamage (eds), *Globalization, Comparative Education and Policy Research: Vol 8. Decentralization, School-Based Management, and Quality*. 53–66, London/New York: Springer.

Caldwell, B. J. and J. M. Spinks (1988), *The Self-Managing School*, London: Falmer.

Çameli, T. (2008), 'Kız Çocukların İlköğretime Erişiminde Türkiye'den Örnekler [Girls' Access to Primary Education – Best Practices from Turkey]', İstanbul: AÇEV, ERG, Kader.

Candaş, A., B. E. Akkan, S. Günseli and M. B. Deniz (2011), *Devlet ilköğretim okullarında ücretsiz öğle yemeği sağlamak mümkün mü? [Is it possible to offer free lunch in state schools?]*, İstanbul: Açık Toplum Vakfı.

Çayır, K. (2007), *Islamic Literature in Contemporary Turkey: From Epic to Novel*, New York: Palgrave Macmillan.

Cemalcilar, Z. and F. Gökşen (2012), 'Inequality in Social Capital: Social Capital, Social Risk and Drop-Out in the Turkish Education System', *British Journal of Sociology of Education*, 35 (1): 94–114.

CNNTurk (2016), 'Anaokulu öğrencileri 15 Temmuz'u sahneledi [Kindergarten pupils staged 15 July]', *CNNTurk*, 22 December. Available online: https://www.cnnturk.com/turkiye/anaokulu-ogrencileri-15-temmuzu-sahneledi?page=1 (accessed 28 January 2022).

Çobanoğlu, Y. (2018), 'Women in the Gülen Movement: Life in a PostmodernDisplay, Enshrined with Sacredness', in M. H. Yavuz and B. Balcı (eds), *Turkey's July 15th Coup What Happened and Why*, 237–61, Salt Lake City: The University of Utah Press.

Connell, R. W. (1987), *Gender and Power: Society, the Person and Sexual Politics*, Cambridge: Polity Press.

Connell, R. W. (2000), *The Men and the Boys*, Cambridge: Polity Press.

Connell, R. W. (2005), *Masculinities*, second edition, Cambridge: Polity Press.

Connell, R. W. (2009), *Gender in World Perspective*, Cambridge: Polity Press.

Connell, R. W. and J. W. Messerschmidt (2005), 'Hegemonic Masculinity: Rethinking the Concept', *Gender & Society*, 19 (6): 829–59.

Connerton, P. (2008), 'Seven Types of Forgetting', *Memory Studies*, 1 (1): 59–71.

Copeaux, E. (2000), *Tarih Ders Kitaplarında (1931–1993) Türk Tarih Tezinden Türk-Islam Sentezine [From Turkish History Thesis to Turkish-Islam Synthesis in History Books]*, second edition, İstanbul: Tarih Vakfı Yurt Yayınları.

ÇV, 'Çocuk Vakfı [Child Association]' (2009), '100 Temel Eser Raporu [Report on the 100 Essential Works]'. Available online: https://www.cocukvakfi.org.tr/wpcontent/uploads/2020/12/11_100_TEMEL_ESER_RAPORU.pdf (accessed 10 August 2022).

D@bbe (2006), [Film] Dir. Hasan Karacadağ, Turkey: J-Plan.

D@bbe 2 (2009), [Film] Dir. Hasan Karacadağ, Turkey: J-Plan.

Dabbe: Bir Cin Vakası (2012), [Film] Dir. Hasan Karacadağ, Turkey: J-Plan.

Dedeoglu, S. (2012), 'The Effects of the Welfare Reforms on Women's Status in the EU Accession Process', in S. Dedeoglu and A. Elveren (eds), *Gender and Society in Turkey: The Impact of Neoliberal Policies, Political Islam and EU Accession*, 125–40, London/New York: I.B.Tauris.

Delaney, C. (1994), 'Untangling the Meanings of Hair in Turkish Society'. *Anthropological Quarterly*, 67 (4): 159–72.

Deringil, S. (2011), *The Well-Protected Domains: Ideology and the Legitimation of Power in the Ottoman Empire 1876–1909*, London: I.B. Tauris.

Dülger, İ. (2004), 'Turkey: Rapid Coverage for Compulsory Education – The 1997 Basic Education Program', *Case Study from Scaling up Poverty Reduction: A Global Learning Process and Conference*, Shanghai, May 25–7, 2004.

Duvar, (2016), 'Öğrencilerine "ip"li poz verdirdi! [He made his pupils to pose with "noose" into the camera]', *Gazete Duvar*, 13 December. Available online: https://www.gazeteduvar.com.tr/gundem/2016/12/13/ogrencilerine-ipli-poz-verdirdi (accessed 28 January 2022).

EBS, 'Eğitim-Bir-Sen' [Union of Educators' Association]' (2013), '"Özgürlük İçin 10 Milyon İmza" Kampanyamıza Yurtdışından Destek [Support from Abroad to Our Campaign for "10 million Signatures for Freedom"]', Available online: https://www.ebs.org.tr/manset/1892/ozgurluk-icin-10-milyon-imza-kampanyamiza-yurtdisindan-destek (accessed 3 February 2022).

EBS, 'Eğitim-Bir-Sen [Union of Educators' Association]' (n.d.), 'Türkiye Özgürlüğe 12 Milyon 300 Bin İmza Attı [Turkey Gave 12 Million 300 Thousand Signatures for Freedom]', Available online: http://www.egitimbirsen.org.tr/manset-haberleri/turkiye-ozgurluge-12-milyon-300-bin-imza-atti/1931/ (accessed 20 January 2022).

Eiseley, L. (1978), *The Star Thrower*, New York: A Harvest Book.

Ercan, F. and F. Uzunyayla (2009), 'A Class Perspective on the New Actors and Their Demands from the Turkish Education System', in D. Hill and E. Rosskam (eds), *The Developing World and State Education: Neoliberal Depredation and Egalitarian Alternatives*, 109–24, Oxford: Taylor & Francis.

Erdoğan, N. (2007), '"Garibanların Dünyası": Türkiye'de Yoksulların Kültürel Temsilleri. ["The World of the Poor": The Cultural Representations of the Poor in Turkey]', in N. Erdoğan (ed.), *Yoksulluk hâlleri: Türkiye'de Kent Yoksulluğunun Toplumsal Görünümleri*, 29–49, İstanbul: İletişim Yayınları.

ERG, 'Eğitim Reform Girişimi [Education Reform Initiative]' (2008), *Eğitim İzleme Raporu 2007*, İstanbul: Sabancı Üniversitesi Yayını.

ERG, 'Eğitim Reform Girişimi [Education Reform Initiative]' (2012), '18 Soruda 4+4+4 Yasa Teklifi. [Explanation of 4+4+4 Law Proposal with 18 Questions and Answers]'. Available online https://www.egitimreformugirisimi.org/18-soruda-444-yasa-teklifi-ve-ergnin-guncel-gerekceli-degerlendirmesi/ (accessed 1 February 2022).

ERG, 'Eğitim Reform Girişimi [Education Reform Initiative]' (2014), *Eğitim İzleme Raporu 2013*, İstanbul: Sabancı Üniversitesi Yayını.

Erman, T. (1997), 'Squatter (Gecekondu) Housing versus Apartment Housing: Turkish Rural-to-Urban Migrant Residents' Perspectives', *Habitat International*, 21 March 1997, 91–105.

Erman, T. (2001), 'The Politics of Gecekondu (Squatter) Studies in Turkey: The Changing Representations of Rural Migrants in the Academic Discourse', *Urban Studies*, 38, June 2001, 983–1003.

Ersanlı-Behar, B. (1992), *İktidar ve Tarih: Türkiye'de Resmi Tarih Tezinin Oluşumu (1939–1937) [Power and History: The Genesis of the Official History Thesis in Turkey]*, İstanbul: AFA Yayınları.

Evrensel (2016), '15 Temmuz piyesinde çocukların eline silah verdiler! [Pupils were given guns in the 15 July play]', *Evrensel Gazetesi*, 19 September. Available online https://www.evrensel.net/haber/290598/15-temmuz-piyesinde-cocuklarin-eline-silah-verdiler (accessed 28 January 2022).

Fortna, B. C. (2002), *Imperial Classroom: Islam, the State, and Education in the Late Ottoman Empire*, Oxford: Oxford University Press.

Fortna, B. C. (2011), *Learning to Read in the Late Ottoman Empire and the Early Turkish Republic*, Hampshire: Palgrave Macmillan.

Fortna, B. C. (2016), 'Bonbons and Bayonets: Mixed Messages of Childhood in the Late Ottoman Empire and the Early Turkish Republic', in B. C. Fortna (ed.), *Childhood in the Late Ottoman Empire and After*, 173–88, Leiden/Boston: Brill.

Foucault, M. (1995), *Discipline and Punish: The Birth of the Prison*, trans. A. Sheridan, New York: Vintage.

Foucault, M. (1980), 'Questions on Geography', in C. Gordon (ed.), *Power/Knowledge: Selected Interviews and Other Writings 1972–1977*, 63–77, Brighton: Harvester Press.

Gallagher, M. (2010), 'Are Schools Panoptic?', *Surveillance & Society*, 7 (3/4): 262–72.

Gamage, D. T. and J. Zajda (2009), 'Decentralization and School-Based Governance: Comparative Study of Self-Governing School Models', in, J. Zajda and D. T. Gamage (eds), *Globalization, Comparative Education and Policy Research: Vol 8. Decentralization, School-Based Management, and Quality*, 3–22, London/New York: Springer.

Gök, F. (1995), 'Women and Education in Turkey', in Ş. Tekeli (ed.), *Women in Modern Turkish Society: A Reader*, 131–7, London: Zed Books.

Gök, F. (2002), 'The Privatization of Education in Turkey', in N. Balkan and S. Savran (eds), *The Ravages of Neo-Liberalism: Economy, Society, and Gender in Turkey*, 93–104, New York: Nova Publishers.

Gök, F. (2005), 'Üniversiteye Girişte Umut Pazarı: Özel Dershaneler [The Market of Hope: Private Tutorial Colleges]', *Eğitim Bilim Toplum*, 3 (11): 102–9.

Gök, F. (2007a), 'The Girls' Institutes in the Early Period of the Turkish Republic', in M. Carlson, A. Rabo and F. Gök (eds), *Education in Multicultural Societies: Turkish and Swedish Perspectives*, 93–105, Istanbul: Swedish Research Institute in Istanbul.

Gök, F. (2007b), 'The history and development of Turkish Education System', in M. Carlson, A. Rabo and F. Gök (eds), *Education in Multicultural Societies: Turkish and Swedish Perspectives*, 249–57, Istanbul: Swedish Research Institute in Istanbul.

Gök, F. and D. Ilgaz (2007), 'The Right to Education', in Z. Arat (ed.), *Human Rights in Turkey*, 123–36, Philadelphia, PA, Pennsylvania: University of Pennsylvania Press.

Gök, F. and A. Şahin (2003), *İnsan Halkarına Saygılı Bir Eğitim Ortamına Doğru [Education and Human Rights]*, İstanbul: Tarih Vakfı Yayınları.

Gökaçtı, M. A. (2005), *Türkiye'de Din Eğitimi ve İmam Hatipler [Religious Education in Turkey and Imam-Hatip Schools]*, İstanbul: İletişim Yayınları.

Gokalp, G. (2015), 'Cıfteler, the First Village Institute (Turkey 1937–1954)', in E. Rodríguez (ed.), *Pedagogies and Curriculums to (Re)imagine Public Education: Transnational Tales of Hope and Resistance*, 127–40, New York: Springer.

Göktürk, D., G. Güvercin and O. Seçkin (2012), 'The New Stream of Trade Unionism: The Case of Eğitim-Bir-Sen in Turkey', in K. İnal and G. Akkaymak (eds), *Neoliberal*

Transformation of Education in Turkey: Political and Ideological Analysis of Educational Reforms in the Age of the AKP, 109–24, New York: Palgrave Macmillan.

Göle, N. (1996), *The Forbidden Modern: Civilization and Veiling*, Ann Arbor: University of Michigan Press.

Gözaydın, İ. (2009), 'Türkiye'de Din Kültürü Ve Ahlak Bilgisi Ders Kitaplarına İnsan Hakları Merceğiyle Bir Bakış [A Look at the Religious Culture and Moral Knowledge Textbooks in Turkey through the Lens of Human Rights]', in G. Tüzün (ed.), *Ders Kitaplarında İnsan Hakları II Tarama Sonuçları*, 167–93, İstanbul: Tarih Vakfı.

Gramsci, A. (1971), *Selections from the Prison Notebooks*, edited and translated by Quintin Hoare and Geoffrey Nowell Smith. New York: International Publishers.

Grauwe, A. D. (2004), 'School-based Management (SBM): Does It Improve Quality?' *Paper commissioned for the EFA Global Monitoring Report 2005*, The Quality Imperative.

Grauwe, A. D. (2005), 'Improving the Quality of Education through School-based Management: Learning from International Experiences', *Review of Education*, 51: 269–87.

Gülen, F. 'editorial' (1991). 'Kutlu Doğum [Holy Birth]', *Sızıntı* (153).

Gülen, F. (2007), 'Kıyamet Âlameti Olarak Anlatılan Dabbetülarzın AIDS Hastalığı ile Alâkası Var mıdır? [Does *Dabbatularz*, described as a Portent of the Apocalypse, Have Anything to Do with AIDS Disease?]', Available online: http://tr.fgulen.com/content/view/550/146/ (accessed 23 January 2022).

Gümüşoğlu, F. (2008), 'Ders kitaplarında toplumsal cinsiyet [Gender in Textbooks]'. *Toplum ve Demokrasi*, 2 (4): 39–50.

Günay-Erkol, Ç. (2013), 'Issues of Ideology and Identity in Turkish Literature during the Cold War', in C. Örnek and Ç. Üngör (eds), *Turkey in the Cold War: Ideology and Culture*, 109–29, London: Palgrave Macmillan.

Güneş, C. (2021), *The Political Representation of Kurds in Turkey: New Actors and Modes of Participation in a Changing Society*, London: Bloomsbury Publishing.

Gürtan, K. R. and G. Tüzün, eds (2005), *Öğretmen ve Öğrencilerin Gözünden Ders Kitaplarında İnsan Hakları: Anket Sonuçları [Human Rights in School Textbooks]*, İstanbul: Tarih Vakfı.

Güven, O. Ö. (2012), 'Gözetimin Neoliberal Risk Bağlamında Dönüşümü ve Mobese Kameraları [The Transformation of Surveillance in Relation to Neoliberal Risk Society and MOBESE/CCTV]', PhD diss., İstanbul University, Istanbul.

Hanioğlu, M. Ş. (2011), *Ataturk: An Intellectual Biography*, Princeton: Princeton University Press.

Harvey, D. (2005), *A Brief History of Neoliberalism*, Oxford: Oxford University Press.

Helvacıoğlu, F. (1996), *Ders Kitaplarında Cinsiyetçilik 1928–1995 [Sexism in Textbooks]*, İstanbul: Kaynak Yayınları.

Hobsbawm, E. (1983), 'Introduction: Inventing Traditions', in E. Hobsbawm and T. Ranger (eds), *The Invention of Tradition*, 1–4, Cambridge: Cambridge University Press.

Huizinga, J. ([1949] 2002), *Homo Ludens: A Study of the Play-Element in Culture*, London: Routledge & Kegan Paul.

Hürriyet (2009), '*Okul Polisi Projesi Tuttu [School Police Project Is Successful]*'. Available online: http://www.hurriyet.com.tr/okul-polisi-projesi-tuttu-12675437 (accessed 3 February 2022).

Hürriyet (2013), 'Dershaneler Konusu Birsonraki Bakanlar Kuruluna Gelecek [Tutorial Colleges]'. Available online http://www.hurriyet.com.tr/erdogan-dershaneler-konusu-bir-sonraki-bakanlar-kurulu-na-gelecek-25168379 (accessed 3 February 2022).

İlhan, Y. (2010), Interviewed on *Merhaba Haftasonu Samanyolu Haber TV* [TV programme] 3 October, Istanbul.

İnal, K. and G. Akkaymak, eds (2012), *Neoliberal Transformation of Education in Turkey: Political and Ideological Analysis of Educational Reforms in the Age of the AKP*. New York: Palgrave Macmillan.

İnce, B. (2012), *Citizenship and Identity in Turkey: From Atatürk's Republic to the Present Day*, London and New York: I.B. Tauris.

İsmail, H. ([1967] 2019), *Minyeli Abdullah [Abdullah from Minye]*, İstanbul: Timaş Yayınları.

Jenkins, G. (2009), 'Between Fact and Fantasy: Turkey's Ergenekon Investigation', *Silk Road Papers and Monographs*, 1–84, Washington, DC: Central Asia-Caucasus Institute and Silk Road Studies.

Kağıtçıbaşı, Ç. (2010), 'Giris: Türkiye'de Kadın ve Eğitim. [Introduction: Women and Education in Turkey]', in B. E. Oder, D. Yükseker, F. Gökşen, H. Şimga (eds), *Türkiye'de Toplumsal Cinsiyet Çalışmaları*, 9–19, İstanbul: Koç Üniversitesi Yayınları.

Kancı, T. (2007), 'Imagining the Turkish Men and Women: Nationalism, Modernism, and Militarism in Primary School Textbooks, 1928–2000', PhD diss., Institute of Social Sciences, Sabancı University, Istanbul.

Kancı, T. and A. Altınay (2007), 'Educating Little Soldiers and Little Ayşes: Militarised and Gendered Citizenships in Turkish Textbooks', in M. Carlson, A. Rabo and F. Gök (eds), *Education in Multicultural Societies: Turkish and Swedish Perspectives*, 51–70, Istanbul: Swedish Research Institute in Istanbul.

Kandiyoti, D. (1987), 'Emancipated but Unliberated? Reflections on the Turkish Case', *Feminist Studies*, 13 (2): 317–38.

Kandiyoti, D. (1989), 'Women and the Turkish State: Political Actors or Symbolic Pawns?', in N. Yuval-Davis and F. Anthias (eds), *Woman-Nation-State*, 126–49, London: Macmillan.

Kandiyoti, D. (1991), 'Women, Islam and the State', *Middle East Report*, 173: 9–14.

Kandiyoti, D. (1992), 'Identity and Its Discontents: Women and the Nation', *Millennium*, 20 (3): 429–43.

Kandiyoti, D. (1997), 'Gendering the Modern: On Missing Dimensions in the Study of Turkish Modernity', in S. Bozdoğan and R. Kasaba (eds), *Rethinking Modernity and National Identity in Turkey*, 113–32, Washington, DC: University of Washington Press.

References

185

Kandiyoti, D. (2012), 'The Travails of the Secular: Puzzle and Paradox in Turkey', *Economy and Society*, 41 (4): 513–31.

Kandiyoti, D. (2013), 'Bargaining with Patriarchy', in C. R. McCann and S. Kim (eds), *Feminist Theory Reader: Local and Global Perspectives*, third edition, 98–106, Oxford: Routledge.

Kandiyoti, D. and Z. Emanet (2017), 'Education as Battleground: The Capture of Minds in Turkey', *Globalizations*, 14 (6): 869–76.

Kaplan, İ. (1999), *Türkiye'de Milli Eğitim İdeolojisi ve Siyasal Toplumsallaşma Üzerindeki Etkisi* [National Education Ideology and Its Impact on *Political* Socialization in Turkey], İstanbul: İletişim Yayınları.

Kaplan, S. (2002), 'Din-u Devlet All Over Again? The Politics of Military Secularism and Religious Militarism in Turkey Following the 1980 Coup', *International Journal of Middle East Studies*, 34 (1): 113–27.

Kaplan, S. (2006), *The Pedagogical State: Education and Politics of National Culture in Post-1980 Turkey*, Stanford: Stanford University Press.

Kaptein, N. J. G. (1993), *Muḥammad's Birthday Festival: Early History in the Central Muslim Lands and Development in the Muslim West until the 10th/16th Century*, Leiden, New York, Köln: Brill.

Kara, İ. (2005), 'İslâmcı Söylemin Kaynakları ve Gerçeklik Değeri [The Sources of Islamist Discourse]', in T. Bora and M. Gültekingil (eds), *Modern Dünyada Siyasi Düşünce Cilt 6 İslâmcılık*, 34–47, İstanbul: İletişim Yayınları,

Karacadağ, H. (2012), interviewed by Yeşim Tabak for *Radikal*, 8 July.

Karaömerlioğlu, M. A. (1998), 'The Village Institutes Experience in Turkey', *British Journal of Middle Eastern Studies*, 25 (1): 47–73.

Karaömerlioğlu, M. A. (2006), *Orada Bir Köy Var Uzakta: Erken Cumhuriyet Döneminde Köycü Söylem [There Is a Village, Far Away]*, İstanbul: İletişim Yayınları.

Kasaba, R. (1997), 'Kemalist Certainties and Modern Ambiguities', in S. Bozdoğan and R. Kasaba (eds), *Rethinking Modernity and National Identity in Turkey*, 15–36, Washington, DC: University of Washington Press.

Katz, M. H. (2007), *The Birth of the Prophet Muhammad: Devotional Piety in Sunni Islam*, London: Routledge.

Kavak, Y., E. Ekinci and F. Gökçe (1997), 'İlköğretimde kaynak arayışları [Fund Seeking in Primary Schools]', *Eğitim Yönetimi*, 3 (3): 309–20.

Kaya, M. A. (2014), 'Breastfeeding the Educational System: Analyzing Women's Unpaid Labor and Voluntary Mother Participation in Schools within the Context of Neoliberal Economic Policies', PhD diss., Boğaziçi University, Istanbul.

Kaymakcan, R. (2007), 'Yeni Ortaöğretim Din Kültürü ve Ahlak Bilgisi Öğretim Programı İnceleme ve Değerlendirme Raporu [New Secondary Education Religious Culture and Moral Knowledge Curriculum Review and Evaluation Report]'. Available online: https://www.egitimreformugirisimi.org/yayin/yeni-ortaogretim-din-kulturu-ve-ahlak-bilgisi-ogretim-programi-inceleme-ve-degerlendirme-raporu/ (accessed 25 January 2022), İstanbul: Eğitim Reform Girişimi.

Kazamias, A. M. (1966), *Education and the Quest for Modernity in Turkey*, London: George Allen & Unwin.

Kenar, C. and D. Gürpınar (2013), 'Cold War in the Pulpit: The Presidency of Religious Affairs and Sermons during the Time of Anarchy and Communist Threat', in C. Örnek and Ç. Üngör (eds), *Turkey in the Cold War: Ideology and Culture*, 21–46, London: Palgrave Macmillan.

Keyder, Ç. (1987), 'Economic Development and Crisis: 1950–80', in I. C. Schick and E. A. Tonak (eds), *Turkey in Transition: New Perspectives*, 296–7, New York and Oxford: Oxford University Press.

Keyder, Ç. (1997), 'Whither the Project of Modernity? Turkey in the 1990s', in S. Bozdoğan and R. Kasaba (eds), *Rethinking Modernity and National Identity in Turkey*, 37–51, Washington, DC: University of Washington Press.

Kirby, F. ([1962] 2010), *Türkiye'de Köy Ensitüleri [Village Institutes in Turkey]*, İstanbul: Tarihci Kitabevi.

Koşar-Altınyelken, H. and G. Akkaymak (2012), 'Curriculum Change in Turkey: Some Reflections', in K. İnal and G. Akkaymak (eds), *Neoliberal Transformation of Education in Turkey: Political and Ideological Analysis of Educational Reforms in the Age of the AKP*, 59–70, New York: Palgrave Macmillan.

Köse, A. and A. Şaşmaz (2014), 'İlköğretim Kurumlarının Mali Yönetimi: Araştırma Raporu [Financial Management of Primary Schools: Research Report]', Available online: https://www.egitimreformugirisimi.org/wp-content/uploads/2017/03/ERG_MaliYonetimArastirmaRaporu.pdf (accessed 22 January 2022).

Kurt, M. (2016), *Türkiye'de Hizbullah: Din, Şiddet ve Aidiyet [Hizbullah in Turkey]*, İstanbul: İletişim Yayınları.

Kuru, A. T. (2003), 'Fethullah Gülen's Search for a Middle Way between Modernity and Muslim Tradition', in M. H. Yavuz and J. L. Esposito (eds), *Turkish Islam and the Secular State*, 116–24, New York: Syracuse University Press.

Kurul, N. (2012), 'Turkey under AKP Rule: Neoliberal Interventions into the Public Budget and Educational Finance', in K. İnal and G. Akkaymak (eds), *Neoliberal Transformation of Education in Turkey: Political and Ideological Analysis of Educational Reforms in the Age of the AKP*, 83–94, New York: Palgrave Macmillan.

Kuzmanovic, D. (2013), 'Imbued with Agency: Contesting Notions of the Extraordinariness of Türkan Saylan', in A. Bandak and M. Bille (eds), *Politics of Worship in Contemporary Middle East: Sainthood in Fragile States*, 171–91, Leiden Boston: Brill.

Lord, C. (2018), *Religious Politics in Turkey: From the Birth of the Republic to the AKP*, Cambridge: Cambridge University Press.

Lordoğlu, C. (2018), *İstanbul'da Bekar Kadın Olmak [Being a Single Woman in Istanbul]*, İstanbul: İletişim Yayınları.

Lyon, D. (2006), 'The Search for Surveillance Theories', in D. Lyon (ed.), *Theorizing Surveillance: The Panopticon and Beyond*, 3–20, Cullompton: Willan Publishing,

Makal, M. ([1950] 2008), *Bizim Köy [A Village in Anatolia]*, İstanbul: Literatür.

Mardin, Ş. (2006), *Religion, Society, and Modernity in Turkey*, New York: Syracuse University Press.

Meltem Gazetesi (2013), 'Eğitim-Sen'den Eğitim-Bir-Sen' Eleştri [Eğitim-Sen Criticized Eğitim-Bir-Sen]'. Available online: http://www.meltemgazetesi.com/egitim-senden-egitim-bir-sene-elestiri/ (accessed 3 February 2022).

Memurlarnet (2012), '120 sivil toplum örgütü 4+4+4 eğitim sistemine destek çıktı [One hundred and twenty NGOs supported 4+4+4]', Memurlarnet, 28 March. Available online: https://www.memurlar.net/haber/default.aspx?id=221290 (accessed 25 July 2022).

METU, 'Middle East Technical University' (2012), *İlköğretim ve Ortaöğretimin Yeniden Yapılandırılması. ODTÜ Eğitim Fakültesi Görüşü [The Opinion of Education Faculty of METU on the New Reformation of Primary and Secondary Education]*.

Milliyet (2006), 'Fethullah Gülen, Hande Yener'i, Gülben'i Solladı [Fethullah Gülen Got Ahead of Hande Yener and Gülben]', *Milliyet*, 17 December. Available online: https://www.milliyet.com.tr/ekonomi/fethullah-gulen-hande-yeneri-gulbeni-solladi-181941 (accessed 25 January 2022).

Moshenska, J. (2019), *Iconoclasm as Child's Play*, Stanford, California: Stanford University Press.

Murakami Wood, D. (2007), 'Beyond the Panopticon: Foucault and Surveillance Studies', in J. W. Crampton and S. Elden (eds), *Space, Knowledge and Power: Foucault and Geography*, 245–63, Aldershot: Ashgate.

Nahmias, R. (2010), 'Arab Song for Kids: Allah Loves Martyrs', *Ynetnews.com*, 22 June. Available online: https://www.ynetnews.com/articles/0,7340,L-3909134,00.html (accessed 5 October 2021).

Navaro-Yashin, Y. (2002a), 'Evde Taylorism: Türkiye Cumhuriyeti'nin İlk Yıllarında Ev İşinin Rasyonalleşmesi (1928–1940) [Taylorism at Home: The Rationalization of Housework during the First Years of the Turkish Republic]', *Toplum ve Bilim*, 84 (Bahar): 51–74.

Navaro-Yashin, Y. (2002b), *Faces of the State: Secularism and Public Life in Turkey*, Princeton and Oxford: Princeton University Press.

Neydim, N. (2001), '80 Sonrası Paradigma Değişimi Açısından Çeviri Çocuk Edebiyatı [Post-1980s and Translated Child Literature]', PhD diss. Istanbul University, Istanbul.

NTV (2013), 'Öğretmenler Serbest Kıyafetle Derse Girdi [Teachers Entered the Classrooms in Casual Clothes]'. Available online: http://www.ntv.com.tr/egitim/ogretmenler-serbest-kiyafetle-derse-girdi,kBfY0K0DA0qm50jQTaD63Q (accessed 3 February 2022).

OECD, 'Organization for Economic Co-operation and Development' (2010), *PISA 2009 Results: What Students Know and Can Do – Student Performance in Reading, Mathematics and Science (Volume I): Student Performance in Reading, Mathematics and Science*, OECD Publishing.

Okçabol, R. (2009), 'AKP'nin Eğitim Karnesi [The Education Report Card of AKP]', *Eleştirel Pedagoji*, 1: 26–32.

Öniş, Z. (2009), 'Conservative Globalists versus Defensive Nationalists: Political Parties and Paradoxes of Europeanisation in Turkey', in S. Verney and K. Ifantis (eds), *Turkey's Road to European Union Membership: National Identity and Political Change*, 35–48, New York: Routledge.

Örnek, C. and Ç. Üngör (2013), 'Turkey's Cold War: Global Influences, Local Manifestations', in C. Örnek and Ç. Üngör (eds), *Turkey in the Cold War: Ideology and Culture*, 1–20, London: Palgrave Macmillan.

Orucoglu, B. (2015), 'Why Turkey's Mother of All Corruption Scandals Refuses to Go Away', *Foreign Policy*, 6 January. Available online: https://foreignpolicy.com/2015/01/06/why-turkeys-mother-of-all-corruption-scandals-refuses-to-go-away/ (accessed 1 August 2022).

Özbay, C., A. Terzioğlu, and Y. Yasin (2011), *Neoliberalizm ve Mahremiyet: Türkiye'de Beden, Sağlık ve Cinsellik. [Neoliberalism and Privacy: The Body, Health and Sexuality in Turkey]*, İstanbul: Metis.

Özdalga, E. (2003), 'Following in the Footsteps of Fethullah Gülen: Three Women Teachers Tell Their Stories', in M. H. Yavuz and J. L. Esposito (eds), *Turkish Islam and the Secular State: The Gülen Movement*, 85–114, Syracuse, New York: Syracuse University Press.

Özdemir, N. (2011), 'İlköğretim Finansmanında Bir Araç: Okul-Aile Birliği Bütçe Analizi (Ankara ili örneği) [A Tool in Financing Primary Schools: The Analysis of the Budget of Parent-Teacher Association]', MA diss. Hacettepe University, Ankara.

Özel, C. (2016), '1980'lerden Günümüze İslamcı Müziğin Sosyolojik Analizi [Sociological Analysis of Islamist Music from the 1980s to Present]', *Ankara Üniversitesi İlahiyat Fakültesi Dergisi*, 57 (1): 145–74.

Ozgur, I. (2012), *Islamic Schools in Modern Turkey: Faith, Politics, and Education*, Cambridge: Cambridge University Press.

Özmen, Ü. (2012), 'The Marketization of Primary and Secondary School Curricula and Textbooks under AKP Rule', in K. İnal and G. Akkaymak (eds), *Neoliberal Transformation of Education in Turkey: Political and Ideological Analysis of Educational Reforms in the Age of the AKP*, 47–57, New York: Palgrave Macmillan.

Özoğlu, M. Ö. (2011). 'Dershaneler: Gölge Eğitim Sistemi ile Yüzleşmek [Tutorial Colleges: Facing the Shadow Educaion System]', *SETA Analiz*, no. 36 Mart.

Özsoy, S. (2004), 'Eşitlikçi Bir Eğitim Deneyimi Olarak Köy Enstitüleri', *Eğitim Bilim Toplum*, 2 (7): 4–25.

Öztürk, Y. N. (2009), 'Kıyamet alâmeti olarak Dabbetül Arz [Dabbetül Arz as a Sign of the Apocalypse]', *Hürriyet*, 25 February. Available online: http://www.hurriyet.com.tr/yazarlar/11077314.asp (accessed 23 January 2022).

Öztürkmen, A. (1996), 'Milli Bayramlar: Şekli ve Hatırası 1 [National Commemorations Form and Plan 1]', *Toplumsal Tarih*, 28: 29–35.

Öztürkmen, A. (1998), *Türkiye'de Folklor Ve Milliyetçilik [Folklore and Nationalism in Turkey]*, İstanbul: İletişim Yayınları.

Özyürek, E. (2006), *Nostalgia for the Modern: State Secularism and Everyday Politics in Turkey*, Durham and London: Duke University Press.

Parla, J. (2008), 'The Wounded Language: Turkey's Language Reform and the Canonicity of the Novel', *PMLA*, 123 (1): 27–40.

Pateman, C. (1992), 'Citizen Male', *Australian Left Review*, 1 (137): 30–3.

Perlman, J. (2010), *Favela: Four Decades of Living on the Edge in Rio de Janeiro*, New York: Oxford University Press.

Pingel, F. ([1999] 2010), *UNESCO Guidebook on Textbook Research and Textbook Revision*, second edition, Paris and Braunschweig: UNESCO.

Radikal (2011), 'İlköğretim öğrencileri Arasından Polis Muhbiri Seçiliyor [Police Informers are Selected from Primary School Pupils]'. Available online: http://www.radikal.com.tr/turkiye/ilkogretim-ogrencileri-arasindan-polis-muhbiri-seciliyor-1038651/ (accessed 20 December 2015).

Reay, D. (1995), '"They Employ Cleaners to Do That": Habitus in the Primary Classroom', *British Journal of Sociology of Education*, 16: 353–71.

Reay, D. (1998), *Class Work: Mothers' Involvement*, London: UCL Press.

Reay, D. (2004), '"It's All Becoming Habitus": Beyond the Habitual Use of Habitus in Educational Research', *British Journal of Sociology of Education*, 25 (4): 431–44.

Reay, D. (2006), 'The Zombie Stalking English Schools: Social Class and Educational Inequality', *British Journal of Educational Studies*, 54 (3): 288–307.

Reay, D. (2009), '"Class Acts": Home-school Involvement and Working Class Parents in UK', in R. Deslandes (ed.), *International Perspectives on Contexts, Communities and Evaluated Innovative Practices: Family-School-Community Partnerships*, 50–63, London and New York: Routledge.

Rutz, H. J. and E. M. Balkan (2009), *Reproducing Class: Education, Neoliberalism, and the Rise of the New Middle Class in Istanbul*, New York: Berghahn Books.

Sakallioglu, U. C. (1996), 'Parameters and Strategies of Islam-State Interaction in Republican Turkey', *International Journal of Middle East Studies*, 28 (2): 231–51.

Sakaoğlu, N. (2003), *Osmanlı'dan Günümüze Eğitim Tarihi* [The History of Education: From Ottoman Empire to Today], İstanbul: İstanbul Bilgi Üniversitesi Yayınları.

Saktanber, A. (1991), 'Muslim Identity in Children's Picture-Books', in R. Tapper (ed.), *Islam in Modern Turkey*, 171–88, London: I.B. Tauris.

Saktanber, A. and F. U. Beşpınar (2012), 'Youth', in M. Heper and S. Sayarı (eds), *The Routledge Handbook of Modern Turkey*, 271–81, London and New York: Routledge.

Şaşmaz, A. (2012), 'Kesintili Eğitim: Şura'dan Kanun Teklifine [Disrupted Education: From Education Council to the Legislative Proposal]'. Available online https://www.egitimreformugirisimi.org/kesintili-egitim-suradan-kanun-teklifine/ (accessed 1 February 2022).

Şaşmaz, A. (2015), 'Politics of Educational Expansion in Turkey', in *Background Paper for the Education for All Global Monitoring Report 2015*, Paris: UNESCO.

Şaşmaz, A., B. Aydagül, I. Tüzün, and İ. Aktaşlı (2011), *Türkiye'de Din ve Eğitim: Son Dönemdeki Gelişmeler ve Değişim Süreci [Religious Education in Turkey: Contemporary Developments and the Process of Change]*, İstanbul: Eğitim Reformu Girişimi.

Sayılan, F. and A. Yıldız (2009), 'The Historical and Political Context of Adult Literacy in Turkey', *International Journal of Lifelong Education*, 28 (6): 735–49.

Schriewer, J. and C. Martinez (2004), 'Constructions of Internationality in Education', in G. Steiner-Khamsi (ed.), *The Global Politics of Educational Borrowing and Lending*, 29–53, New York: Teachers College Press.

Semum (2008), [Film] Dir. Hasan Karacadağ, Turkey: J-Plan and Medya Skala.

Şenler, Ş. Y. (2000), *Huzur Sokağı [Peace Street]*, İstanbul: Timaş Yayınları.

Şenlikoğlu, E. ([1992] 2012), *Bize Nasıl Kıydınız? [How Did You Harm Us?]*, İstanbul: Mektup Yayınları.

Smith, G. J. D. (2004), 'Behind the Screens: Examining Constructions of Deviance and Informal Practices among CCTV Control Room Operators in the UK', *Surveillance & Society*, 2 (2): 376–95.

Şolt, H. B. H. (2014), 'Yerel Yönetimlerin Eğitime Katkı Hizmetleri: Bilgi Evleri Projesi –Zeytinburnu Belediyesi [The Contribution of Local Administrations to Education: BilgiEvleri Project- the Zeytinburnu Municipality Case]', *International Ejer Congress 2014 Conference Proceedings*, 8–13, Ankara: Anı Yayıncılık.

Somel, S. A. (2001), *The Modernization of Public Education in the Ottoman Empire, 1839–1908: Islamization, Autocracy, and Discipline*, Leiden: Brill.

Somel, N. R. O. and A.-M. Nohl (2014), 'Turkey: Education and Social Change – Inquiries into Curriculum Reform', in I. Nadiye (ed.), *Education in Eastern Europe and Eurasia*, 127–48, London: Bloomsbury.

Steiner-Khamsi, G. and I. Stolpe (2006), *Educational Import. Local Encounters with Global Forces in Mongolia*, New York: Palgrave Macmillan.

Straube, P. (2011), 'The Starfish Story: One Step towards Changing the World', Available online: https://eventsforchange.wordpress.com/2011/06/05/the-starfish-story-one-step-towards-changing-the-world/ (accessed 2 February 2022).

Tan, M. (1994), 'Bir Kadın Mesleği: Öğretmenlik [A Woman's Occupation: Teaching]', in N. Arat (ed.), *Kadın Gerçeklikleri*, 37–68, İstanbul: Say Yayınları.

Tanrıöver, H. U. (2003), 'Ders Kitaplarında Cinsiyet Ayrımcılığı', in B. Çotuksöken, A. Erzan and O. Silier (eds), *Ders Kitaplarında İnsan Hakları Projesi*, 106–21, İstanbul: Türkiye Ekonomik ve Toplumsal Tarih Vakfı.

Tansel, A. (2013), *Türkiye'de Özel Dershaneler: Yeni Gelişmeler Ve Dershanelerin Geleceği [Tutorial Colleges in Turkey: New Developments and the Future of the Tutorial Colleges]*, Ankara: Orta Doğu Teknik Üniversitesi Ekonomik Araştırma Merkezi.

Tansel, A. and F. Bircan (2005), Türkiye'de Özel Dershane Eğitiminin Üniversite Giriş Sınavlarında Başarıya Etkisi [Effect of Supplementary Education On University Entrance Examination Performance in Turkey]. Kahire: Economic Research Forum Çalışma Raporu No. 0407 ile Bonn: IZA Çalışma Raporu No. 1609.

Taş, N. F. (2002), 'Türk Meclislerinin Kabul Ettiği Bayramlar [Commemorations Accepted by Turkish Parliaments]', in H. C. Güzel, K. Çiçek, and S. Koca (eds), *Türkler Cilt 16*, 352–62, Ankara: Yeni Türkiye Yayınları.

Taşçı-Günlü, S. (2008), 'Adult Literacy Campaigns and Nation Building', in A-M. Nohl, A. Akkoyunlu-Wigley, and S. Wigley (eds), *Education in Turkey*, 175–94, New York: Waxman.

Taşkın, Y. (2002), 'Anti-Komünizm ve Türk Milliyetçiliği: Endişe ve Pragmatizm [Anti-Communism and Turkish Nationalism: Anxiety and Pragmatism]', in T. Bora (ed.), *Türkiye'de Siyasi Düşünce, Cilt IV: Milliyetçilik*, 618–35, İstanbul: İletişim Yayınları,

Tapper, N. and R. Tapper (1987), 'The Birth of the Prophet: Ritual and Gender in Turkish Islam', *Man*, 21/1: 69–92.

Taussig, M. (2003), 'The Adult's Imagination of Child's Imagination', in P. R. Matthews and D. McWhirter (eds), *Aesthetic Subjects*, 449–69, Minneapolis, London: University of Minnesota.

Taylor, E. (2012), 'The Rise of the Surveillance at School', in D. Lyon, K. Ball, and K. D. Haggerty (eds), *Routledge Handbook of Surveillance Studies*, 225–32, London and New York: Routledge.

Tekeli, Ş. (1982), *Kadınlar ve Siyasal Toplumsal Hayat [Women and Political Social Life]*, İstanbul: Birikim Yayınları.

Toprak, B. (1984), 'Politicization of Islam in a Secular State: The National Salvation Party in Turkey', in A. S. Arjomand (ed.), *From Nationalism to Revolutionary Islam*, 119–33, Albany: State University of New York Press.

Toprak, B. (1988), 'The State, Politics, and Religion in Turkey', in M. Heper and A. Evin (eds), *State, Democracy and the Military: Turkey in the 1980s*, 119–35, Berlin: Walter de Gruyter.

TÖS, 'Türkiye Öğretmenler Sendikası [Turkish Teachers' Union]' (1969), *Devrimci Eğitim Şurası: 4-8 Eylûl 1968*. [The Revolutionary Education Council: 4–8 September 1968], Ankara: Töyko The Revolutionary Education Council Matbaası.

Tremblay, P. (2014), 'Turkish Intelligence Agency (MIT) at center of political storm', *Al-monitor*, 8 January. Available online http://www.al-monitor.com/pulse/originals/2014/01/turkey-mit-akp-gulen-battle-power-struggle.html#ixzz3rg9fvwz8 (accessed 5 February 2022).

Tuğal, C. (2009), *Passive Revolution: Absorbing the Islamic Challenge to Capitalism*, Stanford: Stanford University Press.

Tuğla, K. (2012), 'Türkiye'de İslami İçerikli Televizyon Yayıncılığının Gelişimi Üzerine Bir İnceleme: Çocuk Kanalı Yumurcak TV Örneği. [An Analysis of the Development of Television Broadcasting with Islamic Content in Turkey: The Case Study of Children's Channel Yumurcak TV]', PhD diss., Faculty of Communication, Marmara University, Istanbul.

Turam, B. (2007), *Between Islam and the State: The Politics of Engagement*, Stanford: Stanford University Press.

Türkiye (2017), 'Kutlu Doğum Fetö Projesi [Holy Birth Fetö Project]', 21 April, *Türkiye*.

Türköne, M. (2012), 'Kutlu Doğum ve 28 Şubat [Holy Birth and 28 February]' 19 Nisan, *Zaman*.

Tüzün, G. (ed.) (2009), *Ders kitaplarında insan hakları tarama sonuçları II [Human Right in Textbooks]*, İstanbul: Tarih Vakfı Yayınları.

UNESCO, 'United Nations Educational, Scientific and Cultural Organization' (1990), *World Declaration on Education for All and Framework for Action to Meet Basic Learning Needs Text Adopted by the World Conference on Education for All: Meeting Basic Learning Needs, Jomtien, Thailand, 5–9 March*, Paris: UNESCO Publishing.

UNESCO, 'United Nations Educational, Scientific and Cultural Organization' (2000), *The Dakar Framework for Action. Education for All: Meeting our Collective Commitments. Text Adopted by the World Education Forum Dakar, Senegal, 26–28 April 2000*, Paris: UNESCO Publishing.

UNESCO, 'United Nations Educational, Scientific and Cultural Organization' (2007), *Education for All Global Monitoring Report 2008: Education for All by 2015. Will We Make It?*, Oxford: Oxford University Press.

UNESCO, 'United Nations Educational, Scientific and Cultural Organization' (2015), *Education for All 2000–2015: Achievements and Challenges: EFA Global Monitoring Report*, Paris: UNESCO Publishing.

Ünsal, F. B. (2005), 'Mehmet Âkif Ersoy', in T. Bora and M. Gültekingil (eds), *Modern Dünyada Siyasi Düşünce Cilt 6 İslâmcılık*, 72–89, İstanbul: İletişim Yayınları,

Wacquant, L. (2008), *Urban Outcasts: A Comparative Sociology of Advanced Marginality*, Cambridge: Polity Press.

Walkerdine, V. (1994), 'Femininity as Performance', in L. Stone and G. M. Boldt (eds), *The Education Feminism Reader*, 57–72, London: Routledge.

WB, 'World Bank' (2015), *Supply and Demand for Child Care Services in Turkey: A Mixed Methods Study*. Washington, DC: World Bank Group.

White, J. B. (2002), *Islamist Mobilization in Turkey: A Study in Vernacular Politics*, Washington, DC: University of Washington Press.

White, J. B. (2013), *Muslim Nationalism and the New Turks*, Princeton and Oxford: Princeton University Press.

Williams, R. (1977), *Marxism and Literature*, London: Oxford University Press.

Williams, R. (2001), *The Long Revolution*, Ontario: Broadview Press.

Woodward, M. (2011), *Java, Indonesia and Islam*, London/New York: Springer.

Yabanci, B. (2019), 'Work for the Nation, Obey the State, Praise the Ummah: Turkey's Government-oriented Youth Organizations in Cultivating a New Nation', *Ethnopolitics* 20: 4,467–499.

YADA 'Yaşama Dair Vakıf' (2011), 'Eğitimde Toplumsal Cinsiyet Eşitliği İçin 10 Yıl: "Haydi Kızlar Okula!" Kampanyası'nın Serüveni ve Öğrettikleri [10 Years for Gender Equality in Education]'. Available online https://yada.org.tr/yayinlar/egitimde-toplumsal-cinsiyet-esitligi-icin-10-yil-haydi-kizlar-okula-kampanyasinin-seruveni-ve-ogrettikleri/ (accessed 10 August 2022).

Yavuz, M. H. (2003), *Islamic Political Identity in Turkey*, Oxford and New York: Oxford University Press.

Yavuz, M. H. (2009), *Secularism and Muslim Democracy in Turkey*, Cambridge: Cambridge University Press.

Yavuz, M. H. (2013), *Toward an Islamic Enlightenment: The Gülen Movement*, Oxford: Oxford University Press.

Yelken, E. and T. Büyükcan (2015), 'Gündemin Tuzağına Düşmeden Dershaneleri Tartışmak [A Critical Analysis of Tutorial Colleges]', *Eğitim Bilim Toplum Dergisi*, 13 (50) Spring: 24–47.

Yıldız, A. (2012), 'Transformation of Adult Education in Turkey: From Public Education to Life-Long Learning', in K. İnal and G. Akkaymak (eds), *Neoliberal Transformation of Education in Turkey: Political and Ideological Analysis of Educational Reforms in the Age of the AKP*, 245–58, New York: Palgrave Macmillan.

Yolcu, H. (2007), 'Türkiye'de Ilköğretim Finansmanının Değerlendirilmesi [The Evaluation of the Financing of Primary Schools in Turkey]', PhD diss., Ankara University, Ankara.

Yolcu, H. (2014), 'The Education Agenda in Turkey: Marketing Education in the Context of Neo-liberal Policies', in D. A. Turner and H. Yolcu (eds), *Neo-liberal Educational Reforms: A Critical Analysis*, 50–72, New York: Routledge.

Yolcu, H. and N. Kurul (2009), 'Evaluating the Finance of Primary Education in Turkey within the Context of Neo-Liberal Policies', *International Journal of Educational Policies*, 3 (2): 24–45.

Yörük, E. (2012), 'Welfare Provision as Political Containment: The Politics of Social Assistance and the Kurdish Conflict in Turkey', *Politics and Society*, 40: 517–47.

Yung, K. W. H. and M. Bray (2017), 'Shadow education: Features, Expansion and Implications', in T. K. C. Tse and M. Lee (eds), *Making Sense of Education in Post-handover Hong Kong: Achievements and Challenges*, 95–111, London: Routledge.

Zürcher, E. J. (2004), *Turkey: A Modern History*, London: I.B. Tauris.

Index

A

abis (elder brother) 46, 66, 84, 97, 150
Abu-Duhou, Ibtisam 42–3
ADD (Atatürkist Thought Association, Atatürkçü Düşünce Derneği) 33
afterschool activities. *See bilgi evi*
Ahmad, Feroz 24
Akkaymak, Güliz 29, 30, 41
AKP (Justice and Development Party, Adalet ve Kalkınma Partisi)
  and break of alliance with Gülen community 37–9
  and reconfiguration of civil society 32–4, 113
  and visible relation with Gülen community 35–6
  increasing access to primary education 27–8
  neoliberal education policies 29–30
Akşit, Bahattin 23–4, 75, 103, 151
Aktaşlı, İrem 90
Aktay, Yasin 87, 167n.5
Alevi faith. *See* religious culture and moral knowledge course
Altın Nesil (Golden Generation) 35, 48, 89, 104, 150
Altınay, Ayşe Gül 82–3, 172n.4
Anderson, Benedict 97, 104
Anderson-Levitt, Kathryn M. 41, 148
Apak Kaya, Meral 55–6
Asım (poem) 87–90, 98, 104
Asım'ın Nesli (Asım's Generation) 89, 104, 153
Atasoy, Yıldız 32–3
Atatürk Corners 34, 80–3
Atatürk, Mustafa Kemal (Turkish president) 16, 19, 77, 85–6, 102–3, 153
  and forms of play 78–9, 84–5
  and iconoclastic attacks 86, 102–3, 153
Atatürk's principles and reforms course 23
Aydagül, Batuhan 28, 30, 90
Aydın, Murat (mayor) 69

B

Bahçelik 5–7 (*see varoş*)
Bahçelik municipality
  and Islamist network 61–2, 149–50
  and local policies targeting mothers 126–9, 151
  mobilizing mothers (*see* 'good mothers')
  relations with schools 60–3, 72
  services offered (*see bilgi evi*)
Ball, Stephen 44, 68–9, 73, 149–150
Berkes, Niyazi 16, 19–20
Beşpınar, Fatma Umut 22, 129
bilgi evi (house of knowledge) 60, 69, 88, 95, 127, 149, 154
  and cultural products 88, 169n.12
  and the schools 70–1
  attracting girls 71
  co-curricular activities 69–70
  recreational opportunities 70–1
Boli, John 41
Bourdieu, Pierre 49–51, 60, 72, 150
Bowe, Richard 44, 73, 149
boys 47, 71, 77–8, 85–6, 102–3, 112, 119, 121
  boarding in Hidayet Dormitory 65–6
  resisting teachers 121
Bozan, İrfan (journalist) 24
Bray, Mark 65
Brockett, Gavin D. 19, 21
Buğra, Ayşe 129
Bulaç, Ali 87, 167n.5
Butler, Judith
  on gender performativity 124

C

Caldwell, Brian J. 42–3, 148
Candaş, Ayşe 42–3, 72, 148
Çakır, Ruşen (journalist) 165n.8
CCTV (closed-circuit television). *See* surveillance
Çelik, Hüseyin (education minister) 26, 28

Çiller, Tansu (Prime Minister) 91
compulsory literature canon 31
Conell, Raewyn 123–5, 153, 144–5
crowd 111–112
Çubukçu, Nimet (education minister) 93
cultural capital 49
cultural struggle 76
curriculum reform 30–1
ÇYDD (Association for the Support
    of Modern Life, Çağdaş Yaşamı
    Destekleme Derneği) 33, 113

D
dabbe (the Beast of the Earth, Dabbet'ül
    Arz) 78–80, 85, 166n.1
Day of Commemoration of the Adoption
    of the National Anthem and
    Mehmet Akif Ersoy 87–8, 103–4,
    152, 168n.7
decentralization 26, 29, 42, 147
Dedeoglu, Saniye 129
Delaney, Carol 116
Deniz, Mehmet Baki 42–3, 72, 148
deregulation 24
dershane (tutorial college) 35–6, 38, 147,
    164n.5
DİB (Presidency of the Religious Affairs,
    Diyanet İşleri Başkanlığı) 25, 28,
    70, 128, 138
    and Holy Birth Week 33, 91–2, 169n.11
discipline 66, 121
double-shift system 27, 108–9, 120

E
Education reform '4+4+4' 36–7
EFA (Education for All) 26, 171n.5
Eğitim-Bir-Sen (trade union) 34–5,
    114–118
Eğitim-Sen (trade union) 34, 115
Eiseley, Loren 8
Ekim Akkan, Başak 42–3, 72, 148
Emanet, Zühre 5, 39, 86
emphasized femininity 123–4
    author's use of 130, 138, 144–5, 155
Erbakan, Necmettin (Prime Minister) 7,
    22, 32
Erdoğan, Recep Tayyip (Turkish
    president) 26, 36–9, 126, 129
ERG (Education Reform Initiative, Eğitim
    Reform Girişimi) 31

Ergenekon investigation 33–4
Erkişi, Ertuğrul (composer and singer) 98
Erman, Tahire 5–6
Ersoy, Mehmet Akif (poet, author of
    Turkish national anthem)
    life of 167n.5
    poetry. *See Asım* (poem)
    portrayal in schools 87–88, 103
    significance 86, 88–9
EU (European Union) 25, 27, 41, 90, 92,
    129, 146
exams 35–6, 38, 64, 67, 114, 147,
    164n.5

F
fatherhood 142, 155
    and fathers' involvement in education
        (*see* fathers)
    and paternal violence 142–3
    constructed 139–40 (*see* 'hegemonic
        masculinity')
fathers
    non-involvement in education 126, 145
        (*see* mothers, *see also sınıf annesi*)
FETÖ (Fethullahist Terrorist
    Organization, Fethullahçı Terör
    Örgütü) 26, 38
field 50, 60, 72
Fortna, Benjamin C. 15, 19, 89, 97, 104,
    168n.8
forms of play invented by pupils
    dabbe play 78–80
    spitting play 84
    pretending to be Atatürk 85
Foucault, Michael 105–6
fraternity 66, 84, 154
free textbooks 27, 29

G
Gallagher, Michael 106, 111–112, 121
Gamage, David 42–43
gender equality 51, 154–6
gender order 123–5
    author's use of 125, 129
gender parity. *See* HKO
gender performativity 124
    author's use of 130, 144–5, 155
gender regime 123
    author's use of 129–30, 138, 140–1,
        143–5, 153–5

gender segregation (*see* teachers' dress code) 121, 151–5
gender-segregated spaces 127, 144, 155
gender socialization 47, 67–8
gender stereotypes (*see* songs for children)
gendered habitus 59–60
Gewirtz, Sharon 44, 69, 73, 149
girls 17, 24, 27–8, 37, 47, 50, 101–3, 137, 154
  and after school activities (*see bilgi evi*)
  and forms of play 78–9, 85
Girls' Institutes 17
Gök, Fatma 18, 24, 29, 41, 54
Gökaçtı, Mehmet Ali 25, 75, 103, 151
Göktürk, Duygun 34
Göle, Nilüfer 50
Gözaydın, İştar 90
Gramsci, Antonio 75–6
Grauwe, Anton D. 42–43
Gülen community 163n.20
  and *hizmet* (*see hizmet*)
  and Holy Birth Week (*see* Holy Birth Week)
  and Mehmet Akif Ersoy (*see Altın Nesil*)
  role in education sector 32–9
  teachers affiliated with 47, 49, 51, 73, 112–3, 150, 156
Gülen, Fethullah (religious leader) 97–8, 163n.20, 166n.1, 169n.10
Güneş, Cengiz 101
Günseli, Sevda 42–3, 72, 148
Güvercin, Gökçe 34

H
habitus 49–51, 59–60
  author's use of 51–2, 60, 65, 68, 72, 150
Hanioğlu, Şükrü, 19
Harvey, David 41
health and safety risks. *See* crowd and *see* also double-shift system
hegemonic masculinity 124
  author's use of 138, 142, 144–5, 153, 155
Hidayet Dormitory
  acting in place of the parents 65, 68, 72, 150
  and *abis* (*see abis*)
  and boys (*see* boys)
  and shadow education system 65
  and Zinnur School teachers 67

disrupting Zinnur School (*see* gender segregation)
  services offered in 64
hizmet (service) 47–48, 51, 97, 150, 165n.9
HKO (Hey Girls, Let's Go to School, *Haydi Kızlar Okula*) 27–8
Hobsbawm, Eric 91
Holy Birth Week 91–3
  and posters designed by girls 98–102
  as fundraising event 61–2
  celebration in Bahçelik 96
  controversies 32–3, 92, 93, 169n.9
homework 47 (*see* tutoring)
Huizinga, Joan 77, 84
Human Rights in Textbooks 30
hymns. *See* songs for children

I
iconoclasm 77–8
'iconoclasm as child's play' 77–8 (*see* also forms of play invented by pupils)
İlhan, Yasin (composer and artistic director) 95
illiteracy 18
imagined community 97, 104, 152
imam-hatip (prayer leader and preacher) schools 3, 15–6, 20, 22–3, 25, 31–2, 35–6, 48, 50–2, 75, 103, 114, 151
  and *Asım'ın Nesli* (Asım's Generation) 89–90 (*see* also Education reform '4+4+4')
IMF (International Monetary Fund) 24, 27, 41, 54
İnal, Kemal 29, 30, 41
invention 91
Islamic *tariqa* orders 46, 63, 150, 165n.8
Islamization in education 151–5
ışık evi (house of light) 47, 51, 97 (*see hizmet*)

J
Jenkins, Gareth H. 33
jinn, 79, 103, 152, 167n.3

K
Kağıtçıbaşı, Çiğdem 3, 37
Kancı, Tuba 19, 83
Kandiyoti, Deniz 5, 17, 39, 86, 116, 124, 130, 155

Kaplan, İsmail 76, 103, 151
Kaplan, Sam 24, 76, 103, 151
Kaptein, Nico 168n.8
Kara, İsmail (theologian) 87, 167n.5
Karacadağ, Hasan (film director) 79,
    167n.3
Katz, Marion H. 168n.8
Kaymakcan, Recep 31, 90–1
Keyder, Çağlar 19, 23
Kısakürek, Necip Fazıl (poet) 83,
    168n.5
Köse, Ayşen 42–44, 72, 148
Kurdish conflict 24
    and its repercussions in educational
        domain 24–5
Kurdish Hizbullah (Hizbullah in Turkey)
    101, 113
Kurt, Mehmet 101
Kurul, Nejla 42–3, 148
Kuzmanovic, Daniella 33

L
labour market
    and welfare regime 129–30
    teachers' understanding of 135–6, 154
        (*see* single mothers)
lived culture 2, 76–7, 152
loco parentis (acting in place of the
    parents) 46, 65, 72, 150. *See* Hidayet
    Dormitory
Lord, Ceren 38, 163n.20, 165n.8,
    169n.11

M
male gaze 120 (*see* CCTV)
Mardin, Şerif 22, 25
marketization in education 148–51
Martinez, Carlos 41
MEB (Ministry of Education, Milli Eğitim
    Bakanlığı) 25, 27–31, 34–5, 37,
    42–43, 90, 93, 110
Messerschmidt, James W. 123, 153, 155
mevlid. See Holy Birth Week
Meyer, John W. 41
MHP (Nationalist Movement Party,
    Milliyetçi Hareket Partisi) 134
MİT (National Intelligence Service, Milli
    İstihbarat Teşkilatı) crisis 37
money 6, 43, 53–4, 57, 96–7, 137,
    151

Moshenska, Joe 77–9, 103
motherhood, 123–5
    constructed 128–9, 131, 151 (*see*
        emphasized femininity)
    performed 130–1, 133, 144–5
mothers 55, 72–3
    and 'good mothers' 125, 129, 144
    involvement in education (*see sınıf
        annesi*)
    mobilization of 126–7, 129
    receiving support (*see hizmet* and *see*
        also Bahçelik municipality)
Muhammad (prophet)
    in elective courses 3, 37
    in religious culture and moral
        knowledge courses 90–1
    in songs (*see* songs for children)
    veneration (*see* Holy Birth Week)
Mumcu, Erkan (education minister) 26
music albums by children's choirs 97–8

N
National Sovereignty and Children's Day
    92–3, 96
National Turkish Students Union (*Milli
    Türk Talebe Birliği*) 22
Navaro-Yashin, Yael 77, 102–3
'new Turkey' 153
Nohl, Arnd-Michael 26
Nursi, Said (founding father of Nurcu
    movement) 19 (*see* also Gülen
    community)
Nutuk ('The Speech') 85, 167n.4

O
OAB (the Parent Teacher Association,
    Okul Aile Birliği)
    financing primary schools 43–4
Okçabol, Rıfat 29
Öniş, Ziya 27
Özel, Cemal 98
Ozgur, Iren 19, 49–51, 75, 103, 151
Öztürk, Yaşar Nuri (theologian) 167n.1
Özyürek, Esra 77, 80

P
panopticism 105–6
    authors' use of 113, 120
Panopticon 105–6
    authors' use of 107, 109, 121

parental involvement. *See* mothers and
fathers
Passeron, Jean-Claude 49, 72, 150
Pateman, Carole 129
patriarchal bargain 124, 130
People's Houses 17–18
Peygamberi Görmek İçin ('To See the
Prophet') (song) 96
Peygamberin Gülleri ('Roses of the
Prophet') (music album) 95–6
Peygamberin Gülleri II ('Roses of the
Prophet II') (music album) 97–8
PKK (Kurdistan Workers' Party, Partiya
Karkerên Kurdistanê) 101, 113
play 77, 84 (*see* forms of play invented by
pupils)
portraits of Mustafa Kemal Atatürk
haunted 78–9, 82
rumoured of 62
privatization 12, 24, 26–7, 29, 38–9, 54, 147

Q
Qur'an classes 114
Qur'an courses 4, 7, 25, 31, 67, 70, 95

R
Ramirez, Francisco O. 41
Reay, Diane
on Bourdieu 51
on emprical use of habitus 50
on field 60
on gendered habitus 59
on 'genderless parent' 55–6
religious culture and moral knowledge
course 24, 31, 90, 114
Republican rallies (*Cumhuriyet mitingleri*) 33

S
Safahat ('Stages') 1, 88–9
Sakallioglu, Umit Cizre 24
Saktanber, Ayşe 22
Şaşmaz, Aytuğ, 26, 28, 43–4, 72, 90, 148,
163n.19
Saylan, Türkan (chairwoman of ÇYDD)
33, 163n.18
SBM (School Based Management)
broad definition 42–3
interpretation in the country 43–4 (*see*
OAB)
Schriewer, Jürgen 41

Seçkin, Onur 34
'secure school' framework 107, 170n.2
Selçuk, Ziya (education minister) 30
sexist stereotypes 141
shadow education system 65
Significant Days and Weeks (*Belirli Gün ve
Haftalar*) 31, 93
single mothers 134, 136, 138, 155
sınıf annesi (classroom mother) 55–6, 72,
151
and field 60
and habitus of teachers 58–9
and habitus of mothers 57–8
Smith, Gavin J.D. 108
Şolt, H. Burçin H. 69
Somel, Nazlı, 26, 30
songs for children. *See* music albums by
children choirs
Spinks, Jim M. 148
Steiner-Khamsi, Gita 42, 148
Stolpe, Ines 42, 148
structure of feeling 76, 103, 152
surveillance
and CCTV 108–10
and *nöbet* (guard duty) 110–112
and policing 107

T
Talip School 7–8
and pupils' pocket money 54
budget 45, 53
conflict among teachers 52–3
contact with the municipality 61–2
infrastructural limits. *See* double-shift
system
mothers' role in fundraising. *See sınıf
annesi*
Taş, Necati Fahri 168n.8
Taussig, Michael 85, 103
teachers
power relations 113, 117–20
teachers' dress code
and episodes of protests 114–19
and headcarf ban 118
official regulations 115–6
tevhid (the unity of Islam and Muslims)
98–9, 101
Tevhid–i Tedrisat Kanunu (Law on the
Unification of Education) 17, 75,
156

the idoll 79, 103
The Revolutionary Education Council
    (*Devrimci Eğitim Şûrası*) 21
TÖS (Turkish Teachers' Union, Türkiye
    Öğretmenler Sendikası) 21
TSK (Turkish Armed Forces, Türk Silahlı
    Kuvvetleri) 24, 32–3, 92, 156
Tüzün, Işık 90
Tuğal, Cihan 25, 32
Tuğla, Kader 36
Turam, Berna 33
TÜRGEV (Turkish Youth and Education
    Foundation, Türkiye Gençlik ve
    Eğitime Hizmet Vakfı) 38, 156
Turkish–Islamic Synthesis 15–6, 22–4, 76,
    82, 102–3
Türköne, Mümtazer, 91, 169n.9
tutoring. *See bilgi evi* and Hidayet
    Dormitory, *see also hizmet*

U
ummah (the Muslim community) 32,
    95–8, 102, 104, 153
UNICEF (United Nation's Children Fund)
    26–8, 147
uniform. *See* white coat
unionization. *See* TÖS

V
varoş (low-income neighbourhood) 5–6,
    8, 138
veiling. *See* Qur'an classes.
Village Institutes 15, 17–8, 20
violence
    against children 107, 121, 142–3,
        170n.2
    and hegemonic masculinity 139–43,
        145
volunteer work. *See sınıf annesi*

W
Wacquant, Loïc 51, 60
WB (World Bank) 26, 41, 54, 129
white coat 116, 119, 120, 154
    and concealing 121 (*see* gender
        segregation)
White, Jenny B. 5–6
Williams, Raymond
    on lived culture 2
    on structure of feeling 76, 152
Woodward, Mark R. 168n.8

Y
Yabanci, Bilge 38
Yavuz, Hakan 165n.9
Yetim Kız ('the Orphan Girl') (song)
    94–5
Yıldız, Ahmet 31
Yolcu, Hüseyin 29, 41–4, 55–6, 72, 145,
    147
Yücel, Can (poet) 21
Yung, Kevin Wai-Ho 65

Z
Zajda, Joseph 42–43
Zinnur School 7
    alliance of teachers 52
    and 'partisan freedom' 112–113
    and *hizmet* 47–9, 51–2, 150
    and teachers affiliated with Islamic
        communities 46, 165n.8
    budget 44–5
    donations of parents 45
    mothers' role in fundraising (*see sınıf
        annesi*)
    relation with the municipality 61–3
    relationship with Hidayet community
        (*see* Hidayet Dormitory)
Zürcher, Erick J. 21, 25